FiNALEonline.de

FiNALEonline ist die digitale Ergänzung zu deinem Abitur-band. Hier findest du eine Viel-zahl an Angeboten, die dich bei deiner Prüfungsvorbereitung zusätzlich unterstützen.

Das Plus für deine Vorbereitung:

→ Original-Prüfungsaufgaben mit Lösungen (bitte Code von Seite 4 eingeben!)

→ EXTRA-Training Rechtschreibung
So kannst du einem möglichen Punktabzug bei deinen Abi-Klausuren vorbeugen.

→ Videos zur mündlichen Prüfung

→ Tipps zur stressfreien Prüfungsvorbereitung

→ Abi-Checklisten mit allen prüfungsrelevanten Themen

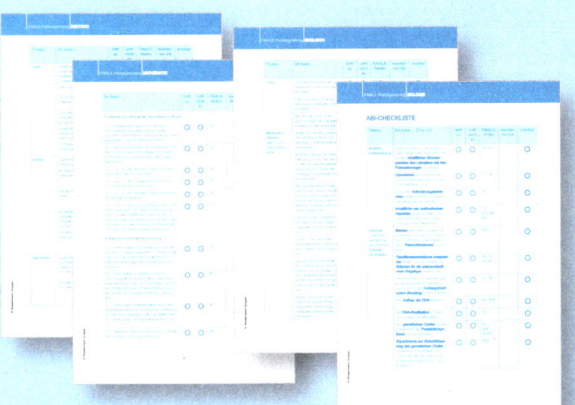

W0192777

Abi-Checklisten
Sie helfen dir, den Überblick über den Prüfungsstoff zu behalten.

Foto: © Peter Wirtz, Dormagen

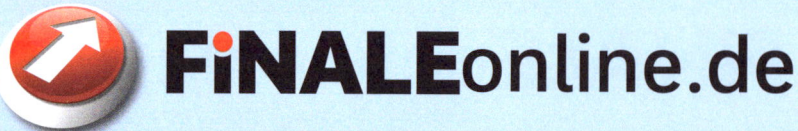

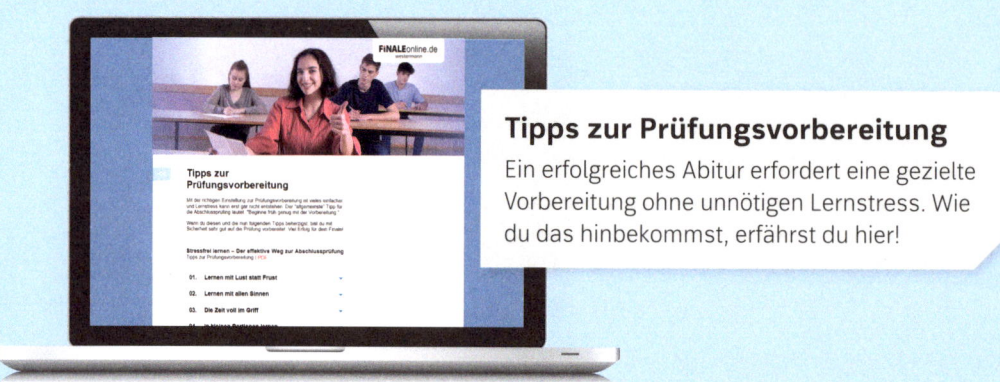

Tipps zur Prüfungsvorbereitung

Ein erfolgreiches Abitur erfordert eine gezielte Vorbereitung ohne unnötigen Lernstress. Wie du das hinbekommst, erfährst du hier!

Videos zur mündlichen Prüfung

Nur wenige Abiturienten wissen genau, wie sie abläuft, die „Mündliche". Die Videos geben dir Einblick in den Ablauf der Prüfung und Tipps für die richtige Vorbereitung.

Die Kombination aus FiNALE-Buch und FiNALEonline bietet dir die optimale Vorbereitung für deine Prüfung und begleitet dich sicher zu einem erfolgreichen Abitur 2024!

www.finaleonline.de

westermann

FiNALE Prüfungstraining

Niedersachsen

Zentralabitur 2024
Englisch

FiNALEonline.de

Liebe Schülerin, lieber Schüler,

sobald die Original-Prüfungsaufgaben zur Veröffentlichung freigegeben sind, können sie unter **www.finaleonline.de** zusammen mit ausführlichen Lösungen kostenlos heruntergeladen werden. Gib dazu einfach diesen Code ein:

EN3Z8A9

Einfach mal reinschauen: www.finaleonline.de

Autorinnen: Anne Böker und Karolin Hofmann
sowie Isabel Wagemann-Steidel und Ortrud-Christine Rotzoll

© 2023 Westermann Lernwelten GmbH, Georg-Westermann-Allee 66, 38104 Braunschweig
www.westermann.de

Bildnachweis:
|Peter Wirtz Fotografie, Dormagen: Titel. |toonpool.com, Berlin, Castrop-Rauxel: Popa Matumula 153.1.

Druck A[1]/Jahr 2023
Alle Drucke der Serie A sind im Unterricht parallel verwendbar.

Redaktion: Federlese GbR – Christina & Boris Kühne, Grevenbroich
Kontakt: finale@westermanngruppe.de
Layout: LIO Design GmbH, Braunschweig
Umschlaggestaltung: Gingco.Net, Braunschweig
Umschlagfoto: Peter Wirtz, Dormagen
Druck und Bindung: Westermann Druck GmbH, Georg-Westermann-Allee 66, 38104 Braunschweig

ISBN 978-3-07-**172437**-2

Inhaltsverzeichnis

Textgestaltung

Ausdrucksvermögen / Verfügbarkeit sprachlicher Mittel

Beispiele für Prüfungsaufgaben

Aufgaben mit Beispiellösungen

Aufgaben mit Bewertungskriterien

Aufgaben zur Sprachmittlung mit Beispiellösungen oder Bewertungskriterien

Original-Prüfungsaufgaben 2022 und 2023

Arbeiten mit FiNALE

FiNALE Prüfungstraining Englisch möchte Ihnen eine praxisnahe Hilfe zur Vorbereitung auf die Abiturprüfung sein. Im Praxis-Teil finden sich daher – neben den Original-Prüfungsaufgaben 2022 – zu allen geforderten Themenbereichen weitere authentische Aufgaben, die in ihrer Form den Vorgaben entsprechen. Wir verzichten hier auf eine Differenzierung nach Kursen mit grundlegendem beziehungsweise erhöhtem Anforderungsniveau. Im Abitur unterscheiden sich die Aufgaben einerseits durch den Textumfang, andererseits durch den Schwierigkeitsgrad des Textes. Auch als Schülerin oder Schüler in einem Kurs mit grundlegendem Anforderungsniveau sind Sie durch den Englischunterricht mit längeren und komplexeren Texten vertraut. Als Schülerin oder Schüler eines Kurses mit erhöhtem Anforderungsniveau können Sie eine Textanalyse auch an kürzeren, einfacheren Texten üben.

Zwei Aufgaben im Kapitel „Beispiele für Prüfungsaufgaben" werden kleinschrittig erarbeitet und schließen mit einer Musterlösung. Dies soll für Sie eine exemplarische Hilfe sein auf dem Weg vom Ausgangstext über das Textverständnis, die Methodik der Textanalyse und die Evaluation hin zur Gliederung und sprachlichen Darstellung des Zieltextes. Den weiteren Aufgabenbeispielen folgen Bewertungskriterien ganz in der Form, wie Ihre Lehrerinnen und Lehrer sie zur Korrektur der Abiturarbeiten an die Hand bekommen. Sie dienen Ihnen zur Selbstkontrolle in Ihrem fortschreitenden Prüfungstraining. Geschrieben wurde dieses Buch im Jahr 2023, damit es frühzeitig zur Vorbereitung auf das Abitur 2024 beitragen kann. Die zu diesem Zeitpunkt aktuellen Abituraufgaben 2022 werden jeweils mit Musterlösung angeboten. Sobald die Original-Prüfungsaufgaben des Jahres 2023 freigegeben sind, können Sie sie unter www.finaleonline.de abrufen.

Das Kapitel „Basiswissen" bietet Ihnen eine kompakte Übersicht über die für das Zentralabitur vorgegebenen Themen. Es hilft Ihnen, das im Unterricht erworbene Wissen zu strukturieren und in seinen Grundzügen abzurufen. Um den Umgang mit dem thematischen Vokabular zu vertiefen, ist dieser Teil in englischer Sprache geschrieben und wird durch Glossare zum thematischen Vokabular ergänzt.

Die sprachliche Leistung spielt in der Fremdsprache bei aller inhaltlich-thematischer Kompetenz immer noch die herausragende Rolle. Ein sicherer Umgang mit den Strukturen und Wörtern der englischen Sprache ist also unabdingbar. Deshalb haben wir in FiNALE ein ganzes Kapitel zur sprachlichen Leistung aufgenommen.

Wir wünschen Ihnen viel Erfolg!

Informationen und Tipps zur Prüfung

Das Kerncurriculum (KC) für die Sekundarstufe II

Mit der Einführung des neuen Kerncurriculums für die gymnasiale Oberstufe entwickelt sich der Englischunterricht auf moderne Weise weiter – so, wie es mit dem entsprechenden Kerncurriculum für die Klassen 5–10 bereits angelegt wurde. Das KC für die Oberstufe führt die im KC für die Sek I angelegten Grundlagen fort, sodass ein nahtloser Übergang in die Qualifikationsphase erfolgen kann. Grundlegend ist auch in der Sekundarstufe II der Gemeinsame Europäische Referenzrahmen *CEFR (Common European Framework)*.

Im Zentralabitur **2024** wird die Prüfung aus folgenden **drei Bestandteilen** bestehen (s. auch S. 10 ff.):

1. Hörverstehen (30 Minuten),
2. Sprachmittlung (60 Minuten), sowie
3. einer Textaufgabe (auf erhöhtem Niveau: 225 Minuten, auf grundlegendem Niveau: 195 Minuten). Für die Textaufgabe besteht weiterhin die Wahlmöglichkeit zwischen zwei Vorschlägen; die Auswahl der Textaufgabe ist in der Prüfungszeit inbegriffen.

Die folgende Zusammenfassung der wichtigsten Anliegen des neuen KC gibt Ihnen eine Orientierung über die im Abitur von Ihnen erwarteten Kenntnisse und Kompetenzen.

Die Kompetenzorientierung

Kompetenzen

Das Abitur in Niedersachsen ist nicht nach Inhalten ausgerichtet, sondern es wird eine kompetenzorientierte Prüfung abgenommen. Inhalte sind selbstverständlich immer noch wichtig, sie ergeben sich aus den im Unterricht verpflichtend zu behandelnden Materialien. Die inhaltliche Grundlage sind die Themenfelder, die das Kerncurriculum für die Sekundarstufe II ausweist.

Der Englischunterricht soll es ermöglichen, Fremdes und Anderes zu erfahren und durch Perspektivenwechsel andere Weltsichten zu verstehen, um Perspektiven zu koordinieren und Empathie zu entwickeln.

Hierzu müssen die Inhalte „meaningful", also für die Lernenden von Bedeutung und außerdem in einem interkulturellen Sinne relevant sein. Hierbei wird ausdrücklich von einer erforderlichen Verstehensanstrengung ausgegangen, sodass Aufgaben nicht einfach nur mit bereits vorhandenem Weltwissen oder Allgemeinbildung gelöst werden können. Gefordert sind somit interaktive fremdsprachliche Prozesse, die sinnvolle diskursive Handlungen notwendig machen. Auf diese Weise sollen Reflexion und Selbstreflexion ermöglicht werden.

Um kompetent sprachlich und interkulturell kommunikativ handeln zu können, müssen Wissen und Können miteinander verknüpft werden. Inhalte werden in ihrer Bedeutung relativiert, da die Kompetenzen zwar an Inhalten erworben werden, dieses jedoch exemplarisch geschieht, sodass in der Abiturprüfung keine speziellen Inhalte wie etwa „India" oder „The American Dream" im Mittelpunkt stehen. Gefragt sind vielmehr methodische Problemlösungsstrategien, denn die erworbenen Kompetenzen werden auf neue Situationen, Themen und Kontexte transferiert. Sprachliche, pragmatische oder soziokulturelle Strukturen müssen in den einzelnen Prüfungsteilen erkannt und im Sinne eines kompetenten Umgangs mit der Fremdsprache beherrscht werden.

Wichtig ist hierbei der Hinweis, dass laut KC der Erwerb interkultureller Kompetenzen nicht mit der erfolgreich bestandenen Abiturprüfung endet, sondern ein Leben lang fortgesetzt wird.
Für Schülerinnen und Schüler bedeutet dies, dass sie laut KC nicht nur auf vorhandenes Wissen zurückgreifen müssen, sondern dass sie sich weiterführendes Wissen selbst beschaffen und entsprechende Zusammenhänge erkennen können. Weiterhin sollen sie in der Lage sein, Handlungsschritte zu planen und Lösungen auf kreative Weise zu erproben. Die verfügbaren Kenntnisse, Fähigkeiten und Fertigkeiten sollen dabei zum Einsatz kommen, das gewonnene Ergebnis soll anhand angemessener Kriterien selbst überprüft/evaluiert werden.

Diese Erweiterung der Kompetenzfelder wird nicht nur in den Unterricht, sondern vor allem auch in die Abiturprüfung einfließen.

TIPP Further reading

1. *Kerncurriculum für das Gymnasium – gymnasiale Oberstufe*
   Herausgegeben vom Niedersächsischen Kultusministerium (2009 und 2017), Schiffgraben 12, 30159 Hannover
   Das Kerncurriculum ist auch als PDF-Datei auf dem niedersächsischen Bildungsserver abrufbar: http://www.cuvo.nibis.de
2. *Gemeinsamer Europäischer Referenzrahmen für Sprachen: lernen, lehren, beurteilen*
   Autoren: John Trim / Brian North / Daniel Coste in Zusammenarbeit mit Joseph Sheils. Langenscheidt, ISBN: 978-3-126-06520-7
3. Materialien für kompetenzorientierten Unterricht, hrsg. vom Niedersächsischen Kultusministerium (2010), und Materialien zur Sprechprüfung (2014) auch online unter www.nibis.de
4. Bildungsstandards für die Allgemeine Hochschulreife, als PDF zu finden unter http://www.nibis.de/uploads/1gohrgs/files/englisch/Bildungsstandards_allg_Hochschulreife.pdf (Zugriff: 01.04.2023)

Kompetenzerwerb

Der Erwerb der für die Abiturprüfung erforderlichen Kompetenzen wird bereits in der Sekundarstufe I grundgelegt. Dennoch ist es ratsam, sich in Bezug auf die Abiturklausur rechtzeitig mit den strukturierten Kompetenzanforderungen vertraut zu machen. Das erworbene Wissen soll in der Abiturarbeit abgerufen und in verschiedenen Zusammenhängen genutzt werden können. Am Ende der Einführungsphase soll hier das Niveau B1+ nach dem Gemeinsamen Europäischen Referenzrahmen erreicht werden. Im Folgenden werden die wichtigsten Kompetenzen kurz dargestellt.

Abitur 2024

In der Abiturprüfung wird es zwei Prüfungsteile geben:

1. a) Hörverstehen (30 Minuten)
1. b) Sprachmittlung (60 Minuten)
2. Textaufgabe (195 Minuten gA / 225 Minuten eA)

Hörverstehen

Im Abitur 2024 wird es einen Hörverstehensteil geben, der 30 Minuten in Anspruch nehmen wird. Sie sollten dabei imstande sein, wesentliche Inhalte eines authentischen Hörtextes zu verstehen.

Als Material für die Prüfung können Hörvorlagen z. B. aus Radiosendungen, Reden, Interviews oder Gesprächen herangezogen werden. Die Länge der einzelnen Vorlagen wird fünf Minuten in der Regel nicht überschreiten. Das Hörverstehen wird mittels geschlossener und halboffener Aufgabenformate überprüft, denkbar wären also diese Aufgabenformate:
– Multiple Choice (mit drei oder maximal vier Alternativen pro *item*)
– Zuordnungsaufgaben
– Kurzantworten (mit 1–5 Wörtern)
– Gelenktes Notizenfertigen (Vervollständigung von Sätzen, Tabellen, …)
Richtig/Falsch-Fragen zum Ankreuzen wird es nicht geben, die Ratewahrscheinlichkeit wäre zu groß.

TIPP zum Punktesammeln

Wichtig: Sollten Kurzantworten gefordert sein, zählen Rechtschreib- und Grammatikfehler nicht, solange erkennbar ist, was ausgesagt werden soll! Die geforderte Wortzahl ist unbedingt zu beachten!

Die Datei mit den Höraufgaben läuft bis zum Ende, ohne angehalten zu werden. Sie enthält daher auch alle Zeitintervalle, die zum Lesen der Aufgabenstellung benötigt werden. Die Texte werden zweimal angehört.

Um 5 Punkte zu erreichen, müssen 45 % der items richtig gelöst werden, für 11 Punkte mindestens 75 %.

Sprachmittlung (Mediation)

Im Abitur 2024 wird im ersten Prüfungsteil auch die Kompetenz Sprachmittlung geprüft. Hier kommt es darauf an, den Inhalt eines deutschsprachigen Textes sinngemäß, zielgruppengerecht und kontextgebunden in englischer Sprache wiederzugeben. Die entsprechenden Merkmale der geforderten Textsorte müssen beachtet werden. Die Adressatin bzw. der Adressat muss in die Lage versetzt werden, den Text für ihre/seine Zwecke nutzen zu können. Je nach Text kann es sinnvoll sein, kulturelle Besonderheiten zu berücksichtigen, indem man zusätzliche Erläuterungen anfügt. Unbekannte Wörter und Wendungen müssen gegebenenfalls umschrieben und sprachliche Strukturen vereinfacht werden. Die Mediationstexte beziehen sich häufig auf Alltagserfahrungen bzw. kulturelle Besonderheiten aus dem deutschsprachigen Raum.

Sprachmittlung (*mediation*) darf also keinesfalls mit Übersetzung (*translation*) verwechselt werden. Entscheidend ist für die Sprachmittlung allein die korrekte Wiedergabe wesentlicher Inhalte in sprachlich angemessener und idiomatisch richtiger Weise.

Für den Prüfungsteil Sprachmittlung gilt als Bewertungsgrundlage: Der Inhalt wird mit 40 %, die Sprache mit 60 % bewertet.

Bewertung für die Aufgabe zur Sprachmittlung

Diese Übersicht ist ein Auszug aus der Bewertungskala des Niedersächsischen Kultusministeriums.[1]

Punkte	Sprache (60 %)	Inhalt (40 %)
15–13	Die Zielsprache wird nahezu durchgängig korrekt und treffsicher verwendet: – Geringfügige sprachliche Mängel beeinträchtigen die Verständlichkeit nicht. – Thematischer und funktionaler Wortschatz werden idiomatisch und treffend verwendet. Die Darstellung enthält alle durch die Aufgaben geforderten charakteristischen Textmerkmale. Bei der Gestaltung des Textes werden die sprachlichen Anforderungen der Situations- und Adressatenorientierung nahezu vollständig umgesetzt.	– Alle Aspekte der Aufgabenstellung werden beachtet. – Alle im Sinne der Aufgabenstellung wichtigen Informationen werden präzise und situations- bzw. adressatenorientiert wiedergegeben. – Ggf. werden relevante kulturspezifische Erläuterungen präzise formuliert, wie z. B die Erklärung von Eigennamen oder kultur-spezifischen Begriffen. – Die Darstellung und die Gliederung sind klar und logisch.

[1] Niedersächsisches Kultusministerium, ANLAGE 1 Bewertungsskala Sprachmittlung Erlass vom 02.11.2015 – 33-82102-03/15 i. d. F. vom 16.2.2017, https://www.nibis.de/uploads/redriedl/moderne_fremdsprachen/20151102_Erlass%2BAnlage_Moderne_Fremdsprachen.pdf (Zugriff: 01.04.2023, gekürzt)

06–04	Die Zielsprache wird in Teilen korrekt verwendet: – Die sprachlichen Erfordernisse der Aufgabenstellung werden teilweise beachtet und umgesetzt. – Zahlreiche Mängel beeinträchtigen die Verständlichkeit so, dass einzelne Aussagen nicht erfassbar sind. – Thematischer und funktionaler Wortschatz werden nur lückenhaft verwendet. Die Darstellung enthält wenige durch die Aufgabenstellung geforderte charakteristische Textmerkmale. Bei der Gestaltung des Textes werden die sprachlichen Anforderungen der Situations- und Adressatenorientierung in Teilen korrekt umgesetzt.	– Die Aspekte der Aufgabenstellung werden teilweise beachtet. – Wenige im Sinne der Aufgabenstellung wesentlichen Informationen werden wiedergegeben; der Situations- bzw. Adressatenbezug wird nur ansatzweise beachtet. – Die Darstellung und die Gliederung sind in Ansätzen logisch und zusammenhängend.

Schreiben

Ausschlaggebend beim Schreiben ist die sogenannte kommunikative Absicht; es muss deutlich werden, welchem Zweck der Text dienen soll. Es wird erwartet, dass die Schülerinnen und Schüler selbstständig Texte verfassen, die zielgruppengerecht und sinnvoll strukturiert sein sollen. Die Abiturklausur wird aus einer großen Bandbreite möglicher Themen ausgewählt, die sich auf fachliche oder auch persönliche Fragestellungen beziehen können. Hierbei müssen Planungsstrategien, beispielsweise die Mindmap, ebenso bekannt sein wie Vorgehensweisen zur Gliederung, Bearbeitung und kritischen Beurteilung der eigenen Texte. Die Grundlage der schriftlichen Abiturprüfung können auch sogenannte mehrfach kodierte Texte sein. Hierzu zählen zum Beispiel Karikaturen, Bilder, Statistiken oder Diagramme.

Auf die Bewertung der sprachlichen Leistung im Rahmen der sogenannten **integrativen Sprachentwicklung** wird später noch eingegangen (s. S. 126).

Leseverstehen

In der Abiturprüfung 2024 wird es keine Aufgaben zum Leseverstehen geben, da man sich bundesländerübergreifend auf das Aufgabenformat „Sprachmittlung" verständigt hat. Dennoch müssen die erworbenen Kompetenzen auf der Niveaustufe B1+ während der Qualifikationsphase dahingehend erweitert werden, dass das Niveau C1 erreicht wird, um selbstständig einen längeren, anspruchsvolleren fiktionalen oder nichtfiktionalen Text zu verstehen, ihm gezielt Detailinformationen zu entnehmen und unbekanntes Vokabular zu erschließen. Die Arbeit mit einem Wörterbuch muss also beherrscht werden, ebenso wie die unterschiedlichen Arbeitstechniken etwa des intensiven und extensiven Lesens. Sie müssen außerdem in der Lage sein, sprachliche und gestalterische Merkmale eines Textes zu erfassen und somit die Wirkungsweise eines Textes analysieren können.

Den Erschließungstechniken wie *skimming* (globales Leseverstehen, Erkennen der Hauptaussage des Textes), *scanning* (detailliertes, genaues Lesen) und *careful reading* (Suchen nach spezifischen Informationen) kommt dabei große Bedeutung zu. Weiterhin sollten unbekannte Wörter auch ohne Zuhilfenahme eines Wörterbuches erschlossen werden können.

Sprechen

Die Kompetenz „Sprechen" ist für die schriftliche Abiturprüfung ohne Bedeutung. In einer P5-Prüfung (oder mündlichen Nachprüfung im schriftlichen Prüfungsfach) werden hingegen sowohl monologisches als auch dialogisches Sprechen geprüft. Beim monologischen Sprechen muss man über einen Zeitraum von ca. zehn Minuten frei und zusammenhängend über ein vorgegebenes Thema reden, das auf der Grundlage von Prüfungsunterlagen, zumeist einem Text, zu erschließen ist. In der Regel wird zunächst eine kurze Zusammenfassung des Textmaterials erwartet, bevor die weiteren Aufgaben abgearbeitet werden. Hierbei soll laut KC korrekt und flüssig gesprochen werden. Der/Die Schüler/-in soll im anschließenden Prüfungsgespräch zeigen, dass sie/er flexibel und spontan auf die prüfende Person reagieren und eigene Argumente begründen kann.

Insgesamt soll das Prüfungsgespräch so natürlich wie möglich und idiomatisch korrekt geführt werden, wobei der/die Schüler/-in zeigen soll, dass sie/er Verständnisschwierigkeiten in der Zielsprache ausräumen und Wortschatz- und Grammatiklücken überbrücken kann. Die mündliche Prüfung dauert in der Regel mindestens 20 Minuten.

> **INFO** Mündliche Abiturprüfung als Präsentationsprüfung
>
> Innerhalb des Abiturs kann Englisch als mündliches Prüfungsfach gewählt werden (P5). Die Prüfung kann auch als Präsentationsprüfung abgehalten werden. Das Thema der Prüfung wird den Prüflingen von Seiten der Prüfenden vorher mitgeteilt. Die Prüflinge erstellen eine Präsentation zu dem Thema und reichen diese vor dem Prüfungstag ein. Neben der auf Englisch zu haltenden Präsentation erfolgt am Prüfungstag ein längeres Prüfungsgespräch zu dem Prüfungsthema in der Fremdsprache.

Verknüpfung der Themenfelder und Lektüren

Die curricularen Vorgaben für die Oberstufe sehen die Behandlung von **verpflichtenden Themenfeldern** vor, die im jeweiligen Abiturdurchgang durch verpflichtend zu behandelnde Materialien ergänzt werden. Die verpflichtenden Materialien sollen vor einem thematisch breiteren Hintergrund erarbeitet und in diesen eingebettet werden.
Die folgende Übersicht hilft, dies zu veranschaulichen.

Verbindliche Themenfelder für 2024

Auf alle genannten Themenfelder muss im Laufe der vier Semester eingegangen werden. Aufgrund von Corona wurde für das Abitur 2024 entschieden, für das Fach Englisch der Behandlung der verbindlichen Materialien sowie der verbindlichen Unterrichtsaspekte Vorrang vor der Behandlung weiterer Themen der Themenfelder zu geben.

Beliefs, values and norms in society: **Tradition and change** – Britishness – the American experience – postcolonial/neocolonial experiences – migration effects on the world of work	Individual and society – identity – ethnic, cultural and linguistic diversity – gender and sexual diversity	Globalisation – effects on the world of work – impact on personal lives – global responsibility concerning e. g. politics, the environment, economy – English as a global language
Erhöhtes Niveau (eA) **Shakespeare** – the world that made him – modern adaptations	**Die Lektüren/ Materialien müssen mit diesen Themen verknüpft werden.**	**Science and technology** – chances and risks – visions of the future – the media, e. g. the influence of the media on public opinion and personal life – the digital revolution

Das Curriculum ist vor allem auf eine Vernetzung der Themen ausgelegt, wie sie sich durch die jeweiligen literarischen Texte, Sachtexte, Songs, Filme oder Dokumentationen ergibt. Im Folgenden werden die verbindlichen Texte für den Abiturdurchgang 2024 aufgelistet und thematisch verortet, sodass Sie in der Lage sind, die sich anbietenden Vernetzungen nachzuvollziehen. Die jeweiligen Niveaustufen werden mit gA (grundlegendes) und eA (erhöhtes) Anforderungsniveau abgekürzt.

Verbindliche Materialien für 2024

Die Reihenfolge, in der die Materialien behandelt werden, ist nicht festgelegt. Auch gibt es keine feste inhaltliche Bindung der Lektüren an die Themenfelder. Die hier genannten Verknüpfungen sind daher nur Vorschläge.

Material	inhaltliche Schwerpunkte	thematische Verknüpfungen
Autobiographie: Sarfraz Manzoor, *Greetings from Bury Park* (2008)	growing up, (ethnic) identity, Britishness and multicultural Britain	Individual and society
		Beliefs, values and norms in society
		Globalisation

Kurzprosa: Camille Acker, „Cicada" (2018)	ethnic identity, discrimination	Individual and society
		Beliefs, values and norms in society
Nafissa Thompson-Spires, „Fatima, the Biloquist: A Transformation Story" (2018)	ethnic identity, discrimination	Individual and society
		Beliefs, values and norms in society
Film: *Pride* (2014)	coming of age, sexual diversity, tolerance and discrimination	Beliefs, values and norms in society
		Globalisation
Kurzdrama: Jasmine Lee-Jones, *seven methods of killing kylie jenner* (2019/2021)	ethnic identity, the influence of social media on personal life and public opinion	Individual and society
		Science and technology
		Beliefs, values and norms in society
zusätzlich für erhöhtes Anforderungsniveau		
Roman: Ian McEwan, *Atonement* (2001)	Britishness, innocence and guilt, perception(s) of reality	Individual and society
		Beliefs, values and norms in society
Kurzprosa: Nafissa Thompson-Spires, „Heads of the Colored People: Four Fancy Sketches, Two Chalk Outlines, and No Apology" (2018)	ethnic identity, discrimination	Individual and society
		Beliefs, values and norms in society
Kurzprosa: Camille Acker, „Mambo Sauce" (2018)	ethnic identity, discrimination	Individual and society
		Beliefs, values and norms in society
Film: *Boy Erased* (2018)	coming of age, sexual diversity, tolerance and discrimination	Individual and society
		Beliefs, values and norms in society
Drama: William Shakespeare, *Hamlet* (ca. 1600)	fate vs. free will, the role(s) of women, questions of morality	Individual and society
		Shakespeare

Hinweis

Die Lektüren werden in diesem Band an der Stelle thematisiert, an der sie inhaltlich am naheliegendsten zu verorten sind. Grundsätzlich bietet jedes der Materialien verschiedene Zugangsmöglichkeiten an, sodass es unter unterschiedlichen Gesichtspunkten behandelt werden kann.

Basiswissen

Das folgende Kapitel gibt einen Überblick über die curricularen Themenfelder des Oberstufenunterrichts ohne konkrete Semesterzuordnung. Das Ziel dieses Vorgehens ist es, einen Gesamtüberblick über die inhaltlichen Kenntnisse zu bieten, die im Zentralabitur z. B. auch für Hörverstehen und Mediation vorausgesetzt werden. An geeigneten Stellen wird darauf hingewiesen, wie die verbindlichen Lektüren thematisch im größeren Kontext verortet werden können. Die Zuordnung in fünf große Themenfelder entspricht den Vorgaben für das Abitur 2024 (s. S. 14). Fast alle Unterkapitel in diesem Buch entsprechen dem geforderten Basiswissen für beide Jahrgänge. Darüber hinaus wird auf weitere Lektüren, Filme und andere Materialien hingewiesen, die in vorherigen Abiturdurchgängen relevant waren und/oder sich als „Klassiker" zur näheren Auseinandersetzung mit dem Thema eignen.

Beliefs, Values and Norms in Society

Britishness

People outside of Britain often refer to the British as the English – two terms which are often falsely regarded as being synonymous. This stereotypical perception may have its roots in the history of the British Isles as well as the history of the British Empire. Here, the dominance of English culture can certainly still be seen. In the following chapter a general overview will be given with regard to the correct terms to use when speaking of "the British" as well as the main cultural values and norms which have shaped British society.

Common Stereotypes

British people, but in particular the English, are considered to be well-mannered and polite. A common example named in this context is that British people apologise both when they accidentally run into someone and when they are run into. The British are also renowned for their sense of irony and for their small talk, which they usually begin by talking about the weather, especially when they meet someone they don't know. Some consider the English to be snobbish and arrogant but also very hospitable. Both the British and the Irish are famous for their pub culture. More stereotypes could be listed, but being what they are – clichés –, all of them must be carefully examined.

> **TIPP** Further reading
>
> The peculiar ways of the English are humorously depicted in *Watching the English* by Kate Fox (2004), a sociological approach to (stereo)typical English behaviour and "Englishness".

Geographical and Political Distinctions

There are several phrases commonly used to refer to the English-speaking area in Europe. They are explained here.

- **Great Britain:** refers to the main island including England, Scotland and Wales
- **The United Kingdom** (of Great Britain and Northern Ireland): the political term meaning England, Scotland, Wales and Northern Ireland; the terms "Britons" and "The British" are commonly used synonymously to describe the nation and its people
- **Scotland, Wales and Northern Ireland** were and are centrally governed by London but have all gained rights of self-government (S & W: 1999, NI: 2006)
- the **Republic of Ireland:** independent from the United Kingdom since 1921; as a result of the independence treaty, the island of Ireland was divided into Northern Ireland (which still belongs to the UK) and the Republic of Ireland
- The **Commonwealth of Nations** is a political association of 56 member states, nearly all of which are former colonies of the British Empire. The Commonwealth was founded in 1931 and its members share political frameworks, a certain extent of history and the use of English as a main language. Elizabeth's II successor King Charles III is king of 15 member states (known as Commonwealth realms), the rest are republics (36) or have a different monarch (5).

English Cultural Dominance and its Historical Roots

- The **name "England"** is derived from the Angles, a Germanic tribe which settled the island during the 5th and 6th centuries.
- On the island of Great Britain, England gained dominance over Welsh and Scottish territories, which had been settled by Celtic tribes; over the centuries, all three parts of Great Britain became a political union which still bears traits of its cultural diversity (this can be observed in language, cultural heritage and political concessions).
- At the beginning of the 16th century, England gained worldwide influence during the **Age of Discoveries:** English merchants followed the great explorers; English settlers founded colonies in North America and other newly-discovered parts of the world, while the British East India Company set out to exploit the wealth of the newly established Asian colonies economically.
- The growing territorial expansion during the 16th and 17th centuries led to the development of the **British Empire,** which – at its height – included approximately one quarter of the world's land.
- The Empire lost its influence as the former colonies began to seek independence.
- The earliest colonies to obtain independence from Britain were the thirteen northern American colonies, which in 1776 formed the United States of America.
- During the 19th and 20th centuries, most of the other colonies gained independence by peaceful or violent means (the most important ones being India, South Africa, Australia and the Republic of Ireland); some former colonies joined the Commonwealth of Nations – an organisation which promotes trade and cultural relations between its members.

Because of the long history of Britain as the world's ruling colonial power, British culture has influenced societies worldwide. Its cultural effects can be observed in many nations: Australia recognises Queen Elizabeth as Queen of Australia, represented by the Govenor-General; driving on the left is the rule in many former colonies and many still use English as their official language, etc.

On 8 September 2022, Queen Elizabeth II died of old age. Her distinctive rule, marked by international respect, neutrality and adaptiveness, felt timeless. In fact, she acted as a steady unifying force for more than 70 years, a time in which Britain faced multiple fundamental challenges. One of them is its colonial legacy, with its detrimental effects on local economies as well as individual and national traumata persisting to this day. Hence, the Queen's death has been met with international mourning and condolences as well as a surge of criticism addressing her complicit role in an empire built on genocide, slavery and exploitation. An overdue discussion had been prevented so far by Elizabeth II's extended reign and popularity. Her successor, King Charles III, will be struggling to replicate the impact and reputation of her rule. The task of transforming the British monarchy would therefore adversely affect Charles's reign, especially since it will likely require the involvement of politics and many of the traditional institutions of British society.

Democracy and Monarchy

Despite being a monarchy, the United Kingdom has a long history of parliamentary structures; indeed, first attempts to assert popular power date back to the Magna Carta of 1215 and the Bill of Rights of 1689. Britain has no written constitution, and its legislature is based on laws passed by parliament. Parliamentary sovereignty is the leading norm and the monarch accordingly no longer plays an active role in legislative processes. Parliament constitutionally consists of the Crown (the monarch formally heads Parliament), the House of Lords (the aristocracy) and the House of Commons. Parliament, however, is controlled by the Prime Minister and his or her cabinet. The Prime Minister and his or her government have therefore gained the executive powers of the monarch and act in his/her name.

The Issue of Class

Britain is generally considered to be an extremely class-conscious society. The definition of "class" can very generally be put as a distinction in social standing which developed in feudal times and became more diversified during the Industrial Revolution. Social differences can be defined in terms of heritage (aristocratic vs. common birth), educational, professional and financial standing. Class distinctions into upper, middle, lower and, since the Thatcher Era of the 1980s, a new upper and an underclass have their origins in the emergence of new working and entrepreneur classes during the Industrial Revolution.

The British class system is no longer "closed", meaning that it offers chances for upward or downward movement (social mobility). Education or professional success allows members of lower classes to move upwards on the metaphorical "social ladder". Thus, people are no longer bound to the class they were born into.

Class is generally associated with certain stereotypical traits. The various classes differ with regard to habits and attitudes, as can be observed in everyday life, for instance, in where people live, what they eat, the way they dress, spend their free time, which newspapers they read and which TV programmes they watch, which schools their children attend, the vocabulary they use and what accent they speak with. British people are very aware of these class differences.

Class differences are most easily observed in the British educational system, which is still divided into public schools (which are, in fact, privately funded) and state schools. British public schools control admission by means of tuition fees and application procedures, but grants and scholarships can in theory be applied for by anyone. Attending one of these schools is still to some extent a requirement for admission to the so-called "Oxbridge" universities. Thus, social mobility is essentially a matter of financial and educational background.

Britain and the EU

The UK was a member of the EU from 1973 to 2020, but during this period the scepticism of certain political and public circles towards Europe never ceased.

On 23 June 2016, a referendum was held about Britain's membership in the EU: 51.9 % voted to leave the EU, 48.1 % to remain. The UK finally left the EU after long and complex negotiations on 31 January 2020. Brexit is the UK's attempt to break free from unwanted EU rules and regulations in order to re-establish national sovereignty. Its supporters hope the UK will shed what they see as its EU-regulated and hampered shell in order to negotiate free trade agreements with other countries that will provide it with a better economic and social future.

Others fear that there will be significant economic drawbacks, as the UK is no longer a member of the European single market. This may lead to higher prices of goods on both sides of the Channel, despite the new EU-UK Trade and Cooperation Agreement. Another problem is the question of Northern Ireland. The Republic of Ireland is still part of the EU, but the Brexit deal avoids a "hard border" between the Republic and the six counties of Northern Ireland and establishes a de facto customs border between the two islands. This is a major problem for the anti-EU Protestants in Northern Ireland. Peace-threatening conflicts between certain elements in the Republic of Ireland and Northern Ireland have rekindled, though such conflicts had been settled by the Good Friday Agreement in 1998. Brexit has partially aroused feelings of insecurity in Northern Ireland concerning its future. A well-wrought solution to Northern Ireland's special situation is yet to come.

In the Brexit referendum Scotland voted with a significant majority to "remain". Some politicians – and many Scottish people – would now like a second referendum on Scot-

tish independence, i. e. to leave the UK in order eventually to rejoin the EU. This is unlikely, however, to be agreed by the present government in London.
In the course of time, Brexit may turn out to be a success story, but the people's will in the referendum vote was strongly influenced by populist politicians. Many British people do not like the new regulations and consequences of Brexit, as they bring changes for the worse, such as visa requirements, export restrictions, reduced research funding or the UK's withdrawal from the Erasmus study programme.

Internationally, Britain has established a strong connection with US foreign policies (for years it had or has been engaged both in Afghanistan and Iraq), which partly results from its alliance with America during the Second World War and the subsequent formation of NATO. However, unlike former American administrations, which often regarded the United Nations as a weak institution, Britain regards the UN as an important framework for promoting international foreign policy. Like the United States, Britain is a permanent member of the UN Security Council.

Glossary of Common Political Terms (Britain)

administration	Verwaltung (im AE auch: Regierung)
Act (of Parliament)	(verabschiedetes) Gesetz
bill	Gesetzesvorlage
chamber	Kammer (z. B. House of Commons)
checks and balances	Gewaltenteilung (in der Politik)
constituency	Wahlkreis
constituent	Wähler/-in
domestic/foreign policy	Innen-/Außenpolitik
Foreign/Home Secretary	Außen-, Innenminister/-in
election	Wahl
electorate	Wählerschaft
representative	Volksvertreter/-in
MP (Member of Parliament)	Abgeordnete/-r
Speaker	Vorsitzende/-r des Unterhauses
(hereditary, life) peer	(erbliches, lebenslanges) Mitglied des Oberhauses
in office	im Amt
to hold office; to take office	amtieren; ein Amt antreten
to stand down	zurücktreten
universal suffrage	allgemeines Wahlrecht

The American Experience

The United States of America came into being as a reaction to a lack of political influence. As colonies of the British Empire, the original thirteen states, which had been settled by British citizens, had to pay taxes to the motherland. Yet their interests were not represented in parliament; hence the famous slogan "No taxation without representation". Instead of granting their overseas citizens a say in their own affairs, the British crown continued to impose taxes, which led to several uprisings that eventually turned into outright war between the colonies and their motherland. The imbalance of power led the American settlers to declare their independence in 1776. The famous document, originally written by Thomas Jefferson and signed by representatives of the American people (today called the "Founding Fathers"), questioned the rights of the British King, George III, and included the following statement, which would later become the basis of democratic thought and popular emancipation from the ruling aristocracy: "We hold these truths to be self-evident, that all men are created equal, that they are endowed by their Creator with certain unalienable Rights, that among these are Life, Liberty and the pursuit of Happiness."

This concept of equality and equal opportunities became the key to America's self-perception and national identity and led the US to emerge from the War of Independence (1771–1776) as the world's first modern democracy. In its time (and long before the French Revolution), the concept of equality, as expressed in these lines, was revolutionary.

The American Constitution

– written in 1787
– new ideas of a democratic state stated in the **preamble** of the constitution: "We the People of the United States, in Order to form a more perfect Union[1], establish Justice, ensure domestic Tranquility, provide for the common defense, promote the general Welfare, and secure the Blessings of Liberty to ourselves and our Posterity, do ordain and establish this Constitution for the United States of America."

The Bill of Rights

– the first ten amendments to the American Constitution
– written because some delegates feared that the new American government would threaten everyone's chance of achieving personal freedom and the pursuit of happiness
– The First Congress of the United States originally proposed twelve amendments in 1789, ten of which were added to the constitution as a preamble.
– guarantee America's citizens certain unalienable rights, e. g. freedom of religion, freedom of speech and the press as well as the right to bear arms

---

[1] Barack Obama took up the idea of "a more perfect union" in a speech he delivered on 28 May 2008, in which he elaborated on the issues of race and inequality in the USA.

The American Dream / American Nightmare

> **Keyword**
> **"The American Dream":** There is no single definition of what the American Dream actually is, as it varies for each and every American. The term was first used by James Truslow Adams, an American historian, in his book *The Epic of America*, in 1931: "[The] American Dream [is] the dream of a land in which life should be better and richer and fuller for every man, with opportunity for each according to his ability or achievement."

In order to understand how people who had grown up in a monarchy and were used to being subjects of a king or queen could come to the conclusion that they possessed equal rights, one must consider the motives which led the early settlers to leave Britain.

The Puritans, religious values, New Canaan

- The first English settlers to arrive on American soil were religious outcasts, Protestants who had wanted to cleanse the Anglican Church from remaining Roman Catholic influence. These **Puritans**, as they called themselves, were persecuted in England and thus left for the colonies. Other religious sects like the Quakers, Baptists and Methodists followed.
- In September 1620, a group of 102 people left England for America, sailed on a ship called the Mayflower, which arrived 65 days later in a bay they called Plymouth Bay.
- Between 1620 and 1640 thousands of Puritans emigrated to New England and founded the first settlements in Plymouth and Massachusetts Bay. To them, America was God's promised land, a **"New Canaan"**, a reference to the biblical country to which Moses led his people to free them from slavery in Egypt. In America the Puritans hoped they would be able to follow their religious beliefs and live freely.
- Puritan values such as integrity, virtue, the right to education, individual freedom and communitarianism still constitute central aspects of American self-perception.
- At the same time, the Puritans imposed strict moral rules on their communities, and today "Puritan" is a term associated with extreme conservatism and prudishness.

American values and beliefs

The key to the image of the United States as the country of unlimited opportunities, where each and every person can turn from "dishwasher to millionaire", from rags to riches, lies in these early visions of individual freedom, opportunity and self-reliance which led millions to emigrate to the former British colonies. These ideals shape the American Dream, which is not one single concept but a combination of individual goals and general values.

- **Individualism/self-reliance:** The underlying belief is that everyone is responsible for their own fate and has the liberty to determine their way of life.
- **Opportunity:** If a person is given the chance to take matters into his or her own hands, he or she will prosper. If that person fails, however, he or she has not worked hard enough.

- **Freedom:** This has two faces. On the one hand, it allows all individuals to pursue their own vision of happiness without being controlled by a central government. On the other, this belief also led to a general scepticism towards any kind of federal interference in individual affairs. Even today, Americans still tend to be sceptical of decisions made by the central administration in Washington, D.C., suspecting it of limiting their communal, state or personal rights.
- **Community:** Individual hardships such as unemployment are seen as personal failures, yet the local communities readily offer help to those in need. Because of this communal spirit, federal programs of social welfare and common health care often meet with opposition as they are seen as an intrusion into personal rights.

The American Dream is still alive, and each year many people come to the United States to pursue it, although the number of people able to obtain a "green card" has always been limited and many immigrants today arrive illegally. After the original settlement period, the main waves of immigration entered the US between the middle of the 19th until the beginning of the 20th century, when the United States was in need of workers and a sufficient number of people to settle new territories in the west. Millions of mostly European immigrants arrived at Ellis Island, New York, were inspected and continued on to the city of New York and later to places across the entire country. German immigrants, for example, settled mostly in the Midwest, as can still be observed when looking at city names on a map.

The first thing many immigrants saw when they came by ship to New York City during the 19th and the first half of the 20th century, was the Statue of Liberty, which is located on Liberty Island.

The Statue of Liberty

- given to the USA as a gift by France in 1886 to celebrate the first 100 years of American independence from Britain (the centennial)
- a robed woman, holding a lighted torch in her right and a tablet in her left hand, showing the date of the Declaration of Independence (4 July 1776)
- underneath her right foot the remains of broken shackles can be seen
- one of the most famous American icons, symbolising enlightenment, independence, liberty and freedom
- the theme of Emma Lazarus's famous poem "The New Colossus" (1883), which can be seen on a bronze plaque inside the statue

Ellis Island

- the place where most immigrants first set foot on American soil
- an island of hopes but also an island of tears for a number of immigrants, as some of them were detained there for legal or medical reasons or even sent back to their home countries; for the majority the gateway to a new – better – life
- a federal immigration station from 1892 to 1954

The American Dream today

- A growing number of people regard the American Dream as an illusion, as not everyone has access to the opportunities usually associated with it.
- Examples of American nightmares include the Vietnam War, 11 September 2001, the financial crisis starting in 2008 and the storming of the Capitol on 6 Janury 2021.

The Frontier Experience

Since its independence in 1776, the country had continually acquired larger territories to the west. To put it simply, both the Pacific and the Atlantic coast had been settled and explored, yet the middle of the vast continent was still mostly open territory which remained unknown. The fringe between the settled and unknown territories, more commonly called the "Wild West", not only refers to the geographical border between wilderness and civilisation but also to the social and political aspects which characterised these areas.

The **westward movement** of the early settlers was not a federally organised enterprise. Instead, the federal government simply assigned the right to obtain land in the west to people who were willing to take on the challenge of discovering these unknown lands. While the **pioneers** moved westward in covered wagons, law enforcement and legal order were slow to follow. This left the frontier zone, which was already inhabited by the Native American tribes, in a state both of lawlessness and seemingly unlimited opportunity. This sense of entitlement, combined with the idea of Manifest Destiny (see below), led to the brutal treatment of the Native Americans. The Indigenous nations were taken full economic advantage of, often via Christian missionaries and by fostering alcoholism. From the early 19th century onward, Native tribes were forced to relocate from their ancestral homelands reservations (most notably, "Trail of Tears").

The Turner Thesis (1893)

Frederick Jackson Turner defined the "frontier experience" as the key which determined the American belief in freedom and unlimited opportunities. The abundance of land in the west and the experience of unlimited space provided the psychological basis for the American conviction that anything can be achieved. Once the west had been explored, the US sought to overcome new frontiers. Thus, the frontier experience was later also considered an explanation for American endeavours to overcome frontiers in a much broader sense (be it in areas of technological advancement or by landing on the moon).

Manifest Destiny

The term "Manifest Destiny" was coined by the American journalist John L. O'Sullivan in 1839.

- stands for the belief that America is the one nation ordained by God to expand across the North American continent
- according to John L. O'Sullivan: "[America is] the nation of progress, of individual freedom, of universal enfranchisement"; according to him, the American people had

been chosen "to establish on earth the moral dignity and salvation of man – the immutable truth and beneficence of God."[2]
- America = a country that is superior to all other countries
- stresses the virtue of the American people, as they are the ones to establish moral rules and values across the globe; American patriotism is deeply rooted in the concept of "Manifest Destiny"

A picture that illustrates the idea of the "Manifest Destiny" is the allegorical representation of the new west in the painting *The American Progress* by John Gast (1872).

The US as a World Power

The United States of America became the foremost world power after the end of the Cold War with the Soviet Union. Because of once having been a colony ruled by a foreign nation, it chose to stay out of global politics for over a century. Its involvement in two world wars in the first half of the 20th century led to a change in its foreign policy from isolationism to interventionism.

When, after WW II, the US and its allies found themselves in a worldwide struggle for influence and power with the Soviet Union, the American ideal of freedom and democracy turned into an outright ideology opposing the communist system. In 1947, President Truman formulated the so-called **Truman Doctrine,** which would define US foreign policy: Truman stated that it was "the policy of the United States to support free peoples who are resisting attempted subjugation by armed minorities or by outside pressure". The main aim of the US in the years 1947–1989 was to restrict the expansion of the Soviet Union. This period also shaped post-Cold War US policy and led it to develop new concepts of preemptive intervention to protect its national security (as in the wars in Afghanistan and Iraq). The key to American foreign policy is its self-image as a nation offering the promise of freedom and democracy; a promise whose roots lay in the concept of Manifest Destiny (see p. 24 f.).

US foreign policy has repeatedly been criticised as being hypocritical in the sense that the nations and peoples the US military supposedly sought to set free from oppressors were then in fact subjected to American interests. Indeed, some overt and covert international interventions, especially in Central and South America and the Middle East, can be seen as mainly motivated by commercial interests and matters of national security (by securing natural resources, controlling the influx of drugs into the US, etc.) rather than the altruistic aspiration of bringing peace and democracy.

From a German perspective, however, the role of the US and its allies during the Second World War must be considered as that of a liberator without whom our nation might never have grown to become an internationally accepted democracy.

---

[2] Source: John L. O'Sullivan, "The Great Nation of Futurity," *The United States Democratic Review*, Volume 6, Issue 23, pp. 426–430.

Glossary of Common Political Terms (USA)

amendment (to the constitution)	Zusatzerklärung zu der Verfassung; die ersten zehn *amendments* sind in der *Bill of Rights* verfasst
constitution	Verfassung
unalienable/inalienable rights	unveräußerliche Rechte
civil rights movement	Bürgerrechtsbewegung
Declaration of Independence	Unabhängigkeitserklärung
equality, emancipation	Gleichheit, Befreiung/Emanzipation
freedom (of speech, of the press, religious freedom)	(Rede-, Presse-, Religions-) Freiheit
from rags to riches	Redewendung: vom Tellerwäscher zum Millionär
the Founding Fathers	die Gründungsväter, die Unterzeichner der Unabhängigkeitserklärung
"In God we trust"	offizieller Wahlspruch der USA: „Wir vertrauen auf Gott."
the Promised Land the land of milk and honey God's own country the New Canaan	das gelobte Land das Land, in dem Milch und Honig fließen Gottes eigenes Land das neue Kanaan alles Bezeichnungen für Nordamerika (später die USA)
pioneer	Pionier
pioneer spirit	Pioniergeist
pursuit of happiness	das Streben nach Glück
to attain self-fulfilment	sich selbst verwirklichen
success	Erfolg
failure	Misserfolg, Versagen
to pledge allegiance to the flag	den Fahneneid leisten Ausdruck des amerikanischen Patriotismus, wird u. a. in Schulen an offiziellen Feiertagen gesprochen: "I pledge allegiance to the flag of the United States of America, and to the Republic for which it stands, one nation under God, indivisible, with liberty and justice for all."
to prosper	Erfolg haben, gedeihen
to settle	(be)siedeln
settler	Siedler
settlement	Siedlung

to be persecuted	verfolgt werden
religious/political persecution	religiöse/politische Verfolgung
to immigrate	einwandern
immigrant	Einwandernde/-r
immigration	Einwanderung
influx of immigrants	Zustrom von Einwandernden
Immigration Act	Einwanderungsgesetz
multiculturalism	Multikulturalität
naturalisation	Einbürgerung
assimilation	Assimilation, Angleichung an Bestehendes

Postcolonial/Neocolonial Experience

This chapter will outline the main aspects of two issues:
- How did Great Britain influence other nations as an empire? What consequences does its role as a former empire have for the UK?
- What consequences does its role as a former colony have for the US? How does its society deal with its minorities?

Keywords

Postcolonialism: term first used in the middle of the 20th century; refers to the time after the British had left the colonies, i. e. after their formal rule over the colonies had come to an end

The withdrawal of the British often caused fresh complications or laid bare problems they sowed during their rule. Many countries thus faced difficulties in setting up a functioning government. In addition, political independence did not necessarily lead to economic independence.

The Commonwealth: a group of 56 states; many former British colonies joined at the end of the decolonisation process; aims at racial equality and national sovereignty; British Queen is head of the Commonwealth

---

From Empire to Commonwealth

- At the beginning of the 17th century, Britain started to expand its empire worldwide.
- In most cases, the British colonisers ruled with brutal force, seizing land at will, ending rebellion in bloodshed, causing widespread famine as well as implementing slavery and exterminating whole ethnic groups.
- After the Second World War the British Empire changed rapidly.
- Most British colonies had become independent from Britain by 1970, but a large number of them stayed closely connected with their former coloniser by joining the Commonwealth.
- While the British ruled the colonies, they regarded their culture, values, traditions and language as superior to those of the colonised. Cultural identities and boundaries were thus often disrespected.
- Now, after independence, they faced the difficult task of recreating their own identity, bridging the gap between their country's native traditions and values and British ones.
- As people from member countries of the Commonwealth were allowed to emigrate to Britain, many people did so in the second half of the 20th century. First they were welcomed, as workers were needed after the Second World War, but in the 1970s, when more and more workers faced unemployment because of the economic crisis, immigration came to be seen more critically.
- Much postcolonial writing – both from the former colonies and Britain – deals with the issue of being caught between two cultures or of trying to find one's identity.

Minorities in the UK

Nationalisation and Immigration Acts

Imperial Act (1914): People from the colonies were given British citizenship.

British Nationality Act (1948): New status of Citizen of the United Kingdom and Colonies (CUKC) came into effect for those living within the Commonwealth. This preserved their existing status as British subjects whilst allowing them national citizenship of their own country of origin. However, this did not apply to countries that had gained independence by that date.

Immigration Act (1962, 1971): These acts, passed to counter increasing immigration, tightened the law on immigration of British subjects from other parts of the Commonwealth. Immigrants had to prove strong links to the UK (partiality) in order to be allowed to live and work in Britain.

British Nationality Act (1981): Today's nationality law differentiates between several forms of citizenship, in particular for those living in the overseas territories. Only those with British citizenship and some Commonwealth citizens are still automatically entitled to reside in the United Kingdom.

- About 12.4 % of the population in the UK were born abroad (2013). The non-UK born population decreased from 9.4 million in 2017 to 9.2 million in 2020, and the non-British population decreased from 6.2 million to 6.0 million. Poland remains the most common non-UK country of birth, taking over from India in 2015 (which reflected longer-term migration trends); Polish has been the most common non-British nationality in the UK since 2007.[3]
- Between the 1960s and 1980s, many Indians, Pakistanis and Bangladeshis immigrated to Britain. They now form the largest immigrant communities.
- Many of them settled in the Midlands or in towns in Lancashire, Yorkshire and Strathclyde, where they worked, for example, in the textile industry.
- The highest percentage of ethnic minorities can be found in the London area.
- In recent years, the UK has constantly tightened its laws on immigration.
- The main immigrant groups to Britain – from India, Pakistan, the Caribbean, Africa, Southeast Asia and Eastern Europe – differ widely in culture, religion and language.
- **Ethnic diversity** enriches Britain, not only when it comes to music, fashion and food.
- Many embrace the opportunities and advantages of ethnic diversity (such as the former Foreign Secretary Robin Cook, who said that chicken tikka masala " is now a true British national dish"[4]).
- Others fear that "Britishness" will eventually be lost; they interpret multiculturalism as meaning that various cultures coexist peacefully but without having a common basis of shared values.

[3] Source: https://www.ons.gov.uk/peoplepopulationandcommunity/populationandmigration/internationalmigration/bulletins/ukpopulationbycountryofbirthandnationality/2017 (accessed on 1 April 2023)

[4] Source: https://www.theguardian.com/world/2001/apr/19/race.britishidentity (published on 19 April 2001, accessed on 1 April 2023)

- **Second-generation immigrants,** i. e. children born to parents who immigrated to Britain prior to (or shortly after) their children's birth, faced and still face a variety of problems:
  - They often experience a clash of cultures. Outside their parents' home they adopt a western lifestyle similar to that of their friends and classmates. At home, however, they live according to values, beliefs and traditions typical of their parents' home countries, which many of these children and teenagers have never visited. Quite often they do not speak their parents' language any more either. For some, the transition between these two different lifestyles is not easy.
  - They face difficulties when it comes to living up to the expectations of their parents, friends, teachers, etc.
  - They often have to face discrimination and overt racism.
  - According to a 2007 poll, about a third of British Asians felt it necessary to "act and think white" in order to fit into British society. About the same number did not feel British but believed they needed to be a "coconut", meaning to be "brown on the outside but white on the inside"[5].
  - Therefore, defining one's identity and becoming confident in both cultures has been a central issue for most second-generation immigrants.

Today, the third or fourth generation slowly but surely become more integrated into British society and have arrived in British politics and public positions like the mayor of London Sadiq Khan.

The large number of immigrants from the EU, mostly coming from Eastern Europe after the opening of the borders in 2004 and subsequent years, have had less problems to adapt to British society. However, their existence in Britain remains the subject of public scrutiny and was one reason for the Brexit vote in the 2016 referendum. In 2023, it is still unclear what their status in Britain will be in the future.

In literature, this clash of cultures is portrayed most prominently by British writers such as Hanif Kureishi, Farrukh Dhondy, Zadie Smith and Salman Rushdie.

Keyword

Postcolonial / New English Literature: the literature which deals with the consequences of the British Empire is called postcolonial literature or New English literature. Its authors reflect their nations' history as parts of the former British Empire and the role of the individual in these contexts.

The main issues which are addressed in postcolonial literature are: social and cultural changes/conflicts, exploitation and the misuse of power, cultural alienation and integration of the individual torn between the values of the former colonisers and his or her traditional values and beliefs.

---

[5] Source: BBC poll, http://news.bbc.co.uk/2/hi/uk_news/6921534.stm (published 30 July 2007, accessed on 1 April 2023)

Examples of Postcolonial Societies: India, Australia, South Africa and Pakistan

At its height, the British Empire encompassed about a quarter of the world's land mass and dominated its crown colonies politically, economically and culturally. One must distinguish two types of colonies:

- those which were mainly colonised by the British and which had a relatively small indigenous population (such as Australia); these are sometimes referred to as the "white" colonies
- those colonies with a large indigenous population (such as India).

The decline of the British Empire resulted from internal demands for more independence from the British crown (the earliest colonies to leave were those in North America, see page 21). In most cases this progression from colonial rule to independence was achieved peacefully. But in those countries with a large indigenous population, the way to independence was often paved with rebellion and violent conflict. In the following, the route to independence of four former colonies of the British Empire will be described briefly.

India

India became independent in 1947 and was the first non-white colony to gain complete independence from Britain.

- British influence in India started as early as the 16th century with the founding of the British East India Company. Because of its spices, cotton and tea, India was mainly a trading colony.
- 1858: The British Crown took over the areas ruled by the British East India Company, and in 1876 Queen Victoria became Empress of India. The time of British rule is also called the "Raj" (Hindu for "reign").
- 15 August 1947: The Indian Empire became independent but was divided into the Union of India and the Dominion of Pakistan.

The case of India is unique in the way it gained complete independence from the British Empire at a rather early date and by non-violent means. In India, the British rulers were by far in the minority, and dissatisfaction with British rule led to a national independence movement headed by Mahatma Gandhi. At first, he demanded equal civil rights for Indians in their own country and accused the British government of mistreatment and oppression of the Indian people. Gandhi's struggle sparked a nationwide independence movement. His key to achieving independence was the revolutionary concept of civil disobedience. Being in the majority, the Indians were able to halt all social and economic life by simply refusing to comply with the British. Gandhi's aim was to achieve independence by non-violent means. After many years of struggle and several years spent in prison, Gandhi achieved his goal. Being unable to rule the country any longer, the British complied with India's demand for independence and thus lost one of their most important colonies.

Gandhi's concept of non-violent resistance became a role-model for other leaders of oppressed peoples and minorities. Leaders like Nelson Mandela (in South Africa) and Martin Luther King (in the US) considered him to be their inspiration to fight peacefully for racial equality and civil rights.

Australia

– dominion status in 1901, formally independent in 1931
– Australia's eastern half was claimed by the British in 1770 and most of the original settlers were prisoners shipped from England to the colony of New South Wales, which was founded in 1788.
– Australia's history as a penal colony for Britain resulted from the fact that the country was relatively poor in resources and from the overflow of criminals in British prisons.
– The Australians did not seek independence from Britain by violent means and indeed kept close political and constitutional ties to the United Kingdom until the last century. Australia gained the rights to self-government in 1901 and is a fully independent nation today although the British Queen is formally still head of state; she is represented by the govenor-general of Australia.
– Most of the Australian population is white and of European descent (mostly British and Irish), but after World War II, Australia opened its borders to immigrants and experienced a large influx of nationals from Europe and Asia. Today, nearly two out of seven Australians were born overseas.

Keyword
The Aboriginals / The Stolen Generation(s): Australia's Aboriginals (or: Aborigines) settled the continent 40,000 years ago. Their number was comparatively small, and the white settlers regarded the indigenous people as inferior and barbaric. Their semi-nomadic way of life and the absence of large settlements made it easy for the settlers to take away their land in order to build their own settlements and farms and raise cattle. The Aboriginals found it increasingly difficult to maintain their traditional way of life. For centuries to come they were oppressed and discriminated against by the white population. This oppression reached its climax in the racist ideology which led to the implementation of a child removal programme executed between about 1880 and 1960. This state-supported programme allowed the abduction of Aboriginal children from their families, supposedly to protect them from bad living conditions. These children were put under church or social care and raised according to white values and traditions, thus eradicating the indigenous traditions. It is estimated that more than 100,000 children were put under such guardianship. Not until 2008 did the Australian government, headed by Prime Minister Kevin Rudd, apologise for these actions, and several redress schemes were initiated by the Australian government to compensate those taken from their families.

South Africa

- after 1750: first German and Boer (Dutch) settlements, combined with a first wave of expulsion/enslavement of indigenous peoples
- 1814: British colony; conflict with Boer settlers, resulting in "Great Trek" of Dutch settlers in order to find their own lands; conflict with indigenous Zulu population
- 1880–1902: Anglo-Boer Wars over Boer independence
- 1910: South Africa given dominion status; independence and limited self-governance as Union of South Africa
- 1931: complete independence from Britain
- 1948: beginning of apartheid, giving white minority power over Black population
- 1961: South Africa becomes a republic
- early 1990s: dismantling of apartheid (key figures: Archbishop Desmond Tutu and future president Nelson Mandela)
- present challenges: unrest, corruption, crime, sexual violence, police brutality
- post-apartheid issues:
  - highly unequal society with respect to wealth and income distribution as well as access to jobs, social services and land ownership
  - limited access to education and high unemployment for people of colour

Pakistan

Pakistan is a country located in South Asia, with a current population of over 230 million people. The majority of Pakistan's population is Muslim (96,5 %), with Sunni Islam being the dominant. However, there are also significant minority communities of Hindus, Christians, Sikhs and others. The country has two official languages: Urdu and English, but there are also many regional languages spoken throughout the country such as Punjabi (39 %), Pashto (18 %), Sindhi (15 %) and Saraiki (12 %). Pakistan is a parliamentary federal republic, with a president as head of state and a prime minister who is the head of government. The country has faced political instability and military rule throughout its history.

Pakistan was formerly part of the British Indian Empire, ruled over by the East India Company as a sovereign power for the British crown. It gained independence in 1947, following a movement led by Muslim leaders who wanted a separate homeland for Muslims in South Asia. Pakistan abolished its monarchy in 1956 while remaining in the Commonwealth. The separation from India and the creation of Pakistan was a traumatic and violent process, which led to the displacement and migration of millions of people. The country has since faced numerous challenges, including conflicts with neighboring India, political instability, economic struggles and ongoing security threats from extremist groups. While Pakistan's history as a British colony has influenced its political and cultural development, the country has also retained its own unique identity and traditions. Today, Pakistan remains a complex and diverse country with a rich cultural heritage and a vibrant, dynamic population. Some of the country's most famous cultural exports include music, poetry and cuisine.

Sarfraz Manzoor, *Greetings from Bury Park* (gA)

A note on the author

Sarfraz Manzoor is a British writer, journalist and broadcaster. He was born in Pakistan, grew up in Luton, England, and later studied journalism. Manzoor is known for his work exploring themes of identity, culture and social justice, particularly in relation to the British Pakistani experience. He has written for a variety of publications and has also worked extensively in television and radio. Sarfraz's memoir *Greetings from Bury Park* was the basis for the 2019 film *Blinded by the Light.*

Synopsis

Sarfraz Manzoor's autobiography *Greetings from Bury Park* explores themes of identity, culture, religion and family. Manzoor was born in Pakistan but raised in the town of Luton, England, where he grew up as a British Pakistani Muslim. The book begins with his childhood, which is marked by Thatcherism and the racial tensions and economic decline of 1980s Britain, e. g. fuelled by E. Powell's "Rivers of Blood" speech, following protests and acts of discrimination. Manzoor struggles with a sense of cultural dislocation as he feels torn between his Pakistani heritage and his British environment. He also deals with the tensions that arise from generational conflicts (especially with his father) and navigates multiple cultural identities. Manzoor finds solace in music and particularly the songs of Bruce Springsteen. Throughout the book, he reflects on the challenges and joys of growing up as a British Pakistani Muslim in a society that often views him as an outsider.

Analysis

In his autobiography, Manzoor functions as author, narrator and protagonist, making the narrative insightful but highly subjective. As the title (*Greetings from Bury Park* alludes to Bruce Springsteen's first album, *Greetings from Asbury Park*) and the quotes at the beginning of each chapter illustrate, Manzoor's love of Springsteen's music serves as a central thread throughout the narrative. After befriending Amolak, his "blood brother", he becomes obsessed, not only because Springsteen shares their experience of an emotionally distant and strict father figure but also because his lyrics speak to the two boys' sense of longing and belonging within the struggles of everyday, blue-collar life. Springsteen's music becomes a way to communicate and connect with others, to bridge cultural divides and to find meaning in life in **multicultural Britain** and beyond. This is especially evident in Manzoor's friendship with Amolak, since they never speak explicitly about their feelings but by talking about Springsteen's songs instead. Consequently, music serves as a catalyst for self-discovery and personal growth, and Manzoor's love of music is a testament to the power of art to inspire and transform.

Another important theme is the tension between **tradition and modernity,** highlighted by the relationships and (first- and second-generation immigrants') conflicts within Manzoor's family, most of whom adhere more closely to traditional Pakistani values. He describes how only the boys have the advantage of an advanced education, while the role of women remains not to be selfish but to work and marry instead, and how his older brother shoulders the entire family's responsibilities after his father's death. Eventually, Manzoor comes to realise that the other family members paid a price for his freedom. **Growing up**, he struggles to reconcile his desire for independence and self-determination with the expectations of his family and community, especially his father. However, over time, they all learn to accept and respect each other's differences, demonstrating the enduring love and resilience of family relationships, especially during times of hardship (e.g. Rasool's stroke, Mohammed's death). Ultimately, Manzoor's decision to marry Bridget, a non-Pakistani, non-Muslim English woman, represents a rejection of tradition and a commitment to forging his own path.

Manzoor grapples with his individual relationship with Islam and his family's expectations around religious practice. He considers himself "comfortably British, occasionally Pakistani, and only technically Muslim" and only abides to some of the most principal religious practices. While is mother regards religion as important, teaching him Arabic and the Qur'an, his father identifies more as a Pakistani than as a Muslim. Thus, Manzoor's experiences as a British Pakistani Muslim reflect the broader challenges of navigating religious identity in a multicultural society, which intensify after the terrorist acts of 9/11 and the London bombings on 7 July 2005. However, the book also highlights the power of religion to provide a sense of meaning, purpose and community for Manzoor and his family.

Additionally, the autobiography is infused with a sense of longing for America, which Manzoor considers a magical land of freedom and opportunity. From an early age, he immerses himself in books, travel guides, documentaries and TV shows of and from the US. He also follows its politics, witnessing American life shaped by people like John F. Kennedy, Martin Luther King, Malcom X and Rosa Parks as well as by the Black Civil Rights Movement and the Freedom Riders. As there were no British Pakistanis advocating better conditions and less discrimination in the UK, Manzoor adopts King and Malcolm X as role models instead.

Growing up, Manzoor feels unable to identify as wholly British or wholly Pakistani. Although experiences of open and indirect racism shape his entire life and the political realities (e.g. the "Rivers of Blood" speech) make it impossible for him to feel welcome, this feeling of confusion gradually changes with the rise of "Cool Britannia" (a slogan associated with the second half of the 1990s, describing the spread of British pop culture and its icons such as Oasis, the Spice Girls and David Beckham), New Labour (a political philosophy spearheaded by Tony Blair advocating welfare, social justice and equality) and the 1996 UEFA cup. Eventually, he realises that his current life and its opportunities were mostly formed by the UK. This acceptance of his **Britishness** represents a significant turning point in his life, as he takes control of his own destiny and embraces not only his Pakistani roots but also his British **identity**. However, with his father deceased and his mother becoming older, the direct link to Pakistan slowly weakens. To counter this, Manzoor writes his autobiography as a "keeper of memories, the teller of stories", to ensure a sense of origin for his own daughters.

Migration and the World of Work

Human migration means that people move from one place to another. They do this temporarily or permanently. In the history of mankind, migration has been an evolutionary necessity, as in the hunter and gatherer societies, where people were nomadic and were always looking for better places to find food, to hunt and find shelter. Freedom of mind as well as better work opportunities have always been driving factors of migration, as in 19th century immigration to the US.

Today, in a more or less fixed system of states with state borders, migration is still a huge factor in the development of a society, but in increasingly wide sections of society – especially in right-wing and nationalist political groupings –, it is also seen very critically (cf. the reference to Enoch Powell's "Rivers of Blood" speech in *East is East*).

In addition to the post-WW II migration to the UK from its former colonies, the past two decades, after Poland and nine other countries joined the EU in 2004, have seen a huge influx of people from Eastern Europe. People from the new EU member states have been more willing to do unskilled and low-paid jobs than their British counterparts. This has caused a political debate in Britain and can be seen as one of the many reasons for some people to favour Brexit. As this is a world of large economic differences, i.e. the so-called North-South divide, migration will remain one of the problems of our times, with societies that are better off facing huge numbers of refugees from poorer countries until a certain measure of equality is reached.

In the US, migration has been the driving factor of the nation's creation. However, attitudes towards migration differ with regard to countries of origin. The southern border of the US has been the subject of fierce political debate for a long time, as a lot of immigrants from Mexico and other Latin American countries cross this border, many of them illegally. The discussion about the so-called "dreamers" (sons and daughters of illegal immigrants to the US – the term probably originates in the abbreviation of the name of a piece of 2001 legislation) was particularly fuelled by former President Donald Trump.

Individual and Society

The following chapter will focus on the various facets of identity – both ethnic/cultural and personal identity. How does identity affect a person's position in society?
Central issues to be tackled are:
- the different roles an individual might assume and the potential conflicts between those roles;
- the connection between one's biologically determined sex and the largely socially defined gender of a person;
- minorities and outsiders.

> **Keywords**
>
> **Individual:** The term derives from the Latin "indivisible" and commonly refers to an individual subject, i. e. a person, who can be distinguished from his or her surroundings. As such, the individual has to position himself or herself vis-à-vis the society in which they are living. The relationship between the individual and his or her society can be difficult if the former comes into conflict with the latter's norms and values.
>
> **Society:** This term refers to a collective of individuals united e. g. by a shared territory, history or ways of living and thinking. In order to be effective and not to fall prey to anarchy, societies are organised according to a set of rules and regulations which can even overrule the interests of the individual for the sake of the community.

Roles and Role Conflicts

- While the individual was traditionally believed to be a unified "whole", the concept of the different roles of a person underlines the fact that one does not just have **one** single identity but actually has to fulfil a number of different roles in different situations and contexts.
- A social role consists of a certain pattern of behaviour, of rights but also of obligations. Social roles are performed in **interaction** with other persons. Roles are mostly to be seen in relation to others (child – parent; teacher – student).
- Whether one's behaviour is in line with one's particular role can be judged by society's **expectations** of that role.
- If an individual shows forms of behaviour that are considered **inappropriate** for the social role in question, he or she may have to face various forms of **punishment** (ranging from being made aware of one's improper behaviour to actual punishment); if the behaviour in question is deemed **appropriate**, there will, in return, be **rewards** from society.
- A role (e. g. doctor, teacher, bus driver) can be **achieved** by or **ascribed** to an individual (e. g. child).

– In certain situations, a person can be faced with a **conflict** between contrasting roles which he or she should take on at the same time. Thus, if a mother happens to be her own child's teacher, she would be expected to be simultaneously strict towards the child in her role as teacher and loving in her role as mother.

Gender Identity and Diversity

A central component of an individual's identities is their[1] **gender**. Unlike the biologically determined **sex** (male/female), **gender** and **gender role** (such as masculine and feminine) are often perceived as being social constructs. Accordingly, a society holds a set of certain stereotypical ideas about how a "real" woman and a "real" man should behave, what they should look like but also what they are capable of.

Traditionally, men are thought of as masculine, strong, rational and powerful, while women are considered to be feminine, weak, emotional and submissive. These assumed characteristics have also been used as a "justification" for men's dominant role in society. With the advent of the Feminist Movement in the 1960s, the validity of conventional gender roles was called into question.

However, the media in particular still present largely conservative images of "typical" men and women, thereby keeping these concepts alive. If a person does not conform to the gender role associated by his or her society with his or her sex, he or she may have to face resentment. Even in the comparatively tolerant Western societies, particularly "masculine" women and "feminine" men are not universally accepted.

However, concepts surrounding sexual diversity have been extended. The word „transgender" is generally seen as an umbrella term for people whose gender identity and expression might vary from cultural expectations based on the sex they were assigned at birth. „Non-binary", on the other hand, refers to a person that does not identify exclusively as a man or a woman or identifies completely outside these categories.

The aim of gender diversity is to represent people of different genders in a fair way. This concerns mostly men and women and their ratio in companies, politics or other fields of life. Traditionally, men have dominated many areas of public life such as politics, engineering, science, medicine or computing. Gender diversity has been widely discussed but progress towards having less male and more female company directors – and indeed bosses in many walks of life – has been slow.

However, after the feminist and post-feminist debates of the past decades, discussions about gender have recently become more open, including transgender and non-binary people. This has meant that more people have had the courage to come out with their particular sexuality or their gender identity.

---

[1] In English-language texts, the pronouns „he"/"she" and their possessives „his"/"her"/"hers" are often substituted with „they" and „their"/"theirs" in order to avoid attributing a gender.

Pride (gA)

Synopsis

Directed by Matthew Warchus, the film *Pride* was released in 2014 as a historical co-medy-drama. It tells the true story of Mark Ashton and a group of LGTBQ activists who raised money for miners financially affected by the UK miners' strike in 1984.

Joe Cooper takes the train to London to celebrate his birthday. After his arrival, he runs into Gay Pride where he meets activist Mark Ashton. He and his group are marching in the parade not only on behalf of gay rights, but also on behalf of economic equality and the miners, whose strike is taking place at that time. Mark spontaneously arranges a bucket collection for the miners, to great success. He then founds "Lesbians and Gay Support the Miners (LGSM)" because he believes that the gay movement might benefit from establishing solidarity with the miners. However, the group's first attempt to donate the money to the union is turned down because of their sexual orientation. Mark's friends feel confirmed in their skepticism towards the miners since many of them have been bullied by them back home. But when Mark and his group decide to give their donations directly to the small mining village Onllwyn in Wales, a member of the committee finally accepts the funds. The resulting newspaper story leads The National Union of Miners to decline LGSM's support because they feel that the story humiliated them but also because they want the strike to come to an end. Frustrated, Mark abandons LGSM. Joe comes out to his family, but because of their prejudiced beliefs, they try to keep him away from the group. At the same time, Mark finds out that one of his former lovers is dying of AIDS. In March 1985, the strike ends and the miners of Onllwyn take up their work again. When he sees the news, Joe sneaks out his parents' house to show solidarity in Onllwyn and is immediately confronted by Mark about hiding his sexual orientation from his parents. During the following Gay Pride Parade, Mark apologises in front of the group for abandoning the cause and leads LGSM to the parade. Soon they are joined by miners who came to march in solidarity.

Analysis

The issue of **sexual diversity** is clearly outlined in the movie. While gender roles are defined in a traditional way in the miners' community (men in the pits, women at home), they are not so clearly defined within the gay community. Also, the women of LGSM resist patriarchal structures and form an exclusively lesbian group in order to fight not only for gay but also for feminist rights. With respect to sexuality, LGSM members are also more open, tolerant and equal in contrast to the miner's community, where sexual intercourse is seen as a male right while women are simply expected to tolerate it.

The exploration of (sexual) identity is also central to the films discussion of **coming of age.** At the beginning of the movie, Joe "Bromley" is shy and simply intends to watch the Gay Pride march since he has not yet publicly come out. He is fascinated by Mark and the LGSM group but joins them secretly and hides the newspaper clippings. His mother finally discovers not only his book but also the fact that he leads a double life. Misunderstood by his mother and somewhat alienated from his father, Joe finally makes his transition to adulthood by taking a stand for himself. He leaves his parents' home, returns to LGSM and proudly marches in front of the parade in London.

Another topic that the film weaves into a moving story is **tolerance.** Beyond each others' reservations and prejudices, both miners and LGSM develop an understanding and learn about each others' community. The **discrimination** aimed at the homosexual community is shown to be deep-rooted due to old conservative and patriarchal attitudes. This is also shown by the police that acts aggressively towards the miners and mocks them for their collaboration with gays. Jokes are made about AIDS, Joe's parents are shocked about his sexual orientation and by turning down LGSM's donations, many miners contribute to an oppressive atmosphere. Historical discrimination and homophobia against minority groups in Britain such as LGBTQ members are clearly shown in the film. However, it also indicates that this intolerance can often be worn down through community action when two minority groups find a common cause.

Background information

Margaret Thatcher	– Conservative prime minister from 1979 to 1990 – championed economic deregulation, social conservatism and privatisation – planned to close inefficient pits and import coal in order to grow economy
UK miners' strikes 1984–1985	– coal miner employment underwent a big decline in the 20th century – by 1984, coal in Britain more expensive to mine than to import – mechanisation replaced many miners – 6th March 1984: announcement to cut output and close pits; loss of 20,000 jobs – 12th March 1984: union of mine workers called national strike against pit closure – frequent violent confrontations with the police – by January 1985: strike began to disintegrate because miners needed their pay
Gay rights in the UK until the 1980s	1533: homosexuality punishable by death 1861: homosexuality punishable by a minimum of 10 years imprisonment 1885: any homosexual act (e.g. love letter) illegal; never explicitly targeted lesbians after 1945: significant rise in prosecution of homosexuality 1951: first UK transgender women undergo surgery 1957: homosexuality no longer regarded as disease 1967: homosexual acts legalized in UK between men over 21 if conducted in private 1970: founding of the UK Gay Liberation Front 1988: prohibition of funding educational materials and projects on LGBTQ rights in schools

HIV and AIDS in the 1980s	1981: first known UK case
	1982: term "AIDS" (acquired immune deficiency syndrome) proposed by gay-community leaders and federal bureaucrats to replace "GRID" (gay-related immune deficiency)
	1983: development of the PCR technique, a milestone in AIDS research
	1984: discovery of probable cause of AIDS: retrovirus
	1985: first commercially available test
	1986: retrovirus named HIV (human immunodeficiency virus)
	1987: development of first antiretroviral drug
	1988: first pamphlet distributed to US households to provide information on AIDS
	1989: Florida court rules that AIDS-positive student could share classroom with others using isolation partitions

Boy Erased (Film, eA)

Synopsis

Boy Erased is a 2018 biographical drama based on the memoir by Garrard Conley. The movie follows the story of 18-year-old Jared Eamons, the son of Baptist preacher Marshall and hairdresser Nancy in Arkansas, who reluctantly agrees to attend a conversion therapy programme named "Love in Action" after being outed as gay. The programme is run by a self-appointed therapist Victor Sykes, who purports to "cure" homosexuality. Jared and the other participants of his group are subjected to extreme emotional and physical abuse until he realises the programme's cruel intentions and slowly comes to terms with his sexuality and identity. He eventually confronts the instructors and begs his mother to get him out. Nancy does so with the help of fellow attendee Cameron and finally stands up to her husband by supporting Jared in his decision. Soon after, Jared learns of Cameron's suicide while still in the programme's care. Four years later, he lives in New York with his boyfriend and writes a book about his experiences. After his article about the programme gets out, he has a clarifying discussion with his father, who reluctantly agrees to change his attitude. In gifting him the pen he used to write sermons with, "from one writer to another", his father tries to take a first step towards reconciliation.

Analysis

One of the central themes of the film is the tension between **individual and society.** The film depicts how Jared's journey towards self-discovery and acceptance challenges the traditional notions of conformity and emphasises the importance of independence. His struggle to reconcile his sexual orientation with his family's strict Baptist beliefs forces him to confront the expectations and social cohesion of the community around him. Furthermore, the film raises important questions about the harm caused by societal expectations and the pressure to conform to narrow gender and sexual norms. It explores the shame and fear that many LGBTQ+ individuals feel when they are not able to live up to these expectations and the often painful consequences of coming out in an unsupportive environment. Despite the trauma and abuse that he experiences, Jared is able to find strength and support from his fellow attendees and ultimately rejects the harmful messages of conversion therapy.

Another significant theme in the film is **coming of age,** which is portrayed through Jared's journey of self-discovery. The film shows how his experiences in the conversion therapy programme, despite being deeply traumatic, ultimately serve as a catalyst for his growth and development as a young adult. Through his struggles Jared learns to assert his independence, confront his fears and embrace his true self. This is illustrated by his increasingly rebellious behaviour when he decides to stick his hand out of the window to "surf the wind" before, during and after "therapy". They thus serve as leitmotifs to portray his coming-of-age process.

Sexual diversity is also a prominent theme in the film, as it highlights the complexities of exploring one's sexual orientation and the impact of societal pressure on the identity and emotional well-being of individuals who identify as LGBTQ+. However, Jared's relationship with Christianity, especially in the light of his sexuality and rape, remains unexplored. The latter remains the only scene of homosexuality, depicted needlessly explicitly, and Jared's way of coping with its trauma is likewise not addressed. The film therefore misses an opportunity to delve into the context of rape culture and homophobia. The circumstances of the other attendees remain mostly unaddressed as well. Additionally, the film brings attention to **discrimination,** as it shows the harmful consequences of prejudice and bigotry towards the LGBTQ+ community, embodied by Marshall, Pastor Wilkes as well as Sykes and his staff. Conversion therapy as their chosen method of discrimination highlights the damaging effects of attempting to force individuals to conform to heteronormative standards. On the other hand, Nancy's development from a meek wife to a protecting mother who eventually comes to terms with her son's sexuality as well as the doctor who, despite being religious herself, believes homosexuality to be a natural phenomenon and in no need to be "cured", illustrate the importance of standing up against discrimination and intolerance.

Outsiders

- If an individual deliberately or unintentionally fails to conform to the rules of the society in which they live, they can easily become socially stigmatised **outsiders**.
- When a larger group of people rejects the conventional norms of mainstream culture, this might lead to the formation of a **counterculture** which openly propagates a set of values significantly different from those of the society in which they live.
- Such countercultures are often associated with younger generations that rebel against their parents' way of life.
- Famous countercultural movements include the "Beat Generation" of the 1950s, the "hippies" of the 1960s, the "punks" of the 1970s and 1980s and the "hip-hop" scene, which developed from the 1970s onwards, all of which included such forms of artistic expression as music, graffiti and dance.
- There are numerous ways of expressing one's dissatisfaction with mainstream culture, e. g. through the use of taboo language (as employed by writers of the Beat Generation), through the open violation of generally accepted moral standards (as in

the form of "free love", practised by the hippies), through one's appearance (clothing and hairstyle of the punks), or by aligning oneself with strata of society that are far removed from the mainstream (e. g. hip-hop culture).
– Often aspects of countercultures are eventually commercialised and assimilated by mainstream culture, thereby losing their originally rebellious impetus.

Minorities in the US

Since its birth in 1776, the United States of America has been a nation of immigrants. Especially during the 19th and early 20th century, millions of people (at first mostly from Europe, later also from other continents) were allowed to enter the country, since the young nation was in need of settlers and workers. The US has therefore always been an ethnically and culturally mixed nation, which has led to discussions about how this society might deal with its diversity and how it can be defined.

> **Keywords**
> **Multicultural society:** a society where various ethnic groups and their cultural heritage are accepted in their own right
> **Salad bowl:** the various ethnicities living in the United States mixing their traditions, cultural values, etc.; the various cultures do not merge into one but stay distinct ("unity in diversity")
> **Melting pot:** The various ethnic groups do not retain their cultural heritage but amalgamate into one new nation. The term first appeared in an essay by Jean de Crèvecœur, entitled "Letters from an American farmer" in 1782.
> The term "salad bowl" is now considered to be more politically correct.

One main group which did not enter the United States voluntarily but was deported to the US is the group of millions of slaves from Africa who were shipped to the British colony and later to the newly founded nation. The descendants of these slaves form the second largest minority in the US (in recent years the number of Hispanic immigrants has exceeded the Black population). Their history is one of discrimination and deprivation, which will be summarised briefly below.

African-American History
– 1619: first documented ship of African slaves bound for Jamestown, Virginia
– 17th–19th century: the **Atlantic slave trade**; by 1860 an estimated 3.5 million enslaved Africans lived in the US; another 500,000 lived freely in the (northern) states or territories
– 1861–65: American Civil War; caused by the separationist movement of eleven slave states which refused to end slavery; the North fought to prevent secession of these states and eventually won
– **Emancipation Proclamation** 1863: during the Civil War, President Abraham Lincoln declared that all slaves in the secession states (South) were free

- **Jim Crow Era**: after the Civil War, slavery was illegal; however, many former slave states passed laws which discriminated against Black people, prevented them from purchasing land and voting and segregated Black from white people in almost all areas of public life
- racial segregation remained into the 20th century; this system of separation and discrimination was met with increasing resistance and led to the formation of the Civil Rights Movement between 1954 and 1968

The Situation of African-Americans during Reconstruction

The former slaves formally gained freedom after the North won the Civil War, but they were far from having equal rights. Especially in the South, repressive laws and regulations prevented them from purchasing land, participating in elections, etc. (see Jim Crow Era above). This led to a number of developments:

- Many former slaves left for the industrialised cities of the North, in which all-Black ghettos developed.
- Freemen who stayed in the South often continued to work as sharecroppers for former slave masters. Unable to buy land, they remained dependent on white landowners and still lived in great poverty.
- Discrimination and racism continued (not only) in the South in an institutionalised form of racial segregation and state legislature. Both in the North and the South, Black people began to put up resistance against all forms of discrimination.

The Civil Rights Movement

- 1909: African-Americans founded the National Association for the Advancement of Colored People (NAACP); the aim was to call attention to discrimination in the South and the cities of the North
- 1954: landmark decision of the Supreme Court in the case of Brown vs. Board of Education, which declared the racial segregation of schools to be unconstitutional
- 1955: Rosa Parks, an NAACP member, refused to give up her seat in a bus for a white person in Montgomery, Alabama and was consequently arrested; led by Martin Luther King, thousands of Black people in Montgomery boycotted public transportation (Montgomery Bus Boycott); in 1956, the Supreme Court declared racial segregation on buses to be unconstitutional
- 1950s and 60s: protests continued on various issues, many of them led by the Southern Christian Leadership Conference (SCLC), formed by Martin L. King; following the example of Mahatma Gandhi, they organised peaceful protests and acts of civil disobedience to stop segregation in other areas of public life
- 1963: March on Washington; an estimated 250,000–300,000 people (about 80 % Black) marched to the Capitol in Washington, D.C. to demonstrate peacefully for jobs, freedom and an end to racial discrimination
- During this march, the most famous leader of the movement, the Reverend Martin Luther King gave his famous speech "I have a dream", which moved millions of people and brought widespread attention to the the Civil Rights Movement. King later received the Nobel Peace Prize in 1964 and was assassinated in 1968.

- Forced by the public to take action, the government passed laws to stop racial discrimination and segregation: the Civil Rights Act of 1964 and the Voting Act of 1965.
- Racial discrimination did not end and exists covertly and overtly to this day; African-Americans still have a higher risk of unemployment, poverty and imprisonment in comparison with the white majority population.
- Systemic racism towards Black people today has motivated new campaigns against violence like the movement "Black Lives Matter" in June 2013 (cf. below).
- Shortly before and after former President Trump's inauguration, a lot of new movements were started, including huge demonstrations for human rights and other issues such as women's rights, immigration reform, healthcare reform, racial equality and freedom of religion. Thousands of women wore pink woollen hats in their march on Washington to accuse Trump, among other things, of using sexist and racist language.

Black Lives Matter

Black Lives Matter is a socially motivated movement internationally known for its spectacular "die-in" actions and street demonstrations. It is a decentralised network of activists without a formal hierarchy, which started its actions and protest marches in order to take a stand against racially motivated police brutality towards Black people.
BLM appeared on the scene in 2013 and entered public awareness in 2016 when the movement became more active in protest against Donald Trump's racist utterances. In May 2020, it gained global attention in denouncing George Floyd's death in Minneapolis (Minnesota), caused by police violence in arresting him. According to BLM, Floyd died from suffocation. The acting officer was found guilty of murder in court in April 2021; the three other policemen were found to have been violating Floyd's civil rights.
The protest marches related to Floyd's death led to lootings and rampage, resulting in curfews and deployment of the National Guard. The police violence shown there brought Amnesty International into the arena, criticising violations of human rights.
Sometimes, BLM is criticised from within its own ranks as supporting racial bias and deepening the divide between Black and white people, as well as sidelining Black women's experiences. So, "Say Her Name" has been created to focus attention on female victims of police violence.

Ethnic identity

- "Ethnicity" refers to shared cultural characteristics such as language, ancestry, practices, feelings, values and beliefs while "race" is a social construct that is not universal; race is not always a defining factor even though it is often connected to ethnic identity.
- An ethnic group can, but does not have to be based on geographic origin.
- Ethnic identity is a personal, highly individual construct which an individual uses to categorise themselves.
- Ethnic identity can be a rarely overtly acknowledged fact of someone's life, while others are deeply influenced by their ethnic identity with respect to their choice of clothing, food, relationships, education or neighbourhood.

- Ethnic identity is not static, but can change over time.
- There are four major components of ethnic identity:
  - ethnic awareness – the way we understand our own and other ethnic groups;
  - ethnic self-identification – the label(s) we use for our own ethnic groups;
  - ethnic attitudes – the feelings we have about or own and other ethnic groups;
  - ethnic behaviours – the behavioural patterns specific to an ethnic group.[2]
- A strong sense of ethnic identity can influence a person's self-esteem, both in a positive or negative way, such as the idea of the "superiority" of one particular ethnicity, thus putting too much emphasis on ethnicity as a defining factor.

Tolerance and Discrimination

- discrimination in general: treating some people differently from others in comparable situations
- Intolerance refers to a lack of respect for someone's practices or beliefs if they differ from one's own and can be expressed in actions ranging from avoidance to physical harm.
- Discrimination is one of the most frequent forms of human rights violations and abuses.
- Discrimination and intolerance are closely related.
- Factors that discrimination can be based on include age, weight, ethnicity, race, culture, disability, political or religious beliefs, sex, gender, sexual orientation and language.
- Discrimination not only affects individuals but also society as a whole.
- The principles of equality and non-discrimination are laid down in the Universal Declaration of Human Rights (UDHR): "All human beings are born free and equal in dignity and rights" (Article 1). This concept of equality in dignity and rights is embedded in contemporary democracy, so states are obliged to protect various minorities and vulnerable groups from unequal treatment. Article 2 enshrines freedom from discrimination: "Everyone is entitled to all the rights and freedoms set forth in this Declaration, without distinction of any kind".[3]
- Discrimination can be practiced in a direct or indirect way: Direct discrimination occurs when a person is openly treated unfavourably; indirect discrimination refers to a requirement that appears to be neutral but in fact is disadvantageous to certain groups.
- Structural/systemic discrimination occurs on a macro level in the way a society is organised. Disadvantages to certain groups appear in the form of norms, attitudes, prejudices and behaviour.
- Discrimination is usually carried out by majorities, but discrimination from minorities also exists.
- Examples of discrimination and intolerance are anti-Semitism, xenophobia, racism and sexism.

2 Source: Jean S. Phinney, "The Multigroup Ethnic Identity Measure: A New Scale for Use with Diverse Groups", *Journal of Adolescent Research* 7 (2), 1992, 156–176.

3 Source: https://www.ohchr.org/en/human-rights/universal-declaration/translations/english (accessed on 1 April 2023)

Critical Race Theory (CRT)
CRT is an academic civil rights movement that began forming in the US in the 1970s. It examines social, cultural and legal issues with regards to race and racism. It argues that racism is institutionalised and favours the interests of white people. Laws, for instance, may seem to be colourblind but still have racially discriminatory effects. Since early 2021, several US states have introduced laws that ban or restrict the teaching of CRT in schools.

Camille Acker, "Cicada" (gA)

A note on the author and the text
Camille Acker spent her childhood in Washington, D.C. Upon completing her education in English and Creative Writing, she taught at various universities and writing organisations, while additionally bringing stories of young Black girls, women and people of colour to life. Currently, she works as a writer, researcher and editor in Philadelphia. Her debut collection of short stories centres around characters who also call Washington, D.C. their home. Throughout the collection, all of them are confronted with their definition of identity and belonging while struggling to attain both respectability and freedom.

Synopsis

Camille Acker's short story "Cicada" is about Ellery Cook, a young Black girl from Washington, D.C. who wins her first piano competition, although her joy is short-lived as she realises the extent of unyielding differences between her situation in life and the ones of her all-white competitors.

The story starts by highlighting Ellery's family's low income and social standing. Despite their struggles to make ends meet, however, her parents spare no effort to support Ellery's talent. Ellery's piano lessons eventually lead to a competition, which her parents likewisse atte. There, Ellery is fascinated by the affluent neighbourhood and the magnificent synagogue, functioning as the recital hall. After entering, her piano teacher, Mrs Hamilton, introduces Ellery to Cara and Lori, two competitors, both of whom are white. While Cara is friendly, Lori makes racist remarks about Ellery's hair and displays a disdainful demeanour. However, Ellery emerges victorious. This feeling immediately turns to exasperation once she realises that her prize is a savings bond instead of a cheque she intended to use to support her family, and they have to return home without having their lives altered for the better, while Lori gets to keep her wealth and privileges despite coming in second. Frustrated and furious, Ellery runs behind Lori's car and throws cicada shells at it.

Analysis

"Cicada" is told by a third-person selective narrator with a limited point of view. This offers insights into Ellery's thoughts and feelings but also leads to a biased interpretation of events. The story is traditionally structured into exposition (setting scene and introducing characters), rising action (competition starts, Ellery and Lori meet), climax

(Ellery plays and winners are announced), falling action (prize is explained, everyone leaves) and denouement/resolution (venting her frustration on the car of Lori's family). Its themes focus on rivalry, growing up, social class, racial differences and discrimination. Throughout the story, Ellery is acutely aware of her **ethnic identity** as the only black participant in an affluent neighbourhood she is not accustomed to. She feels isolated and out of place among the other participants, who are all white and show behaviour that is alien to her.

Lori, the antagonist of the story, is another participant in the piano competition for 9- to 12-year-olds. She is white, has an impeccable appearance (jewellery and clothing, straight teeth, flouncy ponytail), lady-like behaviour (as long as people watch) and leads a life of privilege. She wins second place not because of her talent but mainly as a nod to her becoming a "true lady".

As soon as the two girls meet, the atmosphere changes. Ellery is fixated on Lori's apparent wealth and beauty. Lori on the other hand immediately stresses her feeling of superiority by not introducing herself, making racist remarks about Ellery's hair as well as trying to make Ellery feel as if she was acting inappropriately and unworthy. Even Ellery's triumphant win is only commented on with "Anything can make noise", objectifying her. Although Ellery feels awkward and uncomfortable around Lori, she is generally fearless, confident, knows how to stand her ground and does not pretend to be friendly afterwards, the way Lori does when their families are present. Because Ellery is left with a prize that is worthless to her while Lori continues to enjoy all the privileges that come with being white and rich, the Black girl throws cicada shells at Lori's car to vent her frustration, powerlessness and anger. After doing so, she finally "breathed out and smiled" as she is pleased to have found a way to express herself, elementary to **growing up**.

The story uses cicadas at different times to illustrate the situation that the young protagonist finds herself in: Like the discarded and littered shells, Ellery feels constantly **discriminated against** because of the colour of her skin; the cicadas waiting under ground until they're ready mirror Ellery patiently waiting for her moment to shine; and the tree full of loud cicadas reflects her experience of winning into one buzzing with life. Eventually, the sound of the cicadas becomes a crescendo that leads up to the story's resolution of Ellery throwing cicada shells, which are as empty as she feels, and while throwing them at the car is as ineffective as her win is worthless, the act itself solidifies her transformation. The cicadas thus function as a symbol for personal change, growth, renewal and rebirth.

Nafissa Thompson-Spires, "Fatima, the Biloquist: A Transformation Story" (gA)

A note on the author

Nafissa Thompson-Spires was born in San Diego, California in 1983. After earning a Master in Creative Writing and a doctorate in English, she worked on her first publication, *Heads of the Colored People,* which then won numerous prizes. Its title is a nod to James McCune Smith's ten sketches of mundane, Black middle-class life around antebellum New York. Throughout her texts, she concentrates on Black identity, flawed communication and (the deterioration of) mental health, especially in "white spaces". She is currently teaching as an Assistant Professor at Cornell University.

Synopsis

Nafissa Thompson-Spires' short story "Fatima, the Biloquist: A Transformation Story" follows the life of Fatima, an African-American high school student, who struggles to find her identity. Being torn between fitting in at her predominantly white school and feeling like she is not Black enough, Fatima eventually befriends Violet, a Black teenager with albinism. Violet teaches Fatima different facets of Black (pop) culture, lifestyle and language, which lets Fatima be more assertive. As a result, people like her classmates begin treating her differently. Initially, the friendship between Violet and Fatima benefits both. However, Fatima's desire to separate her Black and white identity leads her to betray her friend. She keeps her white boyfriend Rolf from her for months, albeit introducing him to everyone else, and even shares Violet's most personal insecurities with him. When all of them eventually meet by chance, Rolf immediately references the nickname people used to mock Violet with. Fatima's behaviour, born from vacillation and self-doubt, and Rolf's cruel and tactless comments most likely lead to an irreparable rift in Violet's and Fatima's relationship.

Analysis

Nafissa Thompson-Spires' short story is told by an omniscient third-person narrator and explores the theme of **ethnic identity** as well as the struggles that come with trying to be true to it.

Protagonist Fatima is a shy, nerdy, Black teenage girl who attends a predominantly white private school. Her surroundings have led her to repress her Blackness, causing her to feel detached and invisible and making her insecure about her identity. The title of the story indicates that Fatima is able to speak with two voices – her darker top and pink lower lip – codeswitching between them depending on who she is with. The urge to do so results from the need to influence people's perception of her and consequently their immediate impressions and assumptions they make about her. This can affect tone, intonation, vocabulary, appearance and behaviour. Fatima describes her two lives as "two souls trying merge into a better self", but she remains stuck between them, struggling to pick one or find a way to embrace, combine and reconcile both worlds.

Fatima's frustration is highlighted when she interacts with Wally, a white classmate who seems to have no qualms about appropriating Black culture as his own. His popularity is due to his wannabe-Black behaviour, while Fatima, as an actual Black girl, remains ignored at best. This **discrimination** makes her feel even more invisible and unimportant. Meeting Violet, however, Fatima is confronted with her own adapted behavioural patterns and her transformation begins.

Even though she faces discrimination, mockery and her own insecurities because of her albinism, Fatima's new acquaintance is that of an outwardly confident African-American woman and thus helps Fatima to deepen her sociocultural knowledge on how to be

Black. Consequently, Fatima gradually becomes more self-aware and thus empowered and liberated, beginning to embrace this part of her identity. Their friendship intensifies, both sharing a unique understanding of one another. However, when Fatima begins a relationship with a white boy named Rolf, she is unable to balance her two lives and falls back into her adapted patterns of whiteness to fit in. Eventually, "she wasn't sure which lip she was supposed to use", and her fear of Violet perceiving Fatima's new relationship as a betrayal of Blackness, her teachings and their friendship leads to the ruin of their bond and Fatima returns to a worse version of feeling lifeless again.

Camille Acker: "Mambo Sauce" (eA)

Summary

Constance, a Black woman, meets Brian, a white man, in a bar with mainly white guests. Although she really likes him and agrees on a second date, she feels out of place. Yet, they start dating seriously and move in together when Brian accepts a job in Washington, D.C. The neighbourhood they move into is mostly Black, and Constance worries about being the only interracial couple.

When strolling through the neighbourhood, Constance comes across a chicken joint called *Winging It!*. She orders food and jokes with the staff, trying and liking their mambo sauce. The encounter invigorates her and connects her to her Black identity.

Shortly after, Brian and Constance are invited to dinner at Brian's college friends, Alissa and Mark. Again, Constance feels out of place being the only Black person. Brian tells their hosts about *Winging It!* and the sauce that he in contrast to Constance did not like. Alissa and Mark not only laugh about this but also call it "ghetto sauce", joking about the neighbourhood Brian and Constance live in. Constance is angry about their behaviour, calling them ignorant and snobbish. On their way home, Brian defends his friends and both start fighting.

Sometime later, Constance returns to *Winging It!* and has a little chat with the women serving her. She tells them about herself but does not mention that she is dating a white man. During that conversation, she learns that the store will be closing at the end of the month because the building will be sold to developers.

Back home Constance decides to do something to prevent the shop from closing and to stop gentrification. After calling several newspapers, a live TV interview takes place at the restaurant. After the interview, the owner – who Constance calls "Gina" since she does not know her real name – argues with her because no one asked Constance to talk to the press and that her behaviour was encroaching. "Gina" is scared that the sale will be ruined by Constance's interview because she really wants to sell the shop and help the neighbourhood develop. Also, she confronts Constance for hiding her relationship with Brian and accuses her of acting superior like a white person.

On her way home Constance is consumed with shame. Brian is hurt that she never mentioned him and leaves. Constance feels misunderstood and fears her relationship with a white man is changing her.

Analysis

One main theme of "Mambo Sauce" is **ethnic identity.** Constance struggles with her interracial relationship with Brian because she does not feel comfortable in white-dominated situations, which makes her struggle with her own identity as a Black woman. She frequently thinks about her past and the environment she grew up in and the one she moved to while in New York or D.C. She liked New York because it was multicultural and diverse and she could be herself and feel at home. This changed when she and Brian moved to Washington, D.C. She has lost herself in the new environment and does not fully know who she is anymore. Like her new neighbourhood, she is afraid that her identity is becoming gentrified, that she is betraying her Black self. She starts hiding her relationship with Brian and separating her identity into someone she is around white people and someone she is around Black people. Constance sees her own identity affected by her love for a white man who does not seem to understand the full complexity of these racial issues.

Likewise, the dinner at Brian's white friends points out that **discrimination** lurks everywhere in Constance's life. Mocking mambo sauce and their largely Black neighbourhood, Brian and his friends show that they consider themselves fundamentally superior. Constance feels uncomfortable in the face of this racism. Brian, on the other hand, is incapable of recognising this behaviour for what it is and understanding the identity crisis his girlfriend is struggling with.

Symbols
Mambo Sauce

- title of the short story
- symbolises how Constance reconnects with her Black identity through food
- being sweet and spicy = symbol of interracial relationships
- underlines cultural differences between the couple because Brian neither appreciates it nor understands why Constance is upset when it is referred to as "ghetto sauce"

Winging It!

- symbol of her connection to the Black community in Constance's new neighbourhood
- acts as cornerstone to community but also symbolically to Constance's identity; impending closure feels to Constance like she is losing part of her African-American identity

Nafissa Thompson-Spires: "Heads of the Colored People: Four Fancy Sketches, Two Chalk Outlines, and No Apology" (eA)

Summary

The short story "Heads of the Colored People: Four Fancy Sketches, Two Chalk Outlines, and No Apology" introduces the reader to four characters whose individual stories intersect on a day that two of them are shot by the police. It starts off by introducing one of the protagonists, African-American Riley, a cosplay fan who is on his way to a convention. He is stopped by another Black man, Richard Simmons, who calls himself

"Brother Man" and wants to sell him his dystopian comic series. Riley pushes him aside, which makes Brother Man angry, and the two start fighting.

In the next section, Kevan, a painter, is on his way to a meeting together with his daughter Penny. He finds it difficult to follow their discussion about superheroes because he is preoccupied with his plans for an exhibition portraying African Americans and their struggles.

Next, the reader is introduced to Paris Larkin, who is Riley's girlfriend. After her shift as a tour guide, she is supposed to meet Riley at the convention. When she gets there, she sees that Riley has been shot by police trying to break up the fight between Riley and Brother Man.

The story ends with a news report saying that Riley and Brother Man were shot by the police, however admitting that there might have been shortcomings in the telling of the story. Since the narrator is emotionally involved, she/he says this was the only way the story could have been told.

Analysis

The most eye-catching aspect about the short story "Heads of the Colored People" is its plot, which follows a non-linear structure while weaving together the stories of several people. Hence, Kevan sees the news story of the police shooting in the middle of the narrative, and Paris contributes sketches of Riley to his exhibition quite some time after the shooting. Also, the climax of the story, the death of Riley and Brother Man, is not explicitly narrated but frequently foreshadowed instead. Furthermore, the narrative style is also unusual since the story is told in the third person for the most part, but towards the end a first-person narrator comments on the events and addresses the reader directly.

The question of (**ethnic**) **identity** is crucial for the story because it is explored through each of the characters and their struggles with who they are. Riley's striking appearance with blue contact lenses and bleached hair, the narrator insists, is not an attempt to appear more "white" but a product of his self-confidence. Interested in cosplay, both Riley and Paris enjoy taking on the identities of fictional characters, making them feel seen and confident. Although people react with hostility when they see Paris dressed up as a non-Black character, her identity is acknowledged. Brother Man on the other hand, uses many aliases. His whole appearance triggers people's racial prejudices, causing them to see him as violent even though he regards himself as an intellectual as well as talented and skilled.

In the end, the press also ignores the victims' real identities and only offers a biased portrayal of Riley and Brother Man, based on outdated snapshots: the former is depicted as a thug and the latter is characterised as a criminal peddling indoctrinating material. Kevan, on the other hand, is interested in the individual stories of African Americans and wants to give them a voice in his exhibition.

Discrimination is also a crucial aspect of the short story and the author tries to raise awareness about the Black victims of racist police violence. Although the shooting of Brother Man and Riley is not explicitly described by the narrator and the reader is left in the dark as to what really happened when the police arrived, the narrator's agitation and commentary at the end exposes the officers' action as racially motivated and voices pent-up anger at the frequency and ubiquity of such occurrences in the US.

Innocence and Guilt

- The term innocence can refer to two different concepts: the fact that a person is not guilty of a crime or the fact that a person doesn't have much experience of life.
- Guilt on the other hand is defined as a moral emotion that occurs when a person realises that they have violated universal moral standards of a society. It is closely related to other psychological concepts such as regret, remorse, shame and atonement.
- In law, "guilt" refers to the fact that a person can be held legally responsible for actions (or inaction) that caused harm to others or their property. "Not guilty" does not equal "innocent". A person who did not commit a crime is innocent, while "not guilty" means that the prosecution was not able to prove that a person committed a crime. When charged with a crime, a person is assumed to be innocent until proven otherwise. At the end of a trial, someone is declared "guilty" or "not guilty" instead of "innocent" because an acquittal does not require actual innocence.
- The philosopher Karl Jaspers (1883–1969) defined four dimensions of guilt and responsibility:
  - criminal guilt,
  - political guilt,
  - moral guilt,
  - metaphysical guilt (meaning responsibility that is universally shared across a society).[4]
- The definition of guilt is culture-specific and may vary over time.
- The term "collective guilt" refers to a group of individuals and their emotional reaction to illegitimately harming members of another group and requires a shared social identity.

Perceptions of Reality

- Perception and reality have very different meanings:
  - Perception refers to the way that something is regarded, viewed or understood. It varies from person to person.
  - Reality is the actual existence of something and an absolute truth and does not depend on individual perception.
- While someone's perception occurs mentally, reality in contrast exists outside the mind.
- Other than perception, reality cannot be easily manipulated. Perception is not reality, yet someone's perception can become a person's reality.
- The common misconception is that how we perceive reality is an accurate representation of it. What people believe to be reality is highly subjective. A person's perception is shaped by their past experiences, knowledge, their emotions, attitudes, motiva-

4 Source: Karl Jaspers, *The Question of German Guilt,* Translated by E. B. Ashton, New York: Fordham University Press, 1965.

tions, self-interest and cognitive distortions but also their genetic predispositions, so it is highly complex.

- Severe mental illnesses show a substantial disconnect between perception and reality.
- Controlling the perception of reality has frequently been an important aim in human existence, from suppressing scientific thought to finding spurious justifications for military aggression. Perceptions of reality can thus be powerful and dangerous.

Ian McEwan, *Atonement* (eA)

A note on the author and the text

Ian McEwan (born in 1948 in England) is a British novelist, short-story writer and screenwriter. After spending much of his childhood in the Far East, Germany and North Africa, he studied English literature at the University of Sussex. His central themes include childhood, politics, crisis and transformation. Multiple viewpoints are created in most of his novels, which develop more rounded characters and different interpretations of events. This is also a key feature of *Atonement* (2001), which was a *New York Times* bestseller and shortlisted for the Booker Prize in 2001. In 2007, Atonement was made into an award-winning film, starring Keira Knightley and James McAvoy.

Synopsis

Atonement is a novel written in three major parts and time periods: 1935 England, Second World War England and France, and present-day England, with a final denouement.

The first part of the story, set in the summer of 1935, focuses on the protagonist Briony Tallis, a 13-year-old girl whose wealthy family lives on a country estate in England. Being the youngest of three, Briony has an older sister, Cecilia, and an older brother, Leon and dreams of becoming a writer. Cecilia has recently graduated from Cambridge University with her friend Robbie, who is the son of the Tallis family's housekeeper. The family is joined by Briony's cousins – 15-year-old Lola and her nine-year old twin brothers. When her cousins arrive, Briony decides to stage a play called "The Trials of Arabella", which she wrote herself, to be performed at dinner for Leon's homecoming from Oxford. The play, however, fails as it cannot be rehearsed properly. The same day Briony witnesses a scene between Cecilia and Robbie as they argue in front of a fountain. During their fight a vase breaks and falls into the water. Cecilia undresses herself to her underwear in order to dive in to retrieve the pieces. Watching this from a window, Briony is highly confused by what she sees and believes that Robbie is threatening her sister. The whole situation is worsened when Robbie asks Briony to deliver a letter to Cecilia. He accidently hands Briony an early draft, written in vulgar language. Being worried for her sister's safety, Briony reads the letter and is disgusted. She hands it over to Cecilia, who confronts Robbie, prompting him to confess his feelings to her, and the two end up having passionate sex. Briony witnesses the scene and again, being too young to understand the whole situation, is confirmed in her belief that Robbie is hurting Cecilia.

During a dinner with Leon's friend Paul Marshall, a well-off manufacturer, the twins go missing. The party breaks into teams to search for them. In the dark, Briony finds Lola as she is being raped by a man that neither of the girls can see clearly. Still, Briony accuses Robbie of raping Lola and even announces her suspicions to the police, resulting in Robbie's arrest. Shortly after, Cecilia is so distraught that she abandons her family.

The second part of the novel moves to the beginning of the Second World War. Robbie has served several years in prison and is released on the condition that he enlists in the British Army. He and Cecilia have stayed in touch through letters, while the latter has still cut off any contact with her family and has become a nurse. During one of her lunch breaks, she briefly meets Robbie before he has to leave for France. After they kiss, Robbie promises to return after the war but is soon badly injured. During this time, he concludes that Briony was too immature to be blamed for what she has done to him. In a letter, he advises Cecilia to reconnect with her family. His condition deteriorates and he finally becomes delirious as the German army advances.

In the third part of the novel, Briony is 18 years old and training to be a nurse but also still dedicating herself to her writing. Her past and what she has done to Robbie are haunting her. Now she is convinced that Paul Marshall must have raped Lola. When she learns that Lola is engaged to him, she decides to let the past rest and attends their wedding. Afterwards, she decides to visit Cecilia in London, where she is also surprised to encounter Robbie. Both Robbie and Cecilia refuse to forgive Briony for her mistake, even though the younger sister promises to put things right. After leaving Cecilia, Briony is convinced that she can atone for her mistake.

The epilogue is set in London in 1999. Briony is 77 years old and has finally become a successful writer but has recently been diagnosed with dementia. The text is Briony's diary entry in which she reveals that most of the second part of the novel was actually an invention because Robbie and Cecilia died in the war. While she did attend Lola and Paul's wedding, she failed to visit her sister because she was aware of the pain she had caused her. The reader now learns that Briony is the author of all the preceding sections of the novel. Her writing serves as a lifelong attempt to atone for her mistakes and the fact that Robbie and Cecilia were never reunited.

Analysis

Atonement is a multi-level narrative using a story within the story as its essential technique. The first three parts of the novel are told by an omniscient, seemingly reliable narrator, while the postscript changes to a first-person narrator, the 77-year-old Briony, who is rather unreliable and biased.
Briony admits to having written the previous parts as an act of atonement for the tragic mistake she made in her childhood. **Perceptions of reality** are therefore a central theme: Briony's individual reality is a product of her own assumptions and bias but also of her naive and limited knowledge that leads to her tragic misperception of what happened between Robbie and Cecilia.

Atonement thus raises the question of the relationship between reality and fiction. The story answers this question towards the end when Briony attempts to use her writing skills to correct the mistakes that her imagination made her commit in the past Likewise, the theme of atonement is essential as the title indicates. Briony spends the rest of her adult life trying to make amends for what she has done to Robbie and Cecilia in her childhood. By constructing a whole new reality, she apologises in a way she was never able to in real life.

Another questions that can be raised is the one of **innocence and guilt.** Because of her age and limited view, Briony's false testimony against Robbie is innocent. She cannot be considered guilty because, as a thirteen-year-old, she neither knows enough about adult relationships nor is she capable of fully comprehending the harm her testimony might cause to everyone involved.

Finally, **Britishness** is an important aspect in *Atonement*. British society used to be rigidly divided into working class, middle class and upper class, while there was hardly any upward social mobility. In the 20th century an upper-middle class evolved that often aspired to live a lifestyle similar to the upper class, whose wealth usually stems from their own businesses or careers in the field of banking. The Tallis family and Paul Marshall represent this typical upper-middle class. However, the Tallis' country house is depicted as a rather poor and shallow imitation of an upper-class residence. Its somewhat derelict state parallels the dysfunctional family that inhabits it.

Symbols and motifs
Uncle Clem's Vase

- family heirloom that was given to uncle Clem as a reward for his part in World War I
- damaged vase forms the basis for Briony holding Robbie responsible for Lola's rape
- destruction of the vase symbolises the rupture in the family itself

"The Trials of Arabella"

- Briony's play performed at her 70th birthday by a new generation of the family
- reappearance within the story symbolises that Briony's role is beyond her control
- plot of the play mimics the story of *Atonement*: love story between a heroine and her doctor resembles love story of Cecilia and Robbie; Briony wants to tell story with a happy ending in both cases

Glossary – Individual and Society

alienation	Entfremdung (z. B. von der Ursprungskultur)
assimilation	Anpassung (Aufgabe der urspr. Kultur)
to adapt to sth.	sich an etwas anpassen
to blend in	sich einfügen, integrieren
to integrate	integrieren

immigrant, to immigrate, immigration	Einwanderer/-in, einwandern, Einwanderung
colonialism, coloniser, colonised	Kolonialismus, die/der Besiedelnde, kolonisiert
citizenship	Nationalität, Staatsangehörigkeit
naturalisation	Einbürgerung
to receive / to be granted citizenship	die Staatsbürgerschaft erhalten
refugee, asylum seeker	Flüchtling, Asylsuchende/-r
ethnic minority, ethnicity	ethnische Minderheit, Volkszugehörigkeit
indigenous	einheimisch
integration	Integration
imperialism, imperialistic	Imperialismus, imperialistisch
loss of identity	Verlust der Identität
cultural clash	kultureller Zusammenprall (Konflikt)
melting pot vs. salad bowl	„Schmelztiegel" vs. „Salatschüssel" (unterschiedliche Konzepte, die die Vielfalt der Kulturen in den USA beschreiben sollen)
mutual understanding	gegenseitiges/beiderseitiges Verständnis
open-minded vs. narrow-minded	aufgeschlossen vs. engstirnig
pluralistic society	pluralistische (vielseitige) Gesellschaft
covert/overt discrimination	versteckte/offene Diskriminierung
(racial) segregation	Rassentrennung
gentrification	Strukturwandel, durch den ein ärmliches Stadtviertel auch für wohlhabendere Bevölkerungsteile attraktiv gemacht wird, die oftmals die ursprünglichen Bewohner/-innen verdrängen
deprivation	Aberkennung, Entzug (z. B. von Rechten), Benachteiligung
oppression, to be oppressed by s. o.	Unterdrückung, von jmd. unterdrückt werden
racial equality	Gleichwertigkeit verschiedener Rassen
civil rights	Bürgerrechte
civil disobedience	ziviler Ungehorsam
boycott	Ablehnung etwas zu kaufen oder zu benutzen, um z. B. eine Institution zu schwächen
Pride	öffentlicher Event, oftmals verbunden mit einem Umzug; zelebriert LGBTQ-Kultur und -Identität
union	Organisation von Arbeitnehmerinnen und -nehmern, die deren Rechte und Interessen vertritt

Globalisation

Effects on the World of Work and on Personal Lives

> **Keyword**
>
> **Globalisation:** a worldwide development involving the integration of financial, economic and communications systems; often seen as an unstoppable process, affecting people all around the globe, no matter whether they live in industrialised or developing countries, in big cities or rural villages; transfer of goods, capital and services as well as communications make life easier, but not everyone profits from the development; smaller economies may suffer
>
> The world is said to be getting smaller, i.e. it has become a **"global village"**. The term was coined by Marshall McLuhan, a Canadian philosopher and media specialist.

Economic Challenges

As today's customers wish to buy products at the best cost-performance ratio, the global market has become very **competitive**, with the following (and related) consequences:
- More and more jobs are outsourced or offshored to cut down production costs, thereby severely damaging local labour markets.
- When jobs are outsourced to low-wage countries, the workers often work in so-called "sweatshops" for long hours at a stretch, earning only minimum wages and under working conditions that are often inhumane.
- While "global players" consider efficiency, speed, flexibility and profit most important, employees are increasingly unable to defend their rights.
- Critics like the Canadian journalist Naomi Klein accuse multinational companies of exploiting the poor and indirectly supporting child labour by only having their own profits in mind.
- People in developing countries often live in poor conditions, without a decent education or access to new means of communication. Therefore they cannot reap the benefits of globalisation.
- In order to reduce the number of sweatshops, fair trade is becoming increasingly important. Its aim is to ensure that workers and small-scale producers in poor countries are paid a fair price for their work and products.
- Despite these attempts, the gap between the rich and the poor is widening.

Aspects of the "global village"
- The development of aeroplanes, fast ships and trains has made fast transportation of goods and people from one part of the world to another possible.
- New means of communication, especially the internet, have made collaboration between business partners and private individuals easier.

– Multinational companies have branches all over the world, and cost-effectiveness is a decisive factor when new production sites are set up.

Effects on the way of life

Anyone can experience the effects of globalisation, e. g. when
– travelling (and meeting people from one's own town halfway round the globe);
– keeping in touch with friends or business partners in distant countries with the help of new means of communication, which are faster than ever before;
– buying new goods that come from or were processed very far away; or
– calling a service "hotline" of a company that uses a call-center in India.

Globalisation is not always regarded as a positive process:
– Some people fear that individual cultures will finally blend into a single global culture, thereby losing their identity and the benefits of diversity.
– Despite or because of a globalised world, millions of people in developing countries still suffer from malnutrition or die of incurable diseases.
– Others work under cruel working conditions, producing goods that will be shipped to and sold in industrialised countries at a low price.
– One of the latest financial crises, starting in the USA in 2008, has shown that such catastrophes will ultimately affect other nations as well, as businesses are linked and global trade is now the rule.
– Due to increased mobility, diseases like H1N1 ("swine flu") or the coronavirus (cf. p. 60 f.) can easily spread all around the globe, developing into a pandemic.
– The refugee crisis in Europe can partly be seen as connected to globalisation: People from all over the world want to participate in growing economic wealth. Many people from poor countries want to find a better future and leave their homes – just like people have always done over the centuries (e. g. emigration to America in the last two centuries). At the same time, civil and other wars as well as climate change force people to emigrate. As more and more countries close their borders, problems in many regions are growing. Among these problems are huge refugee camps, pushback policies denying migrants their right to apply for asylum and people drowning and starving during dangerous journeys.
– Terrorism has become an ongoing global threat, which has led to a growing feeling of insecurity in many societies. In some countries (e. g. Israel) terrorist attacks have been a permanent aspect of everyday life for six or seven decades. In most Western as well as Middle Eastern countries, what we know as Islamist terrorism (Al-Qaeda, the "Islamic State") began with the "9/11" attacks on the World Trade Center in New York and the Pentagon in Washington on 11 September 2001. This led to the controversial "War on Terror" on the part of the USA and its allies, most notably in Afghanistan from 2001 to 2021. Since then, the world has seen a large number of terrorist attacks connected with Islamist ideology (e. g. in France, England, Nigeria, Germany) or with the ideology of white supremacy (e. g. in Christchurch in New Zealand or Utøya in Norway).

Many ecological and political movements around the world criticise the levelling and disadvantageous effects of globalisation. This has led to the formation of NGOs and alliances opposing the rule of capitalism over the economy of this increasingly smaller world. In opposition to the G8 summit, these organisations formed the **World Social Forum**.

Global competition

The increasingly globalised working world demands new skills and abilities of each individual. Since not only multinational companies but also smaller firms are outsourcing parts of their production, making use of cheap and well-educated workforces abroad, people in industrialised countries will experience more competition when looking for work as well as on the job. This requires both white-collar and blue-collar workers in the West to:
- acquire skills and competencies that are either very specialised or carried out with special qualities no one else can offer;
- become more flexible; one must be able to adapt to changes on the job and learn new ways of working quickly;
- continue learning throughout one's whole life; it is no longer sufficient to learn a job and expect to stay in it for the remainder of one's career;
- be familiar and keep up with new forms of (computer) technology and communications, since these are constantly changing and improving; and to
- be able to compete with workers from all around the world who can offer the same or similar skills and abilities for lower wages.

Globalisation and the COVID-19 Pandemic

At the beginning of 2020, a highly-infectious and often lethal pandemic caused by the coronavirus started to spread rapidly across the world. Governments worldwide faced a situation threatening health and lives as never before. Harsh measures, including travel bans and stay-at-home-orders which sometimes stretched over several weeks, were imposed to keep the disease at bay, temporarily infringing fundamental rights like freedom of assembly and movement. All kinds of public services and shops were put under lockdown; night-time curfews were even decreed to prevent people from leaving their homes.

As there was initially no vaccine to cope with the virus, the pandemic had the world under control until the first vaccines were developed and administered a year after the original outbreak. The vaccination programme has unfortunately developed into a problem in its own right, with manufacture, distribution and administration obstacles arising on international as well as national and local levels.

The spread of the pandemic can be seen as a negative effect of globalisation: it has definitely been fostered by long-distance travelling from one continent to another.

In economic terms, the epidemic has severely damaged global trade and caused heavy financial losses. Even famous, financially strong brands have suffered because customers have had to stay at home. Online orders have flourished but can hardly cushion the drastic losses to local businesses. Moreover, distortions in global supply and demand – as for FFP2 masks – have demonstrated the vulnerability of global trade to unscrupulous business practices.

The various lockdowns have hit social and cultural life in particular very hard, closing entire entertainment branches like theatres, cinemas and concerts, along with museums and art galleries as well as restaurants, hotels and bars. The restrictions on even informal group and family meetings have made people very lonely. Elderly people and people living on their own who have not been allowed to receive visits or to visit other people have suffered greatly from this situation.

School – and with it family – life has also been massively affected. Teachers and students have had to adjust to digital schooling without any personal presence, and families had to get used to the new discipline of home schooling. Similar conditions have been imposed on university staff and students. Children from underprivileged backgrounds were hit particularly hard as they often lacked the necessary hardware and internet connection as well as their own study space. The natural needs of children and young people to grow up together have been disrupted, and the changing requirements imposed by governments, sometimes relaxing and then reinstating lockdowns, have done nothing to alleviate matters.

As governments and institutions struggled to deal with the COVID-19 health crisis, our globalised world proved shockingly vulnerable to the virus, its economic effects and the spread of misinformation. How we prepare ourselves for future pandemics, with vaccines distributed fairly to all nations, will be a real test of globalisation.

Global Responsibilities

The UN

- 24 October 1945: A group of 51 countries founded the United Nations (UN) as a replacement for / successor to the League of Nations.
- The UN headquarters is located in New York City and the current Secretary General is António Guterres.
- The UN has 193 member states.
- It defends human rights and fundamental freedoms.

Five of the six **main organs** of the UN (General Assembly, Security Council, Economic and Social Council, Trusteeship Council and Secretariat) are located in New York City, while the International Court of Justice is in The Hague (the Netherlands). There are **various programmes** and funds affiliated to the UN. Two of the best known are UNICEF (United Nations Children's Fund) and the UNHCR (Office of the United Nations High Commissioner for Refugees). The latter deals with the needs of refugees and displaced persons in post-conflict countries, e.g. Djibouti.

Aims of the UN

- to preserve international peace and security
- to promote friendly relations between member countries
- to support international cooperation with regard to economic, social and cultural as well as humanitarian issues
- Apart from **peacekeeping** and **peacemaking** operations, peacebuilding has become more and more important.
- Here the UN and its affiliated organisations work to equip national groups with the necessary skills in conflict management to ensure lasting peace.
- Currently (April 2023) the UN is involved in 12 peacekeeping operations, e. g. in Haiti, Mali and South Sudan.
- **Humanitarian aid** is also of major importance, e. g. providing relief for people affected by either man-made or natural disasters and helping refugees and displaced persons.
- Other main concerns of the UN are **international law and development** (e. g. sustainable development, agriculture, international trade).

Global political changes

International peacekeeping is one of the aims of the UN:
- Once peace has been established in a country or region, peacekeepers are sent to the country or region in question to oversee the peace process.
- This can be done by overseeing elections, providing reconstruction aid and supervising the withdrawal of combatants.
- Very often, UN peacekeepers are soldiers, but they can be police officers or other civilian personnel.
- The UN Security Council authorises peacekeeping missions, which are then carried out by the international community.
- Many of these missions are organised and led by the UN itself. There is no UN army. While the troops acting as peacekeepers are under the control of the UN, they still belong to the armed forces of their country of origin. The UN itself is controlled by the Security Council and the UN Secretariat. This reduces the risk of a single peacekeeping party following its own interests.
- Regional organisations (e. g. NATO) can be authorised by the UN to lead peace-keeping missions. These regional organisations can also arrange peacekeeping missions of their own.

Migration – A Global Challenge[1]

- Migration has been a worldwide phenomenon since the beginning of human history.
- People have had a number of reasons for leaving their places of origin: poverty and the dream of a better life elsewhere, climatic reasons, wars and civil wars or religious persecution, to name only the most important.
- One has to distinguish between migrants and refugees:

[1] Source for all figures: https://www.unhcr.org/figures-at-a-glance.html (accessed on 1 April 2023)

- **Migrants** leave their countries of origin for a limited period of time or permanently, usually for economic reasons. They might have job offers in a different country or they might have heard of good opportunities. Examples of this are emigration from European countries to the USA in the 19th century, immigrants from Poland to the Ruhr district also during the 19th century, migrant workers inside Europe today, for example to help on farms, as carers for elderly people or to work in hospitals, and people from Africa trying to find better living conditions in Europe.
- **Refugees** usually flee their homes in order to get away from immediate threats to their survival, such as persecution, wars or climate change. Examples of this at present are the Muslim Rohingya from Myanmar, Venezuelans to other South American and Central American countries, or Syrian or Afghan people to Europe. An important example from the past are the Jews from Germany and other countries who had to flee from the Nazis.
- The International Migration Report of the UN from 2022 states that most migrants worldwide go to countries in Asia, followed by Europe and North America. The countries with the most migrants are the USA, followed by Saudi Arabia and Germany. These migrants for the most part seek – and find – employment in the countries of destination. They are not refugees, but quite a large number of them are illegal immigrants. According to the UN, there were 281 million migrants in 2022.
- The UNHCR (United Nations refugee agency) states in its statistical report for 2021 that the world is now witnessing the highest levels of displacement on record. 82.4 million people around the world have been forced to leave their homes. Among them are over 26 million refugees, over 40 % of whom are under the age of 18. 48 million are internal refugees, i. e. they flee from one part of the country to another (Nigeria is one example). There are 4.1 million asylum seekers worldwide. However, 73 % of refugees stay in neighbouring countries: Syrian refugees mainly flee to Turkey, Jordan and other countries close by. Nearly half the refugees worldwide at present come from Syria, Afghanistan and South Sudan.
- In 2021, Turkey hosted the largest refugee population worldwide, with 3.7 million refugees and asylum seekers, followed by Colombia (1.7 million), Pakistan (1.4 million) and Uganda (1.4 million). Most refugees come from Syria (6.7 million), Venezuela (4 million), Afghanistan (2.6 million), South Sudan (2.2 million) and Myanmar (1.1 million). Over 8 million people have fled the Ukraine in the current war (April 2023).
- There are also millions of stateless people, who have been denied nationality and access to basic rights such as education, healthcare, employment and freedom of movement.
- About 1 percent of the world's population have fled their homes.
- Nearly 1 person is forcibly displaced every two seconds as a result of conflict or persecution.
- The fact that most refugees seek help in neighbouring, not always wealthy countries can cause major problems there: The population of these countries has to share access to education, healthcare and jobs with the refugees. Compared to rich countries like Germany, countries like Jordan or the Lebanon find it far more difficult to cope with the situation. Colombia is another example of these conflicts: it is a country which is

only just beginning to overcome the effects of a civil war. Recently it has also been the destination of over 1 million refugees from Venezuela.

– On the other hand, migration always also means enrichment: The destination country will, with time, integrate the new arrivals. Their culture, beliefs and customs will become part of the country, thus leading to a more diverse culture in general.

– Many migrants and refugees want to return to their home countries if the situation allows them to. Seasonal migrants, for example, usually leave their families behind and return when their work has finished for the year. Many refugees want to return to their old home after the end of a war, others would like to build a new life elsewhere.

The EU

– Currently 27 states belong to the European Union (EU). The newest members are Bulgaria and Romania, which both joined the EU on 1 January 2007, and Croatia which became a member on 1 July 2013.

– After World War II there was a desire for a united Europe in order to prevent extreme forms of nationalism. The European Coal and Steel Community (ECSC), the European Economic Community (EEC) and the European Atomic Energy Community (Euratom) were merged into the European Community (EC) in 1967.

– The EU as we know it came into existence in 1993, when the Maastricht Treaty, which, among other things, initiated the euro as a common currency, was ratified.

– The individual member states came to be regarded as one single global player.

– At present the EU faces the challenge of maintaining its unity – and indeed remaining a union at all – in the face and the aftermath of the refugee crisis. The countries of the EU have very different attitudes to solving the refugee problem.

– In December 2019 the United Kingdom (UK) left the EU, a decision taken by referendum in June 2016. There have already been numerous consequences: businesses have been burdened with significant administrational issues, supply chains have been disrupted and there is a shortage in workers, particularly in the healthcare and hospitality sector.

Aims of the EU

– to promote prosperity and social progress with European citizenship for its peoples while still keeping their diversity alive

– to promote friendly relations between member countries

– to guarantee freedom and justice for the peoples of Europe

– to represent the member states internationally with a single voice, tackling the various challenges of globalisation, as well as respecting human rights

When it comes to defence, the individual member countries are sovereign. However, there is military cooperation in peacekeeping missions.

The three main groups which make up the EU are the Council of Ministers, the European Parliament and the European Commission.

Although the EU has no official capital, the official seat of the European Commission and the Council of the European Union as well as the second seat of the European Parliament are in Brussels, Belgium.

Global Warming and its Consequences

Environmental pollution has been growing rapidly and globally. The following factors in particular create global problems:
- Especially in developed nations, rampant consumerism is still increasing **energy consumption and waste gases** from factories.
- Over the last decades the number of **vehicles** on the roads has steadily increased. Cars are no longer found only in industrialised countries.
- The number of people travelling by plane is also greater than ever, due to the fact that plane tickets have become affordable for a larger number of people. Short-haul **flights** have become particularly popular.
- **food miles:** Whereas some years ago many people bought fruit and vegetables locally and ate seasonal products, they now want to eat strawberries and cherries in December. Hence more goods are transported by plane. Ecologically conscious customers ask themselves whether it is better to buy local product than food (even fair trade) that has been flown across continents. The non-sustainable production of meat and dairy foods is another critical factor in global warming.
- Everyone leaves a **carbon footprint** (emission of greenhouse gases from factories, transportation, food, etc), either directly or indirectly.
- **Greenhouse gases** such as carbon dioxide (CO_2) and methane cause chemical damage to the atmosphere (e. g. holes in the ozone layer) as well as global warming.
- World-wide, pupils have joined the movement *Fridays for Future* started by the Swedish teenager Greta Thunberg in a protest against climate change (see page 67).

After years of heated discussion among scientists and (especially) politicians worldwide, it is now considered common knowledge in most nations around the globe that the world's climate is changing and that these changes are, to a large degree, man-made. This change manifests itself most dramatically in the fact that the global average temperature is rising, and this has many side effects.
The documentary *An Inconvenient Truth* and its follow-up *An Inconvenient Sequel: Truth to Power* lay out the scientific facts on global warming in detail.

Causes of global warming
- Fossil fuel emissions, so-called greenhouse gases, form a layer in the earth's atmosphere which traps the sun's heat and thereby causes the temperature on the ground to rise; this is called "global warming".
- The quantity of greenhouse gases produced worldwide is rising because:
  - more cars, planes and industrial complexes are being built and used;
  - forests are burnt to make way for agriculture, people, roads, etc.;
  - growth in the number of cattle is increasing the emission of methane.

– The global rise in temperature is causing the polar ice caps to melt, diminishing their efficiency as a cooling device and mirror to reflect sunbeams and thus speeding up the heating process in the atmosphere.

Effects and consequences

There are many consequences of climate change. Some may seem rather insignificant at first but turn out to be disastrous in the long run. Although these effects are often spoken of as taking place in the future, many of them are already happening.

– Rising global temperatures are causing more water to evaporate both on land and in the oceans, changing historical patterns of rainfall and drought; many people are unable to adapt to these irregular weather phenomena.
– Oceanic warming is causing hurricanes to become more frequent and violent, as the warm water enhances evaporation and (indirectly) wind speed.
– Changes in temperature also cause natural habitats to change. Plants and animals have to adapt, and if they cannot do, so they will die out. Biodiversity is therefore endangered, limiting the natural resources on which we subsist.
– Diseases are spreading more quickly because parasites like mosquitoes and their animal hosts are affecting populations in previously safe areas.
– As polar ice caps melt, more and more of the earth's landmass is flooded, leaving people homeless.
– If enough polar ice melts, the North Atlantic current (Gulf Stream), which guarantees Europe's warm climate, might stop. In a worst-case scenario, Europe might experience another ice age.
– In other areas, desertification will continue to increase, a phenomenon which is already taking place.
– All these developments will dramatically reduce the area of land on which human existence is possible and will therefore lead to worldwide migration that we will be unable to deal with.

The effects are threatening the entire planet and the way we live today. Because of this, scientists, politicians and citizens worldwide have a duty to seek ways of reducing greenhouse gases in order to slow down climate change. Each individual can participate in reducing greenhouse gas emissions by using better insulation in houses, saving electricity, recycling waste, using public transportation instead of a private car, flying only when absolutely necessary, etc.
The key to saving the environment is "thinking globally and acting locally".

Political efforts to reduce greenhouse gas emissions are still faced with various difficulties and conflicts of interest. Each climate summit therefore only achieves small steps towards stopping or slowing down climate change. Scientists and independent organisations alike argue that these small steps are not enough to prevent the catastrophic consequences of global warming. The main goal remains to cut greenhouse gas emissions, especially those caused by the burning of fossil fuels.

INFO The Paris Agreement and the UN Climate Change Conferences

The international political elite came together in Japan in December 1997 and issued a common declaration, the **Kyoto Protocol**, which came into effect on 16 February 2005. The protocol aimed to reduce the emission of greenhouse gases by an annual 5.2 % by 2012, taking 1990 levels as a basis.

Ever since then, numerous other summits have taken place in order to reduce and slow global warming. In Paris in 2015 a global agreement on the slowing of climate change (the **Paris Agreement**) was reached and adopted by 195 countries. Among the decisions made was the resolution to limit the long-term increase of global average temperature to well below 2°C above pre-industrial levels. The agreement came into effect on 4 November 2016, as enough countries had ratified it. In June 2017, the USA withdrew its consent to the agreement but rejoined in 2021 under the Biden presidency.

In the face of urgently needed action, COP 26 in Glasgow failed to implement significant policies. Participants agreed on reducing coal mining, phasing out cars that run on fossil fuels (a resolution Germany was notably absent from) and halting deforestation. These pledges, however, remain first tentative steps. More significantly perhaps, there was strong disagreement on what kind of financial compensation developed nations need to offer developing countries for their copious contributions to climate change.

Fridays for Future

– In August 2018, Greta Thunberg, a then 16-year-old Swedish climate change activist, started protesting outside the Swedish parliament in Stockholm in order to raise awareness of the dangers of climate change.
– According to Thunberg, politicians are not taking enough action against climate change, which is putting our planet's future at risk. Thunberg's solitary school strikes soon caught the attention of the media in countries all over the world.
– Up to May 2019, an estimated 1.4 million teenagers and young adults worldwide followed her example by going on strike from school every Friday and protesting against climate change. This movement is known as "Fridays for Future". Since the beginning of COVID-19, it has been more difficult to demonstrate for new climate change policies, but the movement has tried to find other ways of protesting.
– Greta Thunberg has delivered several public speeches in which she has put pressure on politicians and world leaders to combat climate change more swiftly and resolutely. She spoke at various important global meetings, e.g. the United Nations Climate Change Conference in Katowice, Poland in December 2018 and at the World Economic Forum in Davos, Switzerland in January 2019.
– The speed of the reaction and the immense sums of money provided by governments during the COVID-19 crisis seem to prove Fridays for Future's point: Immediate global action is possible, but the governments all over the world do not seem to regard an effective fight against global warming as a top priority.

Alternatives to Using Fossil Fuels

Recent discussions on fossil fuels and their effect on the atmosphere have supported the development of technology to make use of renewable sources of energy such as wind, water and solar power. In many European countries, national programmes to subsidise these technologies have been established. The US is also aiming to support these alternative energies more substantially, but this has not been achieved by recent administrations. The Fukushima disaster in spring 2011 led the German government to withdraw from using nuclear energy in future. Other parties urge that nuclear power should be used instead of fossil fuels (which are still the most important sources of energy). However, the use of nuclear energy has always been controversial.

Natural alternative energy sources

In general, the use of wind, water and solar power seems far less risky and also less expensive in the long run. The challenge engineers face is to make these technologies more efficient and find ways to store the energy produced. One main hindrance is posed by companies investing more money in fossil fuel exploration and exploitation and in expanding nuclear power facilities. Since these technologies are well established, their exploitation yields enormous profits, whereas investment in new, ecologically-friendly sources of energy is costly, but could create many jobs.

Non-renewable and/versus renewable energy

– Since the Industrial Revolution, Western societies have been in constantly growing need of energy resources to power industrial production and satisfy communal and household requirements for fuel and electricity.
– This increasing demand for energy has led to various developments:
  – The exploitation of natural resources such as oil, gas and coal has led to the destruction of natural habitats on land and in the oceans.
  – The use of nuclear power plants has created a seemingly safe, cheap and climate-friendly source of power. This view is, however, disproven by accidents like those in Chernobyl and Fukushima as well as the ongoing problem of where to store nuclear waste.
  – New inventions have succeeded in making use of renewable energies such as wind, water and solar power.
– The most immediate result of the use of fossil fuels since the Industrial Revolution is the amount of carbon dioxide and other pollutants emitted into the atmosphere.

Environmental sustainability

It will prove difficult to sustain usable natural resources. Industrialisation and capitalism, together with a continuously growing world population, have led to a massive exploitation of limited resources. Thus, finding ways to make our societies and lifestyles sustainable is one of the most important global challenges.

Global goals

In 2015, United Nations member states formulated 17 objectives - or „Sustainable Development Goals" - for a fairer and better world to be achieved by 2030. These included issues such as gender equality, clean water, physical and mental well-being, international peace and justice.

For example, they aim to end global poverty by ensuring that economic resources and fundamental services such as healthcare are available to everyone and by making sure that even the poor are protected from potential environmental disaster. They also seek to implement policies aimed at promoting equality with respect to income, political inclusion and opportunities, but that also allow developing nations in particular a fairer economical share. With respect to climate change, the 17 global goals commit themselves to raising awareness for this issue, protecting against disasters related to climate change and integrating measures on a national level. They also seek to reduce waste, in particular food waste, manage resources more sustainably and to combat market distortions such as tax reductions and subsidies that reward wasteful consumption.[2]

The signatory states have shown variable speed at implementing these goals in their policies. Germany was one of the first to begin this process in the shape of the „Deutsche Nachhaltigkeitsstrategie" in 2017. Whether, however, these 17 aims can be converted from words on paper to real action is yet to be seen. A first stock-taking in 2020 saw positive developments on a communal level and well as in grassroots movements such as Fridays for Future. On the other hand, the report also notes that povery is still growing, basic needs are still nowhere near being met on a global scale and natural resources and habitats continue to be recklessly destroyed. Clearly, more public pressure and political daring will be required in the coming years.

English as a Global Language

The general importance of English in the globalised world of international trade and politics, science, popular culture and travel is still unrivalled. No matter where you are in the world, a command of English will always help.

Worldwide, 1.348 million people speak English as a native speaker or as a second language, followed by Mandarin, the main language in China (1.120 million), Hindi (600 million) and Spanish (543 million).[3]

Especially in the countries of the former British Empire, English is not just a language universally understood and spoken, it is very often still an official language. In India, for example, more than 3,000 newspapers are published in English, but English is spoken by only about 12 % of the population. There are 1,652 languages and dialects in India, which makes English as a working *lingua franca* even more important. All in all, English is the official language in 55 countries today.

---

[2] Source: https://www.globalgoals.org/ (accessed on 1 April 2023)

[3] Source: https://www.statista.com/statistics/266808/the-most-spoken-languages-worldwide/ (published 30 March 2021, accessed on 1 April 2023)

It has been estimated that about a billion people worldwide speak English as a second language.[4] According to the EU statistical service, 96 % of all students at lower secondary level in the EU study English as a second language.[5] International organisations like NATO or OECD use English exclusively, as do many internationally operating enterprises like Airbus Industries and even Volkswagen in their Shanghai branch.

According to Bill Bryson[6], English differs from other languages in three outstanding respects that make it attractive even to speakers of other mother tongues. First, its rich vocabulary is wider than that of other languages. The latest edition of the *Oxford English Dictionary* lists 615,000 words; 200,000 words are commonly used in English, compared to 184,000 in German and just 100,000 in French. What adds to the wide range of words is the large number of synonyms. The best known collection of synonyms and antonyms, *Roget's Thesaurus*, has over 100,000 entries. Thirdly, there is an almost endless list of words that can be used both as noun and verb.

English as a *Lingua Franca*

A *lingua franca* is a language that can be used by speakers who do not have any knowledge of each other's mother tongue. It is therefore also referred to as a "contact" or "link" language. English used in this context bridges the linguistic gap for non-native speakers of English who do not share a common first language and thus serves as a means of intercultural communication. Since this happens worldwide, English has been called a "global *lingua franca*". The result of this extensive use of English is that it is shaped not only by its native speakers but also by those who use it as a foreign language. Researchers[7] have found that although speakers of English as a *lingua franca* do not always adhere to the rules of grammar and pronunciation, communication is not necessarily inhibited by this. What seems more important in this respect is language awareness, along with a command of communication strategies. Nevertheless, the more closely a person's grammar approximates to Standard English, the more readily they will be understood.

Varieties of English [8]

American English

– American English is relatively homogeneous compared to British English. About 80 % of the population speak with the same accent.– The USA contains four speech groups:

---

[4] Source: https://www.statista.com/statistics/266808/the-most-spoken-languages-worldwide/ (published on 25 September 2014, accessed on 1 April 2023)

[5] Source: https://www.thoughtco.com/how-many-people-learn-english-globally-1210367 (published on 27 August 2020, accessed on 1 April 2023)

[6] Source: Bill Bryson, *Mother Tongue. The Story of the English Language*, London: Penguin, 1990, S. 3 f.

[7] Source: Barbara Seidlhofer, "English as a lingua franca", in: *ELT Journal* 59/4 (October 2005), p. 339 f.

[8] You can find lots of additional information as well as sound examples of these and other varieties of English on video platforms online.

Northern, Midland, Southern and New England. Midland is subdivided into North and South Midland.

- Regional variation due to geographical and historical factors: colonists on the East Coast were in touch with people from England via trade; therefore similarities with British English (e. g. the pronunciation of "Tuesday", "news"; the absence of [r] in "horse", "car").
- Social prestige is linked to pronunciation, e. g. the sound of [r] is carefully produced by upper-middle-class speakers when they want to indicate their social standing.
- There has been some rivalry between England and America as to the question whose language is more correct. On becoming independent, Americans emphasised the differences between British and American English, thus creating some sort of language nationalism.
- Immigrants often try to conceal their origins by overemphasising vowel sounds, e. g. in "coffee". This is called hypercorrection.
- The phenomenon of t-dropping is widely practised. That means that [t] is not pronounced in the middle of a word, e. g. in "winter" or "internet".
- [o] in "clock" is realised like the [a] in British English "car". A British native speaker could therefore mistake the American "clock" for the word "clerk".
- The way Americans speak is often referred to as "the American twang". This most commonly refers to "General American", which is a generalised Midwestern accent used by many TV and radio hosts. (cf. p. 73 for AAVE / Black Vernacular).

British English

- In the Middle English period, Oxford, Cambridge and London shared the same kind of English. Because of the prestige attached to it, London English became the basis for Standard English as early as the time of Chaucer's Middle English and in turn formed the national language.
- One variety of English spoken in London is called Cockney. In the sixteenth century this was not associated with the language of the East End working-class, as it is today, but it was the language spoken by all Londoners outside the court. It was only in the eighteenth century that Cockney became regarded as coarse or low English. One of the reasons for this development was that the City became the centre of commerce and trade, thereby making the old inhabitants move east to Wapping, Shoreditch and Bermondsey.
- Characteristics of Cockney include h-dropping, which means that the [h] at the beginning of a word is not pronounced, and the "glottal stop", which is the result of not pronouncing the [t] in words like "butter" or "bottle". Furthermore, the [g] in word endings is often omitted, for example in "eatin'".
- Standard English as spoken by a mere 2–5 % of the British population has also been labelled "Received Pronunciation" or simply "RP". It was until recently spoken by British middle-class people, especially in the South, and it was used by most TV and radio news presenters.

Australian English

- Like American English, Australian English is fairly uniform in pronunciation.
- Three different social accents can be distinguished: "Cultivated" (similar to British English; 10 % of speakers), "Broad" (working-class accent; 10 %) and "General" (80 %). On the whole, there is not much regional variety in dialects.
- Girls and women tend to speak General or Cultivated Australian, whereas boys and men prefer General or Broad Australian.
- Using a rising tone at the end of a statement, which has become popular with girls and women (not only in Australia), is called "rising inflection".
- Australian English contains various words from the Aboriginals, for instance "billabong", "didgeridoo", "boomerang", "koala" and "kangaroo".
- Usage is also influenced by vocabulary from American English, for example: "cookies", "station wagon", "teller", "mail", "labor" and "dollar".
- Australian English has been influenced by large numbers of immigrants, so-called "New Australians" from Turkey, Greece, Italy, Sri Lanka, etc.

New Zealand English

- It is very similar to Australian English, although New Zealanders regard their way of speaking as more sophisticated and try to be as close to British English as possible.

Canadian English

- In the wake of the American Revolution, Loyalists (supporters of the English) fled to Ontario, providing the basis for "General Canadian" as an urban, middle-class variety.
- Along the Atlantic coast there were many English-speaking settlements.

English in India

- Approximately 70 million people use English in India. About 25 million use English regularly, thus making it an important language of official life.
- English is spoken mainly by the educated ruling classes.
- Many national daily papers are in English (e. g. *The Times of India*).
- All-India Radio broadcasts in English all over India.
- English was used in the fields of government, education and imperial rule.
- In 1857, English-speaking universities were established in Bombay, Calcutta and Chennai (formerly: Madras).
- English has become the language of prestige and of nationalist opposition.
- A large number of Indian words have been integrated into English, e. g. "curry", "bungalow" or "veranda", especially by English administrators in the nineteenth century.

Pidgin

A pidgin is an artificial, auxiliary language without any native speakers. It is used by people with different mother tongues who need a common means of communication. Pidgin English was the traders' and slaves' *lingua franca*. The word "pidgin" is derived from the way the Chinese pronounced the word "business". There are French, English and Portuguese pidgins.

Creole

- If a pidgin is used as a first language, it is called a creole. This process happens gradually and it takes several generations.
- When slaves from many different African tribes with different languages were transported to America by slave ships, they needed a common language. Therefore, they spoke pidgin English, which was accessible to all of them.
- Examples are the Caribbean creole of Barbados, which is based on English, or Haitian creole, which is based on French. The creole of Papua New Guinea (Tok Pisin) has a written as well as a spoken form.

African American Vernacular English (AAVE)

- Formerly called Black English, AAVE has absorbed aspects of African pidgin and Caribbean creole and has a long and distinctive tradition. It has a distinct set of rules, although it is still often misjudged as inferior because certain grammatical structures of English are simplified or do not occur. Nowadays, however, it is considered to be simply another variety of English. It is also called "Black Vernacular".
- The verb "to be" is left out under certain circumstances („She at home.") and habitual "be" is used in place of simple present („He be watching TV every night.").
- On the one hand, AAVE is representative of a disadvantaged past, on the other hand, it is also a means of self-expression.
- Contributions from the African world to everyday English are words and expressions like "voodoo", "banana" or "high five".
- Black Vernacular probably originated even before the slave trade began.
- Due to music and popular films and series, it has achieved wide public attention. Some features of AAVE are apparently unique to this variety, but the structure is often similar to other English varieties spoken in the US and Caribbean. The number of speakers of AAVE is extremely difficult to establish.

South African English (SAE)

English was first brought to the Cape area by British settlers, fortune seekers and missionaries in the late 18th and early 19th century. The minority of about 3 million first-language SAE speakers is outnumbered by second- and third-language speakers because English is seen both as the language of communication and aspiration as well as a 'colonist' language. For many Black parents English is an instrument for their children's advancement. SAE is dominant in public life for reasons of practicality, even though official documents are also translated into the other ten official languages.

In the Soweto uprising in 1976, the question of a teaching language in Black schools was crucial: the students opted for English, as they did not want to study in Afrikaans, the language of their white oppressors. So English has always been seen as opposing Afrikaans, with the Black population preferring to use English and the language of their own cultural origin, whereas many white people have kept to Afrikaans.

Strong influences on SAE vocabulary and pronunciation mainly come from the surrounding African languages as well as from Afrikaans or unclear sources. Due to SAE having different native tongues, the pronunciation tends to vary a lot. In general, pronunciation is closest to NZE (New Zealand English), tending to become more levelled through teaching in urban schools and through modern media.

Glossary – Globalisation

anti-globalist	Globalisierungsgegner/-kritiker
backwardness	Rückständigkeit
company philosophy	Geschäfts-/Firmenphilosophie
competition; to be competitive	Konkurrenz(kampf)/Wettbewerb; konkurrenzfähig sein
corporate identity	Firmenimage
crop diseases	Krankheiten von Pflanzen/Saatgut
debt relief	Schuldenerlass, Entschuldung
desertification	die Wüstenbildung, das Vordringen der Wüste
developing countries	Entwicklungsländer
development aid	Entwicklungshilfe
driving forces of globalisation	die Antriebskräfte der Globalisierung
drought	Dürren, Dürreperioden
earth's atmosphere	die Erdatmosphäre
economic growth	Wirtschaftswachstum
economic prosperity	ökonomischer Wohlstand
emerging markets	Schwellenländer
environmental commitment	Umwelteinsatz
environmental damage	Umweltzerstörung
environmentally friendly	umweltfreundlich
expansion of capitalism	Ausbreitung des Kapitalismus
fair trade	fairer Handel
floods	Hochwasser, Überschwemmungen
global interconnection	globale Querverbindungen
global marketplace	globaler Marktplatz
global player	Weltfirma
global superpower	globale Supermacht
global warming	Erderwärmung
going global	*umgangssprachlicher Ausdruck, der ursprünglich für die globale Expansion von Firmen verwendet wurde*
greenhouse gases	Treibhausgase

human rights	Menschenrechte
increase profit margins	die Gewinnspanne erhöhen
Industrial Age	das Industriezeitalter
industrial nations	Industrieländer/-nationen
international stock markets	internationale Börsenmärkte
labour laws/market	Arbeitsgesetze/ Arbeitsmarkt
lingua franca	eine Sprache, die von Personen mit unterschiedlichen Muttersprachen benutzt wird
low-wage countries	Niedriglohnländer
mass tourism	Massentourismus
microcredits	Kleinkredite
NGO (non-governmental organisation)	Nichtregierungsorganisation
outsourcing	Produktionsverlagerung
political turmoil	politischer Aufruhr, politische Turbulenzen
pollution	Verschmutzung
population overshoot, overpopulation, excess of population	Überbevölkerung
poverty	Armut
greenhouse gas emissions	Ausstoß von Treibhausgasen
cost of production	Produktionskosten
rise in global temperature	ein weltweiter Temperaturanstieg
robotised production	computergesteuerte Produktion/Fertigung
shareholder	Aktionär
supremacy	Vormachtsstellung, Überlegenheit
sustainability	Nachhaltigkeit, Zukunftsfähigkeit
sweatshop	ausbeuterischer Betrieb
trade	Handel
trademark policy	Markenpolitik
undernutrition, malnutrition	Unterernährung; Mangelernährung
unemployment	Arbeitslosigkeit
workforce	Arbeiterschaft
working conditions	Arbeitsbedingungen

Science and Technology

The dawn of science in the modern sense of drawing factual conclusions from empirical, experimental or statistical data can be dated back to ancient Greece, when scholars aimed to explain the world on the basis of observation and elaboration. During the Renaissance, science experienced a rebirth, and in the wake of the Industrial Revolution it evolved to become what it is today: the basis of our modern way of life.

> **Gaining background knowledge**
> The emergence of today's technology-oriented societies can only be understood by studying the Industrial Revolution. The full extent of these changes cannot be presented in this context. Various informative sites can be found online, e.g.:
> – https://www.bbc.co.uk/history/scottishhistory/enlightenment/features_enlighten ment_industry.shtml (accessed on 1 April 2023)
> – https://www.history.com/topics/industrial-revolution/industrial-revolution (published on 29 October 2009, accessed on 1 April 2023)

Chances and Risks

Scientific research aims to explore and explain the world around us and improve the means by which we cope with it. Technology, in turn, is the practical outcome of this research, resulting in the tools and machines we use to make our lives (seemingly) easier. Every new technology, however, harbours risks as well as opportunities and creates new kinds of dependencies unknown before. One simple example will suffice to prove this point: At the end of the 19th century, the first automobiles were produced; eventually they would replace horse-drawn vehicles and other means of individual transport. In contrast to older technologies, cars need fossil fuel. Demand for cars increased during the 20th century, production became cheaper, and today almost every household in Western societies owns at least one car.

The increasing use of cars has had various consequences:
– more demand for fossil fuels: increased drilling for oil on land and at sea,
– demand for larger roads: expansion of highways, parking lots, etc.,
– consequences: growing destruction of natural habitats and resources,
– increasing mobility: the former luxury of owning a car has become a must; some jobs cannot be done without a car, one is expected to own a car; public transport systems aim to meet general mobility needs,
– cars produce exhaust fumes, dramatically increasing the amount of carbon dioxide and other climate-changing fumes released into the atmosphere.

Once limited to the so-called developed countries, cars are now in increasing demand in developing countries such as India and China. This development will further increase the amount of atmospheric pollution and have an effect on the global climate. Recently a lot of research has been done in the field of hybrid and electric mobility.

Of course, the invention of the car has improved our lives in numerous ways by making transport and mobility easier and cheaper. The example of the car represents a simple model of how you should view technological developments: always consider their positive as well as negative potential. One such ambivalent area of current scientific research is genetic engineering.

Visions of the Future

Humankind has always dreamed about the future and keeps seeking to create the world it wants to live in. People have always aimed at new challenges and tried out new ideas. In literature, these attempts have been formulated in utopias and dystopias, positive and negative visions of the future. Technological innovation has fuelled the creation of dystopian visions of societies, often in the form of a science fiction novel. Prominent examples are Huxley's *Brave New World*, Orwell's *Nineteen Eighty-Four* and Ishiguro's *Never Let Me Go*. However, broadly dystopian ideas are also present in popular fiction like *The Hunger Games* by the American novelist Suzanne Collins.

Meanwhile, some social movements are still actively seeking new and positive ways of living with each other, sharing space, goods and skills in community projects and living. In the aging societies of the West, this is proving very important. Increasingly, ideas like urban gardening might also change the city space to create a more liveable environment.

The Media

Keyword

The Media: a collective term that denotes means of mass communication, particularly referring to newspapers, radio, TV and the internet. Communication through these media is characterised by the fact that it is public, reaches a broad audience, is not bound to a particular place and time and that it is largely unilateral, i. e. the audience does not normally interact with the sender of the messages it has received.

In the following chapter diverse aspects of the media will be presented. The central issues are:
– various forms of the the media and their prime functions
– the concept of "media literacy"
– the role of the media in contemporary society
– advertising as an example of a text that makes an appeal to the reader.

Types of Media

Newspapers
- printed publications that appear regularly (most commonly daily or weekly) and that are issued in an inexpensive form, affordable for a broad audience
- normally cover a wide range of up-to-date topics from politics, economics and sport to culture and entertainment, also featuring a certain amount of advertising
- The first newspapers were published in the early 17th century.
- Due to the growing availability of information on the internet, however, the number of printed newspapers has been steadily decreasing.
- One can distinguish between the so-called **quality press**, i.e. newspapers in which well-researched information is offered at a high level of credibility (e.g. *The Times*, *The Guardian*) and the **tabloids** (Am. **yellow press**), in which sensational stories are combined with eye-catching headlines and images (e.g. *The Sun*, *The Daily Mirror*).

Radio
- invented in the late 19th century, originally referred to as "the wireless"
- from the 1920s onwards, more and more radio stations started broadcasting and radios became affordable for an ever growing audience
- "Golden Age" of radio: between the 1930s and the mid-1950s, when radio programmes included not only music, news and advertisements but also shows and radio plays
- with the advent of television, the popularity of the radio started to decline

TV
- first introduced to the general public in the late 1930s
- did not become widely available and popular until after World War II
- originally based on a limited number of state-owned broadcasting stations
- the number of private channels, funded either by advertising or by subscriptions, has increased in the last few decades
- most recently, streaming television has enjoyed a growing audience

Advertising
- Advertising is a vital financial aspect of all forms of the media.
- It is a form of communication that makes an appeal to the reader or viewer and as such tries to persuade her or him to carry out an action (to buy the advertised product or to use the advertised service).
- With the advent of the "new media" (primarily the internet), new advertising opportunities opened up for companies. Nowadays, online advertising – e.g. in the form of pop-ups, banners and advergames (free online games that advertise a certain product) – is a growing market, whereas the rate of advertising in the traditional media has been steadily declining.

- One way of describing the effects which a particular ad might have on the receiver is the **"AIDA"** principle: the ad should first catch **A**ttention, then arouse **I**nterest, create a **D**esire for the advertised product or service and finally lead to **A**ction, i.e. the purchase of that particular product.

– Advertising is often criticised for promoting ideal images of people, thereby putting consumers under psychological pressure by making them feel inadequate.

The internet

– term derives from the longer "interconnected networks"
– system of computer networks which enables users to publicise and access information on a global scale
– originally developed to allow some American universities to exchange data quickly
– was made accessible to a broad public and commercialised in the 1990s
– by 2021, the number of internet users worldwide had risen to 4.9 billion, i.e. 60 %, more than half the global population[1]
– in many areas, the internet is mostly accessed via mobile phone
– **advantages**, e.g.
  – makes it possible to communicate with people over long distances in real time, thereby turning the world into a **"global village"**
  – easy access to almost every kind of information imaginable
– **disadvantages**, e.g.
  – the **degree of credibility** of the information available is **not always clear**
  – the rate of **criminal activities** via the internet (from the violation of privacy to internet fraud) has been steadily rising
  – some countries try to suppress information that collides with their own ideologies, employing **censorship** (e.g. China)

The mass media fulfil a number of **functions**. Originally, its primary use was the transmission of **information** to the broadest possible audience, which made the media a vital means of **education**. Public **entertainment** soon came to be seen as equally **important**. With the advent and ever-growing popularity of online social networks such as Facebook, Instagram and Twitter, forging and maintaining **social relations** independently of time and place has also become a crucial function.

> **Keyword**
> **Media literacy:** This term refers to the ability of a recipient to analyse and evaluate the messages they receive through the media. Thus, one is expected to question the information one is given, e.g. by asking who is the actual creator/sender of the message, what is their aim in sending this message, how does the message try to catch my attention, what is the point of view presented in the message? Ultimately, media literacy is also vital in producing one's own messages.

[1] Source: https://www.statista.com/statistics/273018/number-of-internet-users-worldwide (accessed on 1 April 2023)

The Influence of the Media on Society and Personal Life

- Being **the prime source of information**, the media can influence a whole society's opinion about certain topics.
- With the help of more or less open forms of **censorship**, public opinion can be controlled; this was most famously fictionalised by George Orwell in his novel *Nineteen Eighty-Four*, in which a totalitarian regime represses its people by – amongst other means – **controlling** and **manipulating** the **information** communicated through the media.
- It is still being debated whether **images of violence** presented on **TV** and in **computer games** facilitate adolescent violence.
- In consumer societies, **advertisements** determine to a high degree what is considered to be a desirable lifestyle. This can be seen as a form of **indoctrination** and **social control**.

INFO "Fake news"

"Fake news" refers to false stories appearing as genuine news items on the internet or other media. It is usually created to influence political opinion or as a joke or provocation. Recently, fake news has been used to manipulate public opinion and even, it seems, to affect election results.

Keyword

Social Networking Services (SNS): Social networking services such as Facebook, Instagram and Twitter are online platforms that enable users to build or maintain social and business relationships via a wide variety of communication tools. Users usually create individual profiles and share experiences and opinions by posting texts, photos and videos. These virtual communities allow them to be connected regardless of where they live and across boundaries such as social status, profession, age and gender. Among the benefits of these platforms can be listed the strengthening of interpersonal relationships, increased freedom of self-expression and sense of belonging as well as simplifying grassroots organisation.

In the past few years, however, social networks, in particular Facebook, have come under increased scrutiny. Firstly, the business models of the companies are often based not only on selling advertising space but also their users' data for marketing purposes. In 2018, an investigation uncovered that the British firm Cambridge Analytica had illegally harvested the personal data of millions of Facebook users and resold it for political advertising, potentially even the Brexit vote and Donald Trump's 2016 presidential campaign. Facebook has also become the battleground for systematically disseminating misinformation, often used by lobbying groups and intelligence agencies to try and manipulate elections abroad. In September 2021, leaked documents revealed that Facebook Inc. (now Meta Platforms) was fully aware of the negative impact that its platforms had on the health of its teenage users as well as their product's propensity to help spread misinformation.

Keyword

Twitter: Twitter is a social media platform that allows users to post and interact with short messages known as "tweets". Users can follow other accounts to see their tweets in their feed and can also use hashtags to categorise their own tweets and make them more discoverable to other users. Twitter's popularity is based on allowing users to share their thoughts in real-time and provides a platform for celebrities, politicians and other public figures to connect with their fans and followers. Additionally, Twitter has been used extensively for political activism and social movements, particularly through the use of hashtags to organise and mobilise supporters around specific causes. One of the most notable examples of political hashtag activism on Twitter is the #BlackLivesMatter movement. The hashtag was used to draw attention to issues of police brutality and systemic racism and helped spark a broader conversation around race and social justice. Twitter has also had a significant impact on language, with its 280-character limit and emphasis on brevity and conciseness encouraging users to develop new forms of expression and linguistic shortcuts. However, the platform has also been criticised for contributing to the spread of misinformation and hate speech as well as for its role in amplifying and normalising extremist views and ideologies.

Jasmine Lee-Jones, *seven methods of killing kylie jenner* (gA, eA)

A note on the author

Jasmine Lee-Jones (born 1998 in North London) is a writer and actor of Jamaican heritage whose drama "seven methods of killing kylie jenner" (2019) has been honoured with various prizes, among them the "Evening Standard Award for Most Promising Playwright". She has kept any personal information private, and despite incorporating the power of social media strongly into her works, she deleted her own accounts at the end of 2020, claiming that – while being a powerful tool to finally enable marginalised people to being heard – these media also distorted her image, portraying somebody she did not consider herself to be in real life.

Synopsis

The play's plot is initiated when Forbes magazine declares Kylie Jenner the world's first self-made billionaire. This tweet infuriates @INCOGNEGRO, a Twitter user who argues that Kylie's success is not her own doing since she was born into a wealthy family. As a result, @INCOGNEGRO tweets a series of messages suggesting seven ways to kill Jenner. Each of these tweets is connected to an explanation that contrasts Jenner's privilege with the disadvantages of Black people, particularly Black women. The tweets trigger a Twitter storm that ranges from fascination to outrage and ultimately calls for violence, abuse and doxing. After the identity of Cleo – the person behind @INCOGNEGRO – has been revealed, she uses the medium for a long monologue in which she unfolds her feelings, thereby causing the Twittersphere to explode. In the "IRL" passages, her friend Kara tries to persuade Cleo to stop tweeting. The dialogues between the two women focus on the discrimination against Black women in combination with the dynamics of misogyny, abuse, colourism, gender, sexual orientation and the hurt inflicted by the two women upon one another in the past.

Analysis

The play explores themes of racism, colourism, appropriation, queerness and social media culture through the characters of Cleo and Kara, two Black women. It uses a variety of techniques, including flashbacks and multiple timelines, to tell its story.

The play initially introduces the setting, focusing on the most important headlines of the past two years, as the audience needs to understand the topicality of what is about to come. It then opens with Kara and Cleo dragging and burying something that looks like a body. This scene is a teaser to the post-mortem of the play, creating a sense of dread, mystery and suspense.

The play then flashes a couple of hours backwards in time and immediately introduces its central conflict. Cleo's catalyst is a Forbes tweet that triggers her anger as Kylie Jenner comes from a rich family and has made more by appropriating Black features and turning them into beauty standards for white women, while Black women continue to be considered ugly and are discriminated against because of them. Cleo considers this a form of theft and vents her frustration.

Cleo's anger is complex and multifaceted. She is angry at Jenner but also at the system that not only allows the influencer to profit while Black women are still discriminated against but inherently also perpetuates systematic racism and discrimination. Therefore, Cleo seems to suggest, Jenner should suffer the same negative experiences as Black people have since she already cashes in on their appropriation. Cleo then explores seven methods to kill Jenner, each one being a commentary on the ways in which Black bodies are used, abused and appropriated by white people.

The **1st method** involves Jenner dying from her own lip fillers' poison. Cleo sees this as a form of poetic justice, as full lips are considered beautiful in white women and hideous in Black women. The **2nd method** is a play on "shooting". Instead of Jenner's photo shoots, Cleo alludes to police brutality and the shooting of predominantly Black victims. The **3rd method** involves having Jenner drown in the sea, like thousands of refugees do, instead of in her wealth and images of herself. The **4th method** is perhaps the most provocative. Cleo proposes skinning Jenner's body so she can adorn herself with it, just like white people do with Black features. The **5th method** involves sacrificing Jenner, as if burnt by the flames pinned underneath Jenner's instagram posts declaring her appropriated Black features hot and attractive. In the **6th method,** Cleo wants Kylie Jenner shamed to death the same way Black people have been throughout history, e. g. in minstrel and "freak" shows but also through constant discrimination, slurs, harassment and violence. The **7th** and final **method**, death by displacement, does not reference Kylie Jenner anymore but instead tells Saartje Baartman's story and the suffering she had to endure – urging the audience to remember her story as an epitome of colonial exploitation and racism.

The Twittersphere's reactions evolve from initial amusement to racist behaviour and ultimately calls for violence. Cleo explains that said Forbes tweet not only promotes capitalism, cultural appropriation and exploitation but also the ongoing dehumanisation of Black women, while elevating and idolising white women within oppressive white structures. As Cleo points out, these harmful beliefs have been present for centuries and continue to perpetuate inequality and harm towards marginalised groups, especially Black people.

Additionally, the play touches on the issue of colourism ("shadeism"), e.g. when Cleo claims that her abuse was greater due to her darker skin tone or when the two women speak about being fetishised. She also challenges the image of Martin Luther King Jr., stating that he was just as problematic as every other man she has known. On top of this, the play explores trials of friendship, relationships between homo– and heterosexuals, how social media can amplify hate speech and how Black women are often the target of online harassment.

The play's language draws heavily on internet culture, including acronyms and Jamaican patois, suggesting the characters' cultural background. Its form is defined by an increasing blend of virtual and real spaces, ultimately even breaking the fourth wall. Most importantly, it highlights the complexity of being a Black woman in a world that appropriates and profits from their culture while also fetishising, marginalising and dehumanising them.

Topics:

- (ethnic) identity
- discrimination
- sexual diversity
- influence of social media
- role(s) of women

The Digital Revolution

While the Industrial Revolution changed the way people worked and lived together, the so-called Digital Revolution has done the same by digitalising large aspects of the formerly analogue world. This process started soon after WW II and increasingly accelerated from the moment when data storage facilities became smaller and smaller and when wireless technologies were introduced.

The year 2002 is generally seen as a turning point because since then more data has been stored in a digital than in an analogue way. It was the invention and spread of the internet that have made this process possible. Today, more than half the world's population is continuously online, thanks to the usage of computers and smartphones. This interconnectivity means that everyone who is connected to the internet has the world's information at their fingertips and can communicate worldwide.

The notion of privacy will have to be closely monitored, as more and more people give personal data to a few big companies such as Apple, Google or Amazon. Physically tracking or locating a person has become easy, as smartphones continuously show their position through GPS and wireless technologies.

Digitisation has entered all areas of life: communication, homes, banking, work and industry. The Internet of Things (IoT) – as found in a smart home – means that objects and machines are online and have hardware with sensors that interconnect them and communicate autonomously – i.e. without human interference. The IoT is not without hazards, so far as privacy, data storage and security are concerned. In fact, cybersecurity is an increasingly important issue. People have made themselves dependent on the exchange and storage of data, and hacking into data systems, whether personal, corporate or governmental, has become a real threat to modern society.

Glossary – Science and Technology

genetic engineering	Gentechnik, -manipulation
fossil fuels	fossile (endliche) Brennstoffe (z.B. Öl)
renewable energy non-renewable energy	regenerative (erneuerbare) Energien nicht erneuerbare Energien (Öl, Kohle, Gas)
carbon dioxide (CO_2)	Kohlendioxid
methane	Methan
(exhaust) fumes	Abgase
to contaminate	etw. vergiften, verseuchen
fuel rod	Brennstab (im Kernkraftwerk)
half-life	Halbwertzeit (die Zeit, die es dauert, bis ein radioaktives Material die Hälfte seiner Strahlkraft einbüßt; bis zu mehreren Mio. Jahren)
power station, power plant	Kraftwerk
global warming	globale Erwärmung
climate change	Klimawandel
to have an adverse effect	eine nachteilige Wirkung auf etwas haben
to emit, emission	ausstoßen/emittieren, Ausstoß/Abstrahlung
water supply	Wasserversorgung
drought	Dürreperiode
flooding	Überflutung
soil	Boden, Erde
landfill	Mülldeponie
deforestation	Waldrodung
oil spillage/spill/pollution	Ölverschmutzung/-pest
incineration	Verbrennung
to evaporate, evaporation	verdunsten, Verdunstung
precipitation	Niederschlag
greenhouse effect	Treibhauseffekt
(radioactive, chemical, ...) waste	(radioaktiver, chemischer, ...) Abfall

to reprocess something	etwas wiederaufbereiten
raw materials, natural resources	Rohstoffe, natürliche Rohstoffe
energy-efficient	Energie sparend
subsidise	subventionieren
biodegradable	biologisch abbaubar

Glossary – The Media

primary function	Hauptfunktion
public	öffentlich/Öffentlichkeit
unilateral	einseitig
advent	Aufkommen
spread	Ausbreitung
access	Zugang/Zugriff
credibility	Glaubwürdigkeit
censorship	(politische) Zensur
internet fraud	Internetbetrug
literacy	Lese- und Schreibfähigkeit
indoctrination	Indoktrination / ideologische Beeinflussung
inclination	Bereitschaft

William Shakespeare
(erhöhtes Anforderungsniveau)

The World that Made Him: The Elizabethan Age

> **Keyword**
> **The Elizabethan Age:** named after Queen Elizabeth I, born 1533, crowned 1558, died 1603 (reign of 45 years)

Politics and Economics

- England emerged as a world power; exploration of New World (Drake, Raleigh)
- international trade → the rise of capitalism
- strongest naval force (defeat of the Spanish Armada in 1588)
- internal problems: constant clash between Catholics and Protestants
- establishment of a Protestant Church with Elizabeth as head of the Church of England

Culture

> **Keyword**
> **The Golden Age:** term used for the Renaissance in Britain at the time of Elizabeth I
> - freedom of spirit → imagination
> - Greek and Roman thought
> - domestic study of the Bible, widely read and heard
> - opened new worlds of history and poetry, stimulated English culture
> - cultural flowering: theatre, music, poetry, art, architecture
> - writers: William Shakespeare, Christopher Marlowe, Edmund Spenser
> - architect: Inigo Jones (introduced Italianate architecture to England)
> - composers: Thomas Tallis, William Byrd

The era was dominated by contrast: life for ordinary people could be hard, but economic growth also meant better conditions for many.
negative aspects:
- harsh criminal laws (e.g. whipping and hanging for minor offences)
- illiteracy
- short life-expectancy
- no rights for women
positive aspects:
- public provision for the poor (possible because of economic growth)
- few beggars

The Elizabethan World Picture

Elizabethans still saw the Earth as the centre of the universe (geocentric world view) and therefore as the nucleus around which everything else revolved.

The guiding principle of this world view was universal order, which formed two ideas that crucially shaped Elizabethan society and thought: the **Great Chain of Being** and the **correspondence of microcosm and macrocosm**. Their world view was this a fixed and highly constructed one, deeply rooted in Christianity and concepts such as divine providence.

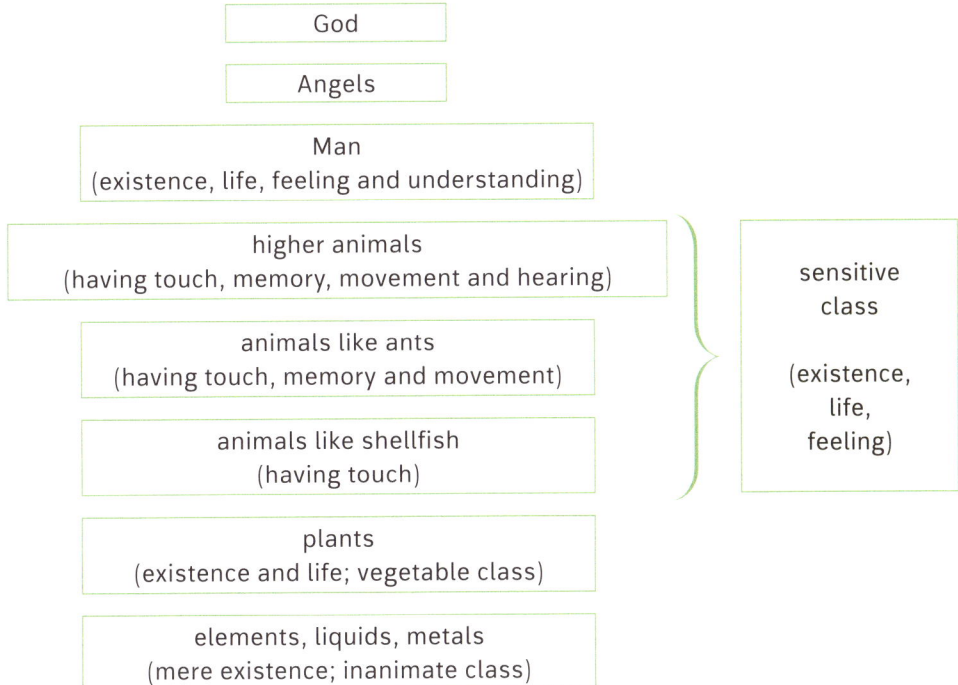

The Great Chain of Being

To Elizabethans, everything that existed was organised in a cosmic order. In this system, everything and everyone has a designated place, as if on a very large ladder: the Great Chain of Being. This hierarchy was based on importance, which in turn was determined by the relative proportion of spirit and matter: the more spirit something or someone had, the higher was its/their place in the chain. At the top of this system sat God, followed by angels, humans, animals, plants and minerals. Each part of the chain was in turn hierarchically structured from most to least important. Each link also had a 'primate' - in the human chain, for instance, this was the king. Being higher in the chain meant natural or God-given authority to rule over those beneath one's position.

As long as all the elements stay in their designated place, the hierarchy and therefore the order of being remain intact. However, if this order is disturbed, the chain is broken and chaos reigns. The attempt to changing one's place on the chain is therefore doomed. Romeo and Juliet, the "pair of star-cross'd lovers" (Prologue), are such a case. The couple falls in love across social boundaries and is bound to fail. Therefore, any attack on the balance has to be rectified - as in a disease of the body - to restore the original balance of the universe.

The corresponding planes

Different segments of the chain are reflected in other segments. This means there is universal interdependence, i. e. there are correspondences.

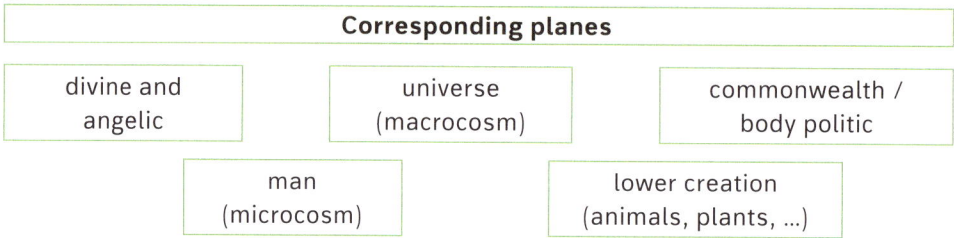

The planes were connected by an immense network of correspondences.

> **Keyword**
> **Correspondences:** Since the planes were interconnected with each other, order and disorder in one plane had the same repercussions in the other planes as well. For instance, the sun governs the other planets as the father rules his children. Elizabethan literature abounds with examples of this idea: for example, King Lear's madness is mirrored in the thunderstorm he walks in, and on the night Macbeth murders the king, horses are seen eating one another. In the same sense, debates between king and council in the body politic are mirrored in the microcosm as commotions in a person's mind.

Elements and humours

Since the human being was seen as a microcosm (literally, a "little world"; cf. John Donne: "I am a little world made cunningly / Of elements"), it reflected the structure of the world as a whole, the macrocosm. The world was composed of four "elements" (earth, water, air, fire), the qualities of which were based on the notions of hot and cold, dry and moist.

Correspondingly, the human body was composed of four substances called "humours", with characteristics corresponding to the four elements. Imbalance among the humours, i. e. when they did not exist in proper proportion to each other, caused illness.

element	humour	common quality
earth	melancholy	cold and dry
water	phlegm	cold and moist
air	blood	hot and moist
fire	choler	hot and dry

Elizabethan Theatre

Theatres in Elizabethan London were venues of mass entertainment.

Performing Shakespeare

Like most companies, Shakespeare and his men performed in theatres situated outside the City of London, on the Southern banks of the River Thames. The quarter was known for its many pubs and brothels. Theatres also acted as venues for bear-baiting, a brutal entertainment popular with Elizabethan in which a bear is tied to a stake and killed by dogs.

Because audiences, who were allowed to smoke, drink and eat in the theatre, were often rowdy, this entertainment was frowned upon by religious people as well as those in power. Common complaints included the accusation that
- the theatre was disorderly,
- the immoral characters on stage corrupted the audience, particularly young people,
- the stories told were depraved and primitive instead of religiously inspiring,
- it kept people away from work and prayer,
- it attracted criminals, for example pickpockets.

After touring through different locations like the Rose Theatre, Shakespeare had his own playhouse built in 1599, the *Globe Theatre*. It is a round, wooden structure with the stage protruding into the audience. Performances were held in the middle of the day, as the Globe had no artificial lighting. Elizabethan theatre also used very few props; instead, actors created the setting by describing it ("word scenery"). They did, however, wear highly elaborate costumes to embellish the characters they were portraying. Women were not allowed on stage, as it was deemed inappropriate for them by the fiercely religious government. Instead, their roles were acted by young men. This fact was frequently exploited by Shakespeare in comedies such as *Twelfth Night,* in which a man played a woman disguising herself as a man.
The Elizabethan theatre was attended by people from all social ranks: Poorer people stood in the space right in front of the stage ("pit"), while those who could afford it took a seat in the circle around the stage. The distance between the actors and the audience was minimal and spectators often interacted with the actors on stage. This had a strong influence on how Shakespeare wrote his plays as there are comic scenes that are purely written to entertain the masses as well as monologues by the protagonists explaining their thoughts and decisions.

Elizabethan Poetry
Sonnets

> **Keyword**
> **Sonnet form:** originally from Italy, 14th century
> Sonnets were made popular by Francesco Petrarca (in English: Petrarch).
> The fashion of sonnet writing spread to France and England.

Important Elizabethan sonnet writers:
- Thomas Wyatt (introduced sonnets to England, translations from Petrarch)
- Sir Philipp Sidney
- Edmund Spenser
- John Donne
- William Shakespeare

The Italian (Petrarchan) sonnet

	rhyme scheme	
octave/octet	a	quatrain
	b	
	b	
	a	
	a	quatrain
	b	
	b	
	a	
turn		turn
sestet	c	tercet
	d	
	e	
	c	tercet
	d	
	e	

Characteristics of the sonnet
- addressed to a beloved
- 14 lines
- clearly defined rhyme scheme (the most common is given above)
- divided into an octet and a sestet
- turn after the octave

The turn after the octave is a shift in thought or feeling, often indicated by "but" or "yet".

Variations in the rhyme scheme within the conventional structure are justified by the function they serve.

The English (Shakespearean) sonnet

	rhyme scheme	
octave/octet	a	quatrain
	b	
	a	
	b	
	c	quatrain
	d	
	c	
	d	
turn		
sestet	e	quatrain
	f	
	e	
	f	
		turn
	g	couplet
	g	

The turn in the English sonnet occurs after the third quatrain. Ideally there should be "three turns of the screw" in the three quatrains, before the point is driven home in the couplet. The couplet therefore offers a conclusion or a summary. However, one should still be aware that there can be the traditional turn after the octave.

Shakespeare's sonnets

- Shakespeare wrote 154 sonnets.
- Sonnets 1 to 126 are addressed to a young man.
- Sonnets 127 to 154 are addressed to a "dark lady".

Main themes: love, beauty, transience, old age, death

The **basic metre** is iambic pentameter, but Shakespeare does not use it slavishly. Metre is used functionally, e. g.
- regular metre: harmony, peace, tranquillity, balance, stability, etc.
- irregular metre: disharmony, confusion, parody

Shakespeare's Plays
The universal appeal

By 1592 William Shakespeare had managed to establish his reputation as a playwright in London. Due to his success, other writers envied him enormously.

A remarkable feature of Shakespeare's time is the complete lack of what we know today as copyright regulations. Authors could not protect their work from being adapted freely or even copied as a whole. Shakespeare himself was engaged in this process of "play-doctoring", modifying existing plays for his acting company. As a consequence, his authorship of a number of plays has been questioned.

From about 1595, however, Shakespeare no longer cooperated with other authors and became the respected playwright with the reputation he has had until today.

The fascination of his plays has not been lost over the more than four centuries since their first appearance. It can at least partly be attributed to the universal appeal of the topics he deals with. Love, happiness, envy, jealousy, treachery, humour – all of these profoundly human emotions and forms of behaviour enter easily into every spectator's heart.

Unfortunately, the dating of the plays, and therefore the order in which they were written, is difficult to determine. Shakespeare did not issue a printed collection of his dramatic works since no copyright existed. *Richard II*, however, appeared in six printed editions from 1597 to 1623, and *Romeo and Juliet* had five printed editions in the same time span. If all the plays had been printed and published in Shakespeare's lifetime, they would have been used by countless actors and authors. As a result, only an approximate order can be suggested. Shakespeare's opus can thus be broadly divided into four periods:

Timeline

Period 1 (1590–1595): The first period is clearly the one that least shows Shakespeare's literary genius. The style and imagery of the plays are rather simple. Although he does use rhyme, there is also a lot of prose. It is a time of experimentation with the genre.

Period 2 (1595–1600): During this period, which is marked by improved characterisation and style, Shakespeare wrote some of his best comedies and history plays, among which are *Henry IV* and *Henry V*. He also wrote his sonnets during this period.

Period 3 (1600–1608): Many scholars consider this to be the most important period. Shakespeare wrote great tragedies like *Hamlet* and the so-called "problem plays"/"bitter comedies".

Period 4 (1608–1613): In this period Shakespeare wrote his romances, which deal with the topic of losing and regaining happiness. The plots are rather melodramatic, but they also display an idyllic atmosphere. Shakespeare's last play was *The Tempest*.

Period	Comedies	Tragedies	History plays
1590–1595	The Comedy of Errors The Taming of the Shrew Two Gentlemen of Verona Love's Labour's Lost	Titus Andronicus	Henry VI
1595–1600	A Midsummer Night's Dream The Merchant of Venice The Merry Wives of Windsor Much Ado About Nothing As You Like It Twelfth Night	Romeo and Juliet	King John Richard II Henry IV Henry V
1600–1608	Troilus and Cressida Measure for Measure All's Well That Ends Well	Julius Caesar Hamlet Othello Timon of Athens King Lear Macbeth Antony and Cleopatra Coriolanus	
1608–1613	Pericles Cymbeline A Winter's Tale The Tempest		Henry VIII

Source: Wilhelm Rotter and Hermann Bendl, *Your Companion to English Literary Texts*. München: Manz, 1991. S. 182 ff. (gekürzt)

Shakespeare's language

The language Shakespeare used is not easy to understand because it differs from the English spoken today. Some words have changed their meaning since the Elizabethan Age, others have been dropped altogether and certain grammatical peculiarities need to be explained. We must also keep in mind that the lines Shakespeare makes his characters speak were intended to be performed on stage. In order to achieve a combined dramatic and artistic effect, he frequently employed blank verse, which is a fixed rhythmical pattern of iambic pentameters, as in this example from *Macbeth*:

Tomórrow ánd tomórrow ánd tomórrow

Especially for the less serious or comic characters, however, Shakespeare used prose, whereas verse is spoken by the noble ones.
Shakespeare's impact on the English language has been immense. He coined more than 500 neologisms (new words), and his works are still appreciated worldwide as

examples of true linguistic genius. It should be kept in mind, though, that Shakespeare never intended his plays to be read as books; they were to be performed on stage. This is where the beauty of their language is most evident.

The following table lists some examples of characteristic vocabulary and grammar used in Shakespeare's plays:

Shakespeare	Modern English
thou	you (used for children, subordinates, ordinary people and friends; Juliet in Romeo and Juliet, however, addresses Romeo as "you".)
ye, you	you (plural); form showing respect
thee	you (object form)
thy/thine	your (determiner) / your (determiner before vowels)
mine	my (determiner) before vowels
doth	does
hath	has
thou canst	you can
thou wilt	you will
I have writ	I have written
I would	I wish
Why call you ...?	Why do you call ...?
The guests are come.	The guests have come.

Hamlet (eA)

William Shakespeare is believed to have written The Tragedy of Hamlet, Prince of Denmark, usually abbreviated to Hamlet, sometime between 1599 and 1601. It is one of his plays that has known continuous success, the tragic role of the Prince of Denmark being interpreted and adapted in countless ways to this day. Even during Shakespeare's own time, the tragedy proved highly popular and was performed regularly.

Questions of morality: 'divine order' vs 'human order'

Perhaps it is the key issue at the centre of Hamlet, namely the **place of the individual within a divine and social order**, that echoes through the ages. Informed about his father's – the king's – murder in rather dubious circumstances, Hamlet is not only forced to verify the allegation against Claudius, his uncle, without raising suspicion, but also to make the crucial choice of whether to avenge his father. In order to find out the truth, Hamlet simulates madness and has actors put up the murder as a play. However, having assured himself, he is stalled by the question of whether it is right to kill Claudius.

It is this ethical question that takes centre stage for most of the play. Unlike a medieval morality play, Hamlet does not impose an idea of right and wrong on the audience but leaves the matter open to debate. It lays bare the prince's conscience, verbalising his thoughts, fears and resolutions, particularly in the soliloquies, thus involving its spectators in his dilemma. Hamlet effectively becomes a **play of inaction** as its protagonist fails to make a choice since, as he points out to Rosencrantz and Guildenstern, "there is nothing either good or bad, but thinking makes it so" (II, ii). Accordingly, Hamlet's only notable actions either occur off-stage – fighting the pirates – or are forced upon him in death, namely killing Claudius and avenging his father.

Hamlet was conceived during a time of **significant political chaos**. The Wars of the Roses, a bloody conflict of two families fighting over the throne, had been settled little more than a decade ago, and the monarch's – particularly a female one's – position was uncertain. In addition, religious tensions were bound up with the ruler's beliefs, often costing lives and livelihoods. Accordingly, intrigue and suspicion prospered at the royal court of Queen Elizabeth. This is duly mirrored in the play, in which – with the exception of Hamlet's and Horatio's friendship – all relationships are at least to some degree strategic alliances. For instance, Claudius uses Rosencrantz and Guildenstern to try and find out whether Hamlet knows anything about the murder. This paranoid atmosphere is also the reason why Hamlet cannot discuss his suspicions about his father's death and which forces him to pretend madness.

However, it is not only fear for his own life that lets Hamlet hesitate. He is also very aware that he is putting **private interests before public ones** in seeking revenge. This is a fatal flaw in various Shakespearean protagonists (e. g. Macbeth and Lear) and was a very real threat in the eyes of the Elizabethan public. As prince, Hamlet primarily has to fulfil a role that ensures the continuation of power and the state. He is not free to speak his mind or to fall in love with a woman of his choice, as is expressed by Laertes when he warns Ophelia that Hamlet's "will is not his own [...], for on his choice depends / The safety and health of this whole state" (I, iii). This warning gives the audience an insight into Hamlet's situation in terms of the political restrictions on his personal affairs. It also establishes Ophelia's position in society. She is considered too 'common' for marriage into the royal family, so the state (in this context, the king) must forbid this marriage for the greater good of the country. Both lovers' free will is restricted by their birth, and it is little wonder that Hamlet regards the court as a "prison" (II, ii).

Like everyone else, Hamlet is thus bound to his social rank as well as his place in the **Great Chain of Being**. He knows that acting out of personal motivation and killing his uncle in revenge would lead to chaos: Claudius is, after all, the king, a position that usually carried God's grace with it. Hamlet's revenge plot therefore threatens not only human order but also the divine plan.

Finally, *Hamlet* also asks of its audience the troubling question of who is **the better monarch**: a rightful one or one that is able to govern. On the one hand, Elizabethans' various ideas of divine order favoured a hereditary succession to the throne – i. e. usually of the deceased monarch's oldest son. On the other hand, the nation had seen a large number of conflicts arise out of this rule. Hence, British scholars of the time frequently discussed the book *The Prince* by the Italian historian Niccolò Machiavelli, which favoured a monarch that governed by force and, if necessary, by dishonest and immoral means in order to provide stability. These two conflicting ideas are obvious over the course of the play. While Hamlet's indecision and melancholy mark him out to be clearly unfit for kingship, Claudius remains an unsympathetic character throughout the play. Moreover, while the ending nominally restores order to the Danish kingdom, in Fortinbras, they effectively crown the enemy.

"Get thee to a nunnery!": the role of women in Hamlet

Despite having a female monarch, Elizabethan society was highly **patriarchal**: women were largely dependent on men and usually confined to the house as well as to providing a number of children to their husbands. They were also subjected to a very strict behavioural code, as is made obvious by the lengthy double sermon of both Laertes and Polonius in Act 1, Scene 3. Delivered in the shape of brotherly love on the one and fatherly wisdom and unshakeable assurance on the other hand, these rules enforce silence and repress female sexuality. The latter point is starkly illustrated by Hamlet demanding of his mother Gertrude that she subdue her libido (cf. III, iv). Likewise, his joke in the play-within-the-play scene, referring to the female genitalia as "[n]othing" (III, ii) – indeed a common synonym in Shakespeare's time –, reveals the usual position of women in Elizabethan society: silenced, belittled and best not seen at all.

Ophelia therefore cannot have a will of her own but is determined by where she comes from and by her **predetermined role** in society, especially by her gender. Her earlier scene with her brother (cf. I, iii) depicts her as a rather independent, witty person. However, she is put under so much pressure and her emotions are manipulated from so many directions that she eventually descends into madness.

While it can be argued that both Ophelia's and Hamlet's madness – pretended or not – mainly served as a spectacle and humorous relief to the Elizabethan audience, their conditions are fundamentally different. To the people of Shakespeare's time, Ophelia suffered from pathological **hysteria**, regarded as a typical 'female' illness, that ultimately causes her to lose her mind and makes her speak nonsense. Hamlet, on the other hand, is affected by **melancholy**, a fashionable condition in Renaissance England, particularly among intellectuals and men of high standing. Furthermore, his words are not merely nonsense but often constitute witty wordplay, leading Polonius to observe that if "this be madness yet there is method in't" (II, ii).

Modern Adaptations

Shakespeare's works have often reached the cinema or TV screen. One has to differentiate here between straight versions and modern adaptations. Concerning storyline, characters and setting, a straight version keeps close to the original by adopting the text and usually historical costumes and stage set as well. Moreover, the characters keep their original names.

An adaptation – generally also in some way a modernisation of the play – is typically based on the original but may present storyline, characters and setting in a different manner. It may be put in a contemporary setting or an historical setting later than Shakespeare's time – e.g. Richard Loncraine's 1995 version of *Richard III* or Julie Taymor's 1999 film *Titus*, with their references to recent European fascism. Likewise, the characters can be transplanted into different social or ethnic groups (as in the 1948 musical *Kiss Me, Kate* or in Baz Luhrmann's 1996 Californian *Romeo & Juliet*). Such modernisations often also aim at developing a market for a potential audience that might be attracted by the lightness of a musical version or an animated cartoon such as *The Lion King* (1994/2019), a loose adaptation of the Hamlet story. In such modern presentations the original poetic language, with its distinct metric scheme, is either not adopted at all or strongly abridged.

The catalogue of *Hamlet* versions currently runs to about 50 films. They range from very close straight versions to more or less loose adaptations that only adhere to the rough storyline. The first theatrical release of the story was in 1948, in which Laurence Olivier directed and also starred as the prince. The black-and-white film won four Oscars and is iconic to this day, even if it cut out political aspects of the play in favour of psychological ones. Franco Zeffirelli deliberately cast action star Mel Gibson in the titular role for his 1990 version, focussing less on the contemplative nature of the play and more on its action. In 1996, Kenneth Branagh attempted a definitive version of *Hamlet*, again both as director and actor. His film does not cut a single line from the text and thus runs to four hours, even portraying scenes that only occur offstage in the text. Set in the 19th century, the movie uses a vibrant, exquisite setting and an all-star cast. Although it proved a failure at the box office, critics regard the film as one of the best Shakespeare adaptations of all time. Finally, Michael Almereyda's version (2000) may be the most accessible to modern audiences. It translates the setting into the big-city "Denmark Corporation" and stars Ethan Hawke as the prince, who delivers his "To be or not to be" monologue in a video rental shop while cardboard signs scream "Action" at him.

Methoden der Textarbeit

Anforderungen von Aufgaben mit Textbezug

Alle im Abitur gestellten Aufgaben sind textbasiert. Sie können auch Bildmaterialien sowie audio-visuelle Materialien umfassen, auf die sprachlich reagiert werden muss. Zu den typischen Aufgabenformaten, die bei fiktionalen sowie nicht-fiktionalen Textvorlagen im freischriftlichen Teil gestellt werden, zählen die Zusammenfassung, die Analyse und der Kommentar bzw. kreative Aufgaben, die unterschiedlich ausgeprägt sein können (vgl. Hinweise zu den Operatoren, S. 99 f.). Neben diesen freischriftlichen Aufgaben werden auch neue Aufgabentypen zur Mediation vorkommen, die im Einleitungskapitel bereits thematisiert wurden. An dieser Stelle erhalten Sie Hinweise zu den üblichen schriftlichen Aufgaben, die weiterhin Teil der Abiturprüfung sind.

Aufgabenarten und Anforderungsbereiche

Aufgabenart	Anforderungsbereich
u. a. *summary* Operatoren: *describe, outline, state, summarise*	**I – comprehension, orientation, context** – Wiedergabe der zentralen Aussagen eines Textes – ggf. auch Einordnung des Textes in einen bekannten Kontext, aber üblicherweise ist die Aufgabe rein auf Basis des Ausgangstextes zu beantworten
u. a. *analysis* Operatoren: *analyse, examine, compare, explain, contrast*	**II – analysis** – Anwendung von Fachmethoden: textanalytische Verfahren, exakte Arbeit am sprachlichen Detail, Belegen und Zitieren, problemlösende Argumentation – gezielte Anwendung von Kenntnissen und Wissen – z. B. soziokulturelles Wissen oder Wissen über Sprache
u. a. *comment* Operatoren: *comment, discuss, justify, evaluate* u. a. *write* Operatoren: *write, imagine, continue, find*	**III – comment, evaluation, re-creation of text, creativity** für die analytisch-interpretierende Aufgabenstellung: – Bewertung der Textvorlage auf Basis der vorher gewonnenen Erkenntnisse, Einordnung des Textes in einen größeren Zusammenhang – persönliche Stellungnahme, eigene Meinung für die produktionsorientierte/kreative Aufgabenstellung: – Umsetzung, Bewertung, Reflexion der Problematik des Ausgangstextes bzw. der Analyse in einem kreativen Kontext: z. B. Perspektivwechsel (Sicht einer Figur) – Füllen von Leerstellen (Weitererzählen, neues Ende) – Textsortenwechsel (Brief an Protagonisten, Leserbrief, Brief an *agony aunt*, Tagebucheintrag, Dialog usw.)

Die Bedeutung der Operatoren[1]

Für die Formulierung der Aufgaben gibt es klare Vorgaben. Verben für die Arbeitsanweisungen (= Operatoren) müssen in ihrer exakten Bedeutung verstanden werden. Eine ungefähre Ahnung, was gefordert ist, reicht keinesfalls aus. Die folgende Operatorenübersicht ist der Website des Ministeriums entnommen. Die mittlere Spalte definiert die genaue Wortbedeutung der Anweisung, die dritte Spalte gibt jeweils ein Beispiel für eine mögliche Aufgabenstellung.

Operatoren	Definitionen	Beispiele
(schwerpunktmäßig) Anforderungsbereich I		
describe	give a detailed account of something	Describe the soldier's appearance. Describe the situation …
outline	give the main features or the general principles of a text/topic, omitting minor details	Outline the author's views on love, marriage and divorce and point out how …
state	specify clearly	State briefly the main developments in the family described in the text.
summarise, write a summary	give a concise account of the main points	Summarise the information given in the text about the hazards of cloning.
(schwerpunktmäßig) Anforderungsbereich II		
analyse, examine	describe and explore in detail certain aspects and/or features of the text and how they are presented	Analyse the views on class held by the two protagonists. Examine the author's use of language … Examine how the author characterises …
compare	show similarities and differences	Compare the attitude of the two characters towards war.
explain	show causes and effects in a given context	Explain the protagonist's obsession with money. Explain XYZ's attitude towards …
contrast	emphasise the differences between two or more things	Contrast the author's idea of human aggression with the theories of aggression you have read about.

[1] Quelle: https://www.nibis.de/uploads/mk-bolhoefer/2021/EN_2021Abi_Operatoren.pdf (Zugriff: 01.04.2023; verändert)

(schwerpunktmäßig) Anforderungsbereich III		
comment	state clearly your opinion on the topic in question and support your views with evidence	Comment on the suggestion made in the text that a "lack of women in the armed forces demonstrates a weakness in the role of women in society".
discuss	investigate by giving reasons for and against	Discuss the implications of globalisation as presented in this text.
justify	present reasons for decisions, positions or conclusions	You are the head boy / head girl of your school. Justify a decision taken by the pupils' council when you meet with your headmaster.
assess/ evaluate	consider in a balanced way points for and against something	Evaluate the author's view of the impact of the American Dream … Assess the importance of standards in education.

Kreative Aufgaben

Der **Anforderungsbereich III umfasst auch kreative Aufgaben**, für die jedoch keine allgemein verbindlichen Operatoren formuliert werden können. Folgende Aufgabenstellungen sind möglich:

– Write a letter, email to a friend / to the the editor / of complaint / of enquiry … .
– Write a dialogue / the dialogue between X and Y / a script (film, play …) based on / XYZ's diary entry … .

– Write an article (for …) / a report (for …).
– Continue the story … / Find a suitable ending … / Imagine you are XYZ. Continue/Tell the story … from her/his point of view … .

TIPP zum Punktesammeln

Befassen Sie sich intensiv mit den Operatoren. Nur wenn Sie genau wissen, was in der Aufgabenstellung gefordert ist, können Sie eine gute Lösung schreiben.

Grundlegende Hinweise zu den Aufgaben: *summary, analysis, comment*

Summary

– Hier soll gezeigt werden, dass der **Textinhalt** verstanden wurde.
– Aus diesem Grund ist es entscheidend, sich von der Textvorlage zu lösen und in eigenen Worten die Hauptinhalte wiederzugeben; das heißt auch, dass weder Passagen übernommen noch Zitate integriert werden dürfen.

- Sprachlich ist Folgendes zu beachten: Bei Zusammenfassungen von **fiktionalen Texten** ist durchgehend das **Präsens** zu verwenden (bei Vorzeitigkeit kann vereinzelt das *present perfect*, bei Nachzeitigkeit das *will future* eingesetzt werden, auf keinen Fall aber eine Vergangenheitsform).
- Bei **nicht-fiktionalen Texten** (z. B. Zeitungsartikel) sind die Hauptaussagen des Autors ebenfalls im Präsens wiederzugeben; nur in Einzelfällen ist es zulässig, für Ereignisse, die in der Vergangenheit tatsächlich stattgefunden haben, das *past tense* zu verwenden.
- **Autorenbezug herstellen:** Besonders bei **nicht-fiktionalen Texten** ist es wichtig, immer klarzustellen, wer welche Aussagen trifft (vor allem bei Zeitungsartikeln, in denen verschiedene Meinungen wiedergegeben werden).
- Je nach Operator kann eine pointierte oder umfassende Zusammenfassung verlangt werden (vgl. Operatoren, S. 99 f.).

Analysis

- Inhaltlich soll hier gezeigt werden, inwiefern die **Form des Textes** dessen Inhalt, Aussageabsicht oder die Haltung des Autors beeinflusst.
- Hier wird verlangt, dass die sprachliche Form des Textes genauer untersucht wird (z. B. im Hinblick auf Sprachebenen, stilistische Mittel, Erzählhaltung etc.) und dass daraus Rückschlüsse auf den Textinhalt bzw. dessen Wirkung gezogen werden; auch hier wird der Text im Präsens verfasst.
- Für eine sprachliche Analyse genügt es nicht, lediglich Stilmittel zu identifizieren und aufzulisten; es kommt vor allem darauf an, deren Wirkungsabsicht zu erkennen.
- Typische Analyseaspekte sind bei **fiktionalen Texten**: *point of view, character analysis, analysis of atmosphere/setting, analysis of tone,* usw.
- Typische Analyseaspekte bei **nicht-fiktionalen Texten** sind: *the use of language/ structure, the intention or attitude of the author, the intended effect on the audience (i. e. in speeches), the use of language to achieve the text's aim (e. g. to convince, to provoke, to educate, etc.),* usw.
- **Autorenbezug herstellen:** Es ist sinnvoll klarzustellen, welche Aussageabsicht dem Autor oder dem Erzähler oder einer der Figuren zuzuordnen ist und welche Wirkungsabsicht damit verfolgt wird.

Comment (Evaluation)

- Inhaltlich soll hier gezeigt werden, dass der Textinhalt reflektiert werden kann.
- Diese kritische Auseinandersetzung mit dem Text kann in unterschiedlicher Form gefordert werden:
    - persönlicher *comment*: Hier wird eine persönliche Stellungnahme zum Material verlangt, die fachlich-argumentativ begründet sein muss und in der Regel auch Hintergrundwissen erfordert; das reine Feststellen der eigenen Meinung reicht nicht; sie muss erläutert werden und fundiert sein.
    - argumentativer *comment*: Hier wird in der Regel eine sachlich-distanzierte Gegenüberstellung von Vor- und Nachteilen bzw. Pro- und Kontra-Argumenten verlangt, die in einem abwägenden und schlüssigen Fazit enden muss.

– *comment* aus der Sicht einer anderen Person: Unter Umständen ist gefordert, dass Sie sich in die Situation einer Figur des Textes oder einer anderen Person versetzen, um aus deren Vorstellung heraus den Inhalt zu kommentieren; hier kann es sinnvoll sein, auch die Sprache / den Ausdruck dieser Figur zu übernehmen, um den Kommentar authentischer wirken zu lassen (insbesondere bei kreativen Aufgaben wird diese Form häufig verlangt).

Hinweise zu kreativen Aufgaben

Typische Formen

– formeller oder persönlicher Brief, E-Mail
– Tagebucheintrag, *blog entry, interior monologue*
– eine Geschichte erzählen (ein Ende für einen Text verfassen, eine Geschichte zu einem Bild erfinden, die Erzählperspektive wechseln etc.)
– einen Artikel schreiben, einen Leserbrief verfassen
– einen Dialog zwischen zwei Figuren eines fiktionalen Textes entwickeln etc.

Wichtige Aspekte für die Bearbeitung

– Zentral ist, dass Sie auf das Material eingehen und dieses einbeziehen. Unabhängig davon, welche Art von kreativer Produktion verlangt wird, sollte der Ausgangstext oder das Ausgangsbild nie aus den Augen verloren werden.
– Der selbst produzierte Text muss den formalen Anforderungen entsprechen (z. B.: Adresszeile, Anrede, ggf. Betreff, Datum, Abschlussformel bei Briefen) und muss als Brief, E-Mail, Zeitungsartikel o. Ä. klar erkennbar sein.
– Sprachlich sollte der Text den Ton der Vorlage bzw. der Figur treffen: Ein Brief aus der Sicht eines Kindes kann nicht in stilistisch gehobenem Englisch verfasst werden, ein Brief an einen Redakteur nicht mit Umgangssprache durchsetzt sein.
– Hier ist es also entscheidend, dass man das eigene Sprachrepertoire durch ein anderes ersetzen bzw. ergänzen kann, damit der Text glaubwürdig wird.
– Auch hier ist es wichtig, dass der Inhalt nicht zu oberflächlich bleibt (auch ein Tagebucheintrag eines Jugendlichen sollte emotionale Tiefe zeigen und nicht lediglich beschreibend sein).
– Insgesamt sollte der Text so verfasst werden, dass er die Lesenden überzeugt und authentisch wirkt.

Literarische Texte

Narration

Keyword
Narrative texts: Narrative texts can have many forms, among them short story, novel, fairy tale, satire, parable, legend, etc.
The ones that are most relevant for your final exam are the short story and the novel.

When asked to analyse a narrative text, you will have to focus on particular elements that are characteristic of short stories or novels.

Elements of narration

Plot

INFO Elements of a complete plot

exposition → rising action → climax / turning point → falling action → ending

A **plot** need not necessarily be complete (there may be an open ending).
The **sequence** need not necessarily be chronological.
There may be foreshadowing or flashbacks or there may be reverse narration (umgestelltes Erzählen).
In particular, an excerpt from a longer text, which is the most common sort of text in the final exam, may not contain all the elements of the plot.
Certain **key events** within the action of a story will increase the tension; they will create suspense, rising to a climax or turning point. After that there will be falling tension or relief.

INFO Tension curve

rising tension → climax or turning point → falling tension or relief

Theme
The **theme** of a story is always abstract. Themes can be love, poverty, racism, childhood, etc. The **subject matter** of a story is the concrete realisation of a theme.

Example:
Two stories may have the same theme: racism. The subject matter of one may be the murder of an African American, of the other the bullying of a Black schoolgirl.

Characters
When asked to characterise a figure from a narrative text, you must be aware of different aspects. There are key questions that can guide you.

Direct characterisation
– What does the narrator say about the character?
– What do other characters say about the character?
– What does the character say about himself/herself?
– How objective is what they say? Be aware of words with negative or positive connotations.

Indirect characterisation
- How does the character act?
- What does the character say?
- What kind of language does he/she use?

It might help to fill in a table with the following headings:

Character's outward appearance	Character's language	Character's actions	What the character says	Other characters' statements (or actions)
...	...	...	...	...

Narrator / Point of view

INFO Narrator

The narrator is either a first-person or a third-person narrator.
The first-person narrator is NOT the author!

limited point of view	unlimited/omniscient point of view
first-person narrator	third-person narrator (neutral omniscience, God-like knowledge of all the facts)
third-person narrator (one character's point of view, "selective omniscience")	third-person narrator (several characters' points of view)

Modes of presentation

Narratives can be presented in two ways: the panoramic and the scenic mode.
Panoramic presentation is used to pay great attention to detail, immersing the reader in the events, while **scenic** presentation condenses the action and can summarise the events of several years into a few lines.

Interior monologue is a particular kind of scenic presentation in which the thoughts and feelings passing through a character's mind are depicted. In **reported thought**, thoughts are presented as reported speech.

This is closely connected with the concepts of **narrated time** and **narrating (or acting) time**:

narrated time longer than narrating time	usually summary of events
narrated time identical with narrating time	e.g. direct speech
narrated time shorter than narrating time	e.g. stream of consciousness, interior monologue, detailed description of a scene, comparable to slow motion in a film

INFO Function of mode of presentation and point of view

A neutral, omniscient narrator, who observes the action and the characters from above and who uses a panoramic mode of presentation, is more detached and thus creates a distance between the reader and the action. On the other hand, a narrator who takes a character's point of view creates immediacy and directly involves the reader in what happens.

Setting

The place and time where the action is set is called the setting. It is especially important for *atmosphere* and *symbolism*.

Atmosphere

Atmosphere is created by means of setting, objects, colours, light and darkness but also by reference to a character's mood or the use of language.

Symbolism

Symbols are part of the setting of the narrative. They are objects, characters or even actions that suggest something beyond their mere meaning. For example, the colour white often symbolises purity.

INFO Established symbols

These are conventional symbols which have long been used and have a certain, traditional significance that everybody knows. Examples of established symbols: a rose, a cross, the colour white.

INFO Created symbols

Something becomes symbolic within a certain context because it is closely connected to an event, a situation or a character.

INFO Symbols

Symbols are NOT metaphors!
Symbols are a factual physical part of the story. Metaphors or similes are figures of speech without an actual representation in the narrated world.

Examples:
She was a rose, so beautiful. → metaphor
She was like a rose, so beautiful. → simile/comparison
They fell in love when they first met in her father's rose garden. → symbol

Language and style

In order to determine the style of a text, it is necessary to examine aspects such as register, diction (choice of words), tone and also sentence structure.

Register is the level of language used in a particular situation. It may be formal, neutral, informal, or vulgar. There may be a lot of slang words, even taboo words as well as technical terms or jargon.

The **tone** may be ironic, sarcastic, sad, humorous, serious, playful, angry, etc., depending on the emotional attitude it expresses. This depends on the choice of words, level of speech, rhythm, sentence length, etc.

Stylistic devices will be considered at length in the chapters on drama and non-fictional texts (p. 111 f. and 116 f.).

Poetry

Poetry focuses on the **aesthetic function** of language; it appeals to the senses. It is to be enjoyed for its beauty, its cleverness, its wit, its impact.
This is achieved by
- the sound of words,
- the rhythm of the words and phrases,
- the choice of words,
- the structure of the sentences,
- the composition of the poem,
- the visual arrangement of words and lines,
- and, above all, by means of imagery.

In your final exams, however, you will be asked not so much to enjoy the poem but to examine its meaning and the effect of the language the speaker uses.

How to proceed

Questions to be asked

- Who is the speaker of the poem?
- Where is the speaker?
- Does the speaker address somebody?
- Does the speaker contemplate something?
- Does the speaker describe something or somebody?
- Does the speaker tell a story?
- Does the speaker explain something?
- Does the speaker argue against or in favour of something?
- What is the speaker's attitude? What is he/she saying?
- How is the poem composed? Is it structured by a rhyme scheme, by the division into stanzas or by some other device?
- Is there a correspondence between the structure of the poem and the structure of the speaker's thoughts?
- What is the significance of the title?
- What words does the speaker use? What do they mean?
- What is the structure of the sentences? Simple? Complex?
- What poetic devices does the speaker use?
- And what is the effect of all this? What is the experience of reading the poem?

In order to understand and describe poetry, you need to be familiar with its most important elements.

Elements of poetry

INFO Speaker and author

The speaker of the poem is NOT the author. Poems may be autobiographical, but you must still refer to the "speaker in the poem".

Poems are composed of **stanzas** and **lines**.
Stanzas may have a certain **rhyme scheme.**

Rhyme

Rhyme schemes

pair rhyme	a a b b
alternate rhyme	a b a b
embracing rhyme	a b b a

Types of rhyme

masculine rhyme (one syllable)	kiss/this
feminine rhyme (two syllables)	dreary/weary
true rhyme	kiss/this, dreary/weary
slant rhyme assonance (same vowel) consonance (same consonant)	comb/coat hope/heap

Lines and rhythm

Lines may have a certain rhythm. The smallest unit that determines rhythm is the foot, consisting of at least one stressed and one or two unstressed syllables. The pattern of stressed and unstressed syllables is called **metre.**
A sequence of stressed and unstressed syllables is not something artificial. It is the natural rhythm of the English language. It is the poet's skill to choose words in such a way that this pattern constitutes a regular metre. Types of foot:

foot	stresses	example
iamb/iambic	–/ (da-**dum**)	compare
trochee/trochaic	/ – (**dum**-da)	lovely
spondee/spondaic	// (**dum dum**)	drop dead
anapest/anapestic	– –/ (da-da-**dum**)	lemonade
dactyl/dactylic	/ – – (**dum**-da-da)	whispering

The number of feet or stressed syllables in a line determines its metre. The most common types are shown here:

number of feet	metre	example
1	monometer	"And **find** / What **wind**" (John Donne, "Song", ll. 7 – 8)
2	dimeter	"Why **dost** thou **thus**" (John Donne, "The Sun Rising", l. 2)
3	trimeter	"**Go**, Soul, the **bo**dy's **guest** / U**pon** a **thank**less **er**rant" (Sir Walter Raleigh, "The Lie", l. 1 f.)
4	tetrameter	"**Bu**sy old **fool**, unruly **sun**" (John Donne, "The Sun Rising", l. 1)

| 5 | pentameter | "If **mu**sic **be** the **food** of **love**, play **on**" (William Shakespeare, *Twelfth Night,* l. i) |
| 6 | hexameter | "And **in** your **dread**ful **verse** in**grav'd** the **prophe**cies" (Michael Drayton, „Poly-Olbion", l. 33) |

INFO Most important metre in English poetry

Iambic pentameter:
"But **thy** e**ter**nal **sum**mer **shall** not **fade**" (Shakespeare, Sonnet 18).

Types of lines

end-stop lines	The meaning requires a pause at the end of the line.	"Shall I compare thee to a summer's day**?**" (Shakespeare, Sonnet 18)
run-on lines (enjambement)	The meaning requires no pause between the lines.	"When yellow leaves, or none, or few, do **hang** **Upon** those boughs which shake against the cold" (Shakespeare, Sonnet 73)
caesura	The meaning requires a pause in mid-line.	"Let me not to the marriage of true minds Admit **impediments**; **love** is not love" (Shakespeare, Sonnet 116)

TIPP Watch out!

The word *imagery* is an abstract noun. There is no plural. You can only talk about single *images*.

Imagery

A writer or speaker using language beyond its dictionary meaning makes use of **imagery.** All figurative use of language is imagery. Imagery appeals to all the senses; it is meant to stimulate the reader's or listener's imagination.

Important types of imagery are: metaphor, simile/comparison, personification and symbol (cf. p. 111 f.).

Drama

When asked to analyse a dramatic text, you will have to focus on particular elements that are characteristic of plays.

Elements of drama
Plot

exposition → rising action → climax or crisis → falling action → dénouement or catastrophe

The action is presented to the audience on stage or on a screen directly. There is no narrator. Yet one can identify the same elements of plot as are found in narration.
In tragedy, the opponents of the hero gain the upper hand in the falling action, which ends in the catastrophe. Comedy has a happy ending, in which conflicts are resolved (dénouement).

Stage directions

The dramatic text consists of **two kinds of text:** the more important kind of text is spoken by the characters (i. e. dialogue, monologue, soliloquy and asides).
The **stage directions** are the second kind of text. They give instructions concerning the stage design, about sounds to be heard, visual effects, the characters' outer appearance and actions and also the way some of the dialogue has to be spoken.
The following visual and acoustic elements will have to be considered in your analysis of stage directions. They will help to characterise the dramatis personae, to create a specific atmosphere or they will function as symbols (cf. p. 111 f.).

concerning the actors		concerning the stage	
visual	acoustic	visual	acoustic
size	voice	scenery	music
facial expressions	intonation	stage design	background noise
gestures	language of the play	lighting	sounds
costumes	non-verbal noises	props	

Characters

The characters are not mediated via a narrator but present themselves through action, interaction and dialogue and, of course, their outward appearance on stage (see above). There are **flat** characters, types that act in a predictable way and do not develop over the course of the action, and **round** characters that appear and act lifelike and non-stereotypical and often undergo some form of inner development during the play.

Language/Dialogue/Communication

When analysing the language of a play, you have to keep in mind that it works on two levels:
1. the inner system of communication, i. e. the communication among the characters
2. the outer system of communication between the playwright and the audience

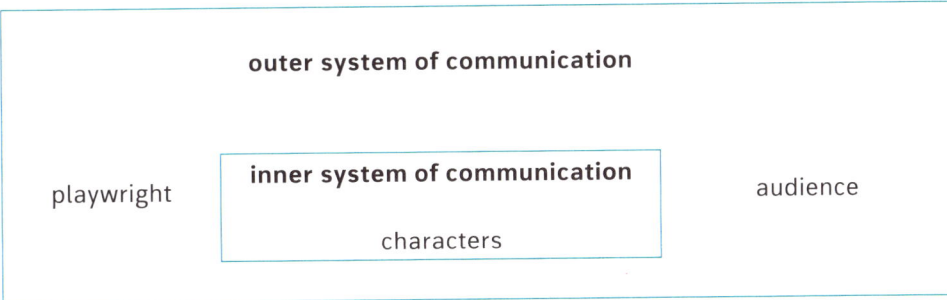

Dramatic irony

Dramatic irony is an important effect that is created by these two levels of communication. It arises when there is a sharp contrast between what the audience knows and what a character knows or utters. Dramatic irony often serves to great comic effect as well. Shakespeare, for example, puts it to great effect in his comedies when he introduces cases of mistaken identity.

Example:

In Shakespeare's Macbeth, King Duncan praises the peaceful atmosphere at Macbeth's castle, whereas the audience knows that Duncan is going to be murdered.

Aside

In an aside, an actor speaks to the audience in order to provide information on his thoughts and feelings or intentions. The other characters on stage supposedly do not hear what she/he says.

TIPP

As many of Shakespeare's plays are written in verse, you may approach their language in the same way as poetry.

Language and style

Important stylistic devices

device	definition	example
alliteration	repetition of a sound (usually a consonant) at the beginning of neighbouring words	"From forth the fatal loins of these two foes" (Shakespeare, *Romeo and Juliet,* Prologue)
allusion	direct or implied reference	Poetry is great. Just think of the most famous writer of sonnets in English.
analogy	establishing a resemblance between two things that are basically unlike	The heart is simply a pump propelling the blood round the body.

anaphora	neighbouring sentences starting with the same word(s)	"We shall not flag or fail. We shall go on to the end. We shall fight in France" (W. Churchill)
antithesis	contrasting ideas using a parallel syntactic structure	"It's a story that hasn't made me the most conventional candidate. But it is a story that has seared into my genetic make-up the idea that [...]" (B. Obama)
assonance	repetition of internal vowel sounds in neighbouring words	How now, brown cow?
blank verse	poetry without rhyme but with a regular metre: iambic pentameter	"The king has happily received, Macbeth, / The news of thy success, and when he reads" (Shakespeare, *Macbeth*)
chiasmus	the reversal of word order in two parts of a sentence	"Fair is foul, and foul is fair" (Shakespeare, *Macbeth*)
climax	an enumeration of arguments that become stronger	Friendship, affection, love.
ellipsis	incomplete sentence	A good choice!
enumeration	list of arguments	Macbeth is disloyal, greedy and obedient to his wife.
euphemism	replacing an unpleasant expression with a more agreeable one	"Civilising" Australian Aboriginals meant forcibly removing the children from their families.
hyperbole	exaggeration	I've told you a thousand times.
inversion	reversal of word order	Not only did he like chocolate, he also ate a lot of it.
metaphor	indirect comparison without "like" or "as"	Love is a red, red rose.
metonymy	name of a thing or concept is replaced by a part of it or by s.th. associated with it	"wheels" for "car" / "turf" for "horse-racing"
onomatopoeia	word that imitates the sound that it stands for	Bang! Swoosh! Ding-dong.
paradox	an apparent contradiction	This statement is true and false at the same time.
parallelism	same syntactic structure of two or more sentences	"One small step for man, one giant leap for mankind." (Neil Armstrong)
personification	inanimate objects / abstract ideas presented as if human beings	The flowers are begging for water.

rhetorical question	a question that does not require an answer	Do you think I'm stupid?
simile	comparison using the words "like" or "as"	Your love is like a red, red rose.
telling name	a name that represents character traits	"Doolittle": she is too little, or: she does too little (Shaw, Pygmalion)

Glossary – Analysing Literary Texts

the narrator tells of / shows / relates / reveals
the narrator takes xy's point of view
the narrator is omniscient
the story is told in the first-person/third-person form
the narrator uses / employs / makes use of metaphors/similes/comparisons
this metaphor shows / stands for / suggests
the narrator speaks in an ironic/satirical/detached/matter-of-fact/serious tone
the story deals with / treats of / concentrates on / focuses on …
atmosphere is created
tension/suspense is created/built up
the poem is written/composed
the poem is read/spoken/recited
the recital of a poem
the poem is by Shakespeare / it is a song by Genesis
the speaker of the poem / the poetic I / the poetic persona
the poem consists of / is composed of / is arranged in stanzas
the comedy ridicules/mocks/satirises
the exposition sets the action in motion
the action moves towards and culminates in a turning point
the play has a simple/complex/tight plot
it has a happy/unhappy ending
the main/major/minor character(s) is/are
the protagonist is in conflict with an opponent
the antagonist fights the protagonist
the spectator/audience follows the play
the play is performed/produced/staged
the scenery is shifted
actors perform/play/enact
an actor enters / makes an entrance / exits / makes her/his exit

Sach- und Gebrauchstexte

Argumentative Texts: How to Deal with (Political) Speeches

> **Keyword**
> **(Political) speeches:** aim at convincing *(überzeugen)* the audience of the speaker's position, winning them over to his/her side. Very often, the speaker tries to persuade *(überreden)* the listener by appealing to his/her feelings. In some cases, the orator may even attempt to manipulate *(manipulieren)* his/her audience.
> You should always keep in mind that the speaker wants to present his/her opinion / conviction / point of view as positively as possible.

When asked to analyse a political speech, you will have to focus on the topic as well as characteristic features.

How to proceed

Reading the text
1. Read the speech (or, more likely, an extract from it) as a whole, trying to identify the main topic (reading for gist).
2. Re-read the speech/extract several times, paying close attention to certain characteristic features of such speeches. Mark words or phrases in the text and take notes (intensive reading).

Pay close attention to
- key words and phrases
- references to historical events
- the use of symbols, key words, slogans
- references to famous people
- references to works of literature
- stylistic devices (see below)

Questions to be asked
When it comes to analysing a speech, you should always ask yourself the following questions:
- What is the main topic of the speech?
- What is its political, historical and social context?
- What do I know about the speaker (biography, political orientation)?

Elements of a (political) speech
Structure

Speeches can usually be divided into an **introduction**, a **main part** and a **conclusion**. These parts serve different purposes:

INFO Introduction to a speech

In the introduction the orator announces the topic/purpose of the speech and explains its importance. He/She also wants to attract the audience's attention so that they will follow the speech closely and accept his/her opinion.

There are several ways to make listeners interested:
- The speaker can open by telling the audience **something about their personal history / recent experience**, thereby underlining the fact that the topic of the speech is of personal importance to them. By relating a **little story** to the audience, the speaker will also appear more human and less remote.
- Another common way of starting a speech is to **open it with a question** that refers to the main topic and which will be answered later in the speech. By asking the audience a question, the speaker actively involves them, indirectly asking them to think more deeply about an issue.
- A speaker may **present visual material to the audience,** e.g. pictures, concrete objects or a short extract from a film. This also helps to attract the audience's attention: listeners will become curious about how the object or visual material is related to the content of the speech.

INFO Main part of a speech

In the main part of the speech the orator needs to keep the audience interested and to make sure that they can follow the train of thought.

Again, there are several ways to do this. The following techniques are particularly effective:
- **using short and simple sentences**, developing the argumentation step by step and ensuring that the audience can follow,
- quoting reliable sources/experts, referring to statistics and **providing the audience with facts and necessary background information**, which shows that the speaker is well-informed and has researched the subject,
- **pointing out problems** but also providing solutions to them, thus showing that the speaker is competent, and
- **including personal experiences** and vivid, specific events, again aiming for a personal relationship with the audience, often using personal pronouns like "we", "us", "our".

Towards the end of a speech the speaker might
- take up a question posed at the beginning of the speech,
- appeal once more to both the audience's heads and hearts,
- ask for support, giving the listeners the feeling that their support is of major importance, and
- develop a vision for the future.

Language and style

There are certain stylistic devices which are often used in speeches. They aim at making the speech more lively and interesting.

Important stylistic devices

analogy	A resemblance is established between things which are dissimilar.
simile	This is a direct comparison using the words "like" or "as", e.g. *He fought like a lion in the battle.*
metaphor	This is an indirect comparison without using the words "like" or "as", e.g. *He was a lion in the battle.*
alliteration	A consonantal sound is repeated in two or more adjacent words, e.g. *We will win; "We must understand that ties of trade bind nations in closest intimacy"* (Warren G. Harding: Inaugural address, 4 March 1921).
repetition	Repeating certain words or phrases puts emphasis on their meaning, e.g. *"The answer to the slavery question was already embedded within our Constitution – a Constitution that had at its very core the ideal of equal citizenship under the law; a Constitution that promised its people liberty, and justice"* (Barack Obama: *A More Perfect Union*)
parallelism	Two or more parts of a sentence (or two or more sentences) have the same (or similar) syntactic structure. Like repetition, parallelism serves to emphasise the parts of the sentence in question, intensifying the force of the statement and encouraging the audience to think about its meaning, e.g. *"Let us be our sister's keeper. Let us find that common stake we all have in one another, and let our politics reflect that spirit as well."* (Barack Obama: *A More Perfect Union*)
antithesis	Two ideas are opposed to one another, using a parallel syntactic structure to achieve the desired effect, i.e. establishing a contrast, e.g. *"It's a story that hasn't made me the most conventional candidate. But it is a story that has seared into my genetic make-up the idea that this nation is more than the sum of its parts – that out of many, we are truly one."* (Barack Obama: *A More Perfect Union*)

rhetorical question	A rhetorical question is one to which no answer is expected; instead, the listener is asked to think about the question and its relevance, e.g. *"How long should this suffering continue?"*
irony	Irony is the use of a statement in which the literal meaning is very different, often even the opposite of the intended meaning; usually, the recipient is made aware of the intended meaning through context or verbal and non-verbal cues, e.g. *hugging oneself in a thunderstorm, saying, „Lovely weather!"*

Glossary – Vocabulary for Analysing Speeches

By telling the listeners something about himself he attempts to establish a personal relationship with his audience.	Er bemüht sich, eine persönliche Beziehung zu seinen Zuhörern aufzubauen, indem er seinem Publikum etwas über seine persönliche Geschichte erzählt.
She attempts to win her listeners over to her side.	Sie versucht, das Publikum auf ihre Seite zu ziehen.
He draws a comparison between ... and ...	Er zieht einen Vergleich zwischen ... und ...
He puts emphasis on the meaning of his words by using parallelism/ repetition in line X.	Durch den in Zeile X verwendeten Parallelismus / die in Zeile X verwendete Wiederholung verleiht er seinen Worten Nachdruck.
He refers to well-known historical events such as ...	Er bezieht sich auf allgemein bekannte historische Ereignisse wie z.B. ...
He wants to call/draw the audience's attention to the fact that ...	Er möchte die Aufmerksamkeit des Publikums auf die Tatsache lenken, dass ...
His frequent use of rhetorical questions is intended to show that ...	Sein häufiger Gebrauch rhetorischer Fragen soll verdeutlichen, dass ...
His use of metaphorical language is intended to make his speech more lively and interesting.	Sein metaphorischer Sprachgebrauch soll seine Rede interessanter und lebendiger machen.
In line X he directly criticises his political opponents.	In Zeile ... kritisiert er offen seine politischen Gegner.
The frequent use of personal pronouns such as "we", "us" and "our" gives the audience the impression that he does not regard himself as superior to them but as one of them.	Der häufige Gebrauch der Personalpronomen „wir", „uns" und „unser" soll dem Publikum das Gefühl geben, dass er sich als einer von ihnen und nicht als eine höher gestellte Person sieht.
The speaker appeals to the audience's emotions by ...	Der Redner / Die Rednerin spricht die Gefühle des Publikums an, indem er/sie ...

The speaker begins by ...	Der Redner / Die Rednerin beginnt mit ...
The speaker makes frequent use of metaphors/similes/symbols/examples to point out / to underline that ...	Der Redner / Die Rednerin macht regen Gebrauch von Metaphern/Vergleichen/Symbolen/Beispielen, um herauszustellen / zu unterstreichen, dass ...
The speaker tries to convince his/her audience of his/her point of view by ...	Der Redner / Die Rednerin versucht sein/ihr Publikum von seinem/ihrem Standpunkt zu überzeugen, indem er/sie ...
The speaker aims to convince/persuade/manipulate the audience.	Es ist das Anliegen des Redners / der Rednerin, das Publikum zu überzeugen/überreden/manipulieren.

Expository Texts: How to Deal with Essays

Keyword
Essay: There are various kinds:
a) essays which reflect the author's opinion on a certain topic (**comment**)
b) essays in which the author weighs up the pros and cons of a particular subject (**argumentative essay**)
c) essays in which a topic is presented in a clear and logical way and which do not contain the author's opinion (**expository essay**)

How to proceed

First you have to find out which kind of essay you are being asked to analyse.
For details on how to analyse **comments** you can refer to the section on **political speeches** above.
Here we will focus on the **argumentative essay.**

Structure

- In the **introduction** the author expresses the main idea of the essay. Instead of giving a personal opinion, she/he might choose to provide the reader with some background information or start with a question which will serve as a guideline and be answered in the course of the essay.
- For the **main part** of the essay, the author can decide on a dialectical or an enumerative approach.
- In an **enumerative approach** the author will enumerate all the aspects of the topic in a neutral way. A **dialectical approach** can either present all the arguments in favour of a position before focusing on the counterarguments (or vice versa), or it can present the pros and cons alternately. The latter is usually considered more skilful.
- Each **new aspect** is usually presented in a new paragraph. The various **arguments** can be backed with examples from real life, established facts, an expert opinion or

other reliable sources. These pieces of evidence are very important as they enable the author to make his/her argument convincing and thus to persuade the reader.

- In the **conclusion** the author sums up the arguments, frequently also restating his/her own opinion and referring to what could happen in the future.

Glossary – Vocabulary for Analysing Essays

The author discusses the pros and cons of …	Der Verfasser / Die Verfasserin diskutiert die Vor- und Nachteile von …
The author gives his/her personal opinion on the problem of …	Der Verfasser / Die Verfasserin äußert seine/ihre eigene Meinung zum Thema …
He/She believes / is convinced / presumes that …	Er/Sie glaubt / ist überzeugt / nimmt an, dass …
She/He wants to persuade the reader …	Sie/Er möchte die Lesenden überreden …
One can easily follow his train of thought.	Man kann seinen Gedankengang leicht nachvollziehen.
At the end of her essay she draws / comes to the conclusion …	Am Ende ihres Essays kommt sie zu dem Schluss …
His/Her arguments are (not) convincing/well-chosen.	Seine/Ihre Argumente sind (nicht) überzeugend/gut gewählt.
The main topic of the essay is …	Das Hauptthema des Berichts ist …
The tone of this essay is humorous/neutral/ironic/serious.	Der Ton des Berichts ist humorvoll/neutral/ironisch/ernst.
The author uses real examples to convince her readers.	Die Verfasserin verwendet reale Beispiele, um ihre Leserschaft zu überzeugen.
The author's choice of words shows/emphasises that he is for/against …	Die Wortwahl des Verfassers zeigt/unterstreicht, dass er für/gegen … ist.
In the introductory paragraph of her essay, she asks a rhetorical question, which serves as a thread.	Im einleitenden Abschnitt ihres Berichts stellt sie den Lesenden eine rhetorische Frage, die sich wie ein roter Faden durch den Bericht zieht.
The author uses adjectives with positive/negative connotations to support his/her point of view.	Der Verfasser / Die Verfasserin verwendet Adjektive mit einer positiven/negativen Konnotation, um seinen/ihren Standpunkt zu verdeutlichen.
Her attempt to persuade the readers backfires / works very well.	Ihr Versuch, die Leser zu überreden, misslingt/gelingt.

Narrative Texts: How to Deal with Reports

> **Keyword**
>
> **Report:** This is a special kind of newspaper article.
> It provides answers to the five "W" questions *(Who? What? Where? When? Why?),* as well as the *How* question. Its aim is to inform its readers and NOT to manipulate or influence them.
> A report deals with current events and only contains facts.

Sometimes students have problems when it comes to differentiating between a *report* and an *article,* which can also deal with current events but which is usually a mixture of both fact and opinion.

The style of an **article** is usually more personal and its main aim is to entertain the reader. This is ensured by using many adverbs and adjectives to make the article lively and by addressing its readers directly, often by asking them a hypothetical question, e. g. *How would you feel if you discovered that someone had stolen your brand-new car?* The main characteristics of a **report** are outlined below.

Elements of a report
Structure

- To arouse the reader's curiosity, reports have **headlines** containing basic information without providing too much detail.
- The basic information is generally provided in the first paragraph, which serves as an **introduction.**
- The **main body** of a report consists of a number of paragraphs, which contain one piece of information each.
- The last paragraph serves as a kind of **conclusion.**

Language and style

- A report is written in a factual style and neither reflects the author's personal opinion nor contains any kind of speculation.
- Individual paragraphs are relatively short and consist of short sentences, aiming to ensure that the reader understands the information presented.
- Experts – or people who have first-hand experience of the topic in question – are often quoted, but no authorial comment is given on what they say.

Glossary – Vocabulary for Analysing Reports

The report [title] written by [author] deals with / is about / relates to / describes ...	Der Bericht [Titel] von [Verfasser] beschäftigt sich mit / handelt von / berichtet von / beschreibt ...
The topic(s) of the report is (are) ...	Das Thema / Die Themen des Berichts ist/sind ...
In the introduction the reader learns about / gets to know ...	In der Einleitung erfährt der Leser / die Leserin ...
The report can be divided into ... paragraphs.	Der Bericht kann in ... Absätze gegliedert werden.
The report consists of ... paragraphs.	Der Bericht besteht aus ... Absätzen.
It is the author's aim to inform the reader about ...	Es ist das Anliegen des Autors / der Autorin, die Lesenden über ... zu informieren.
The 2nd/3rd paragraph contains information on ...	Der zweite/dritte Absatz enthält Informationen über ...
The author quotes an eye-witness/ expert who says that ...	Der Autor / Die Autorin zitiert einen Augenzeugen/Experten, der sagt, dass ...
The author describes how ...	Der Verfasser / Die Verfasserin beschreibt, wie ...
The author does not give his/her personal opinion on the topic/problem/question but merely relates facts.	Der Verfasser / Die Verfasserin äußert nicht seine/ihre eigene Meinung zum Sachverhalt / Problem / zu der Frage, sondern gibt Fakten wieder.
The factual style of writing shows that it is the author's aim to inform the reader and not to entertain him/her.	Der sachliche Sprachgebrauch verdeutlicht, dass es das Anliegen des Autors / der Autorin ist, die Leser zu informieren und nicht, sie zu unterhalten.

Visuelle Materialien

Any kind of picture can be considered a type of text: it contains information that can be read and interpreted. This requires knowledge of the language of pictures, which is different for each medium: a cartoon must be approached differently from a photograph, for example. A complete account of every kind of visual material cannot be offered here, but some central aspects will be listed and explained.

> **INFO** A note on visual texts in the Abitur
>
> Pictures have often been used in the Zentralabitur. They generally appear as additional material illustrating a certain text and picking up its issues or introducing new aspects for the student to react to. During the written exam, visual texts are limited to printable material; oral exams may occasionally also feature short video sequences.

Common Types of Pictures Used

- **photographs:** often illustrate an issue or problem; their aesthetic qualities should be considered
- **advertisements:** mostly use photographic material combined with text to promote a certain product/service; the intention of the ad must be considered and reflected on; political ads also belong to this category
- **cartoons:** reflect an issue from a critical point of view; the cartoonist's intention to criticise a social or political problem plays a central role
- **works of art:** rarely used; can reflect a society's state of mind and ideals during a certain period (e. g. early American paintings); their aesthetic qualities are essential to an understanding of their message
- **film stills:** a special type of photograph which enables the viewer to analyse the composition of a scene and its meaning/intention
- **films/videos:** this may include formats such as movie scenes, vines and vlogs; for legal reasons these are not likely to be shown in the Abitur but are used in the classroom for film analysis as well as comprehension tasks and as central study texts
- **statistics:** used to prove or explain a certain issue scientifically

Steps for Approaching Visual Material

Step 1: Describe the picture and its content. Do not begin by analysing or interpreting it, but state clearly and briefly what can be seen in the picture. The central question to be answered is, "What type of picture are you dealing with and what can be seen?"

Step 2: Analyse the content and form. The method of analysis depends on the picture. Ask yourself: "What information does the picture convey?" and (except for statistics) "Why was the picture created in this way and not differently?" End by stating what the picture aims to reveal, illustrate, criticise or otherwise convey.

Step 3: Interpret and evaluate the meaning or importance of the picture and the possible intention(s) of its creator. You may ask yourself whether the picture gives a truthful reflection of a certain issue or aspect, whether it distorts or exaggerates reality or whether it is meant to manipulate the viewer.

> **INFO** A note on tasks given to discuss pictures in the Abitur
>
> Many tasks in the Abitur that involve the use of pictures do not specifically ask for an analysis or interpretation but imply that this must be provided. Usually, visual materials have been used to illustrate an issue already introduced in a longer text. In such cases, you will be asked to react to the picture and relate it to the text or to a certain general topic discussed in class.

Examples of Types of Picture

Cartoons

When analysing cartoons, pay attention to the following aspects:

context: the circumstances in which it was created: when and in what type of magazine or newspaper it was published (historical, political context), connection to a particular article or reference to a current topic, position of its creator

content: the details of what it shows:

- **target:** who or what is it aimed at, what issue does it discuss/criticise?
- **message:** what point does the cartoon aim to make or what ideas does it propose?
  - Has the cartoonist taken sides? Is he/she biased?
  - Is the cartoon's humour ironic, satirical, aggressive …?

style: How is this message put across? Consider visual and textual elements.

visual elements	textual elements
Do visual items display incongruities by means of size, contrast, exaggeration, distortion, personification, etc.?	Has the cartoonist used labels/speech bubbles/captions? What words are made up to convey sounds? (onomatopoeia)
What facial features are used to convey expressions?	Does the cartoon use formal or informal language?
Do the images have symbolic meaning?	Does it play with words?
Does it use contrasts to convey certain issues of the main topic?	Does it use technical or specific terms?
Note: Almost every form of humour is based on incongruity. Things that are juxtaposed or compared in a strange way make us laugh.	

Key elements of cartoons

- **visual metaphors:** Cartoons use simplified visual symbols to carry meaning. The viewer can usually quickly decode them without any effort, e. g. when seeing a grey, dissolving shape one can imagine that this represents smoke.
- **caricature** (noun/verb): usually an exaggerated drawing or picture of a well-known person that makes them seem ridiculous but also easy to recognise
- **onomatopoeia** (noun): a word that sounds similar to the thing it describes, for example "hiss", "bang", "pow" (adj: onomatopoeic)

Advertisements

When analysing ads, pay attention to the AIDA principle (see below) and ask how the ad achieves the following points:

Attention: Ads aim to attract the consumer's attention quickly, for example by showing an appealing, provocative or shocking image or message.

Interest: This initial attention must be kept, thus the ad must create a further interest in the product.

Desire: Once the consumer is interested, the advertisement must spark a desire to buy the product which is advertised.

Action: The desire to own or use the product must lead to action by the consumer; he/she must seek ways to buy or access the product.

These aspects apply to all ads in general even if they do not directly aim to sell a specific product. Campaign ads in politics aim to "sell" a programme or candidate, whereas campaigns published by organisations such as Greenpeace seek to make viewers change their way of living or become politically involved. One must always consider the context in which an ad tries to affect its audience.

Photographs

When analysing and interpreting photographs, it is important to remember that even if a photograph shows a real environment at a certain time, it is still a fabrication of sorts. All photography is influenced by a) the photographer's choice of perspective, frame and timing and b) the camera itself, which can only show a limited view.

Photographers make choices when taking a picture in order to convey a specific effect or impression of their object. So a photograph must be considered in the same way as a painting – always ask yourself why the photographer chose this specific object, perspective, frame (what can and cannot be seen), moment in time and rendition (e. g. colour, black and white, sepia).

Modern means of digital photography have also led to increasing manipulation. Thus, even though we still tend to believe that pictures show reality, it can no longer be taken for granted that a photograph shows an aspect of the real world and/or has not been digitally altered.

Glossary – Vocabulary for Analysing Visual Material

viewer	Betrachter
picture, image	Bild
painting, drawing	Gemälde, Zeichnung
photograph/photo	Fotografie (Vorsicht: nicht Fotograf)
photographer	Fotograf
portrait	Porträt
landscape painting/photograph	Landschaftsgemälde/-fotografie
bird's eye view	Vogelperspektive
worm's eye view	Froschperspektive
incongruity	Widerspruch, Widersprüchlichkeit
background	Hintergrund
foreground	Vordergrund

Basic phrases for a description

In the picture/advertisement one can see …
In the foreground/middle ground/background …
The theme / topic / main motif of the advertisement is …
It's an image of … (place, person, scene)
The picture shows … (place, person, scene) close up / from a medium/long distance view.
You look at … (place, person, scene) from … (above/behind/…)
The picture was taken in/at … (place)
Above/On top of … one can read / it says / one can see a short text …

Basic phrases to express intention/message/aim

The picture/advertisement is aimed at / is meant to attract / is intended to / appeals to a / shows a/an (exaggerated, illustrative, provocative, unrealistic, flattering/beautified) depiction/image of …
It expresses/criticises/suggests/reveals/claims/manipulates/influences …

Basic phrases to express stylistic means / how aims are achieved

The photographer/painter/cartoonist achieves his/her aim by presenting … in an objective / artistic / exaggerated / limited / digitally manipulated way/style.
By using contrasts / incongruities such as … / differences in colour/focus, … the artist/photographer/cartoonist illustrates/emphasises/shows …
The perspective / point of view suggests that …
The motif was chosen deliberately because it illustrates the issue well / evokes emotions / stands for / represents a larger, more complex issue …

Die sprachliche Leistung im Abitur

Die integrative Sprachbewertung

Mit der **integrativen Sprachbewertung** entfallen sowohl die früher getrennte Bewertung von Ausdrucksvermögen und Sprachrichtigkeit als auch die entsprechenden Fehlerindex-Tabellen.

Nun gibt es nur noch eine Gesamtzensur für die sprachliche Leistung, wobei sich die Bewertung an klar umrissenen Kriterien orientiert. Hierbei hat sich ein grundlegender Wandel vollzogen. Wurden früher insbesondere die fehlerhaften Äußerungen einer Klausur als Bewertungsgrundlage herangezogen, so steht jetzt eine sogenannte **Positiv-Korrektur** im Vordergrund. Zwar werden die Mängel der sprachlichen Leistung nach wie vor rot markiert, jedoch sollen besonders gelungene Teile einer Klausur in grüner Farbe hervorgehoben werden. Beispiele für eine positive, grüne Markierung wären etwa der richtige Gebrauch von Präpositionen, Gerundien oder Konnektoren (zur Satzverknüpfung).

Es wird bewertet, ob und in welchem Umfang die Verstöße gegen die sprachliche Richtigkeit die Kommunikation zwischen der/dem Schreibenden und der/dem Lesenden der Klausur beeinträchtigen und ob die Häufigkeit den Gesamteindruck des Textes bestimmt, inwiefern die Fehler störend wirken und ob sie auf eine Nichtbeherrschung grammatischer Regeln schließen lassen.

Zur integrativen Leistungsbewertung im sprachlichen Bereich werden folgende Kriterien betrachtet:

Texterstellung

– Ist der Text übersichtlich gegliedert und für die Leserschaft damit leicht zu erfassen?
– Ist der Textumfang angemessen?
– Werden sogenannte *linking words* (Konnektoren) zur Verknüpfung von Satzteilen und Ideen sinnvoll und abwechslungsreich eingesetzt?
– Ist das Ausdrucksvermögen anspruchsvoll und wird evtl. das Risiko von möglichen Fehlern akzeptiert, um einen flüssigen und idiomatisch ansprechenden Text zu produzieren?
– Werden textsortenspezifische Formulierungen verwendet (z. B. wird eine private E-Mail anders formuliert als ein Leserbrief)?
– Werden Zitate sinnvoll integriert (treffend gewählt, nicht zu lang)?

Syntax

– Wird der Satzbau variiert oder werden hauptsächlich gleiche Strukturen verwendet?
– Wird auch komplexerer Satzbau beherrscht oder werden bei den Versuchen, nicht nur einfache Strukturen zu verwenden, viele Fehler gemacht?

Lexik

– Sind sowohl der allgemeine als auch der themenspezifische Wortschatz reichhaltig?
– Wird der Wortschatz treffsicher eingesetzt?

Grammatik

– Ist die Fehlerzahl eher gering und beeinträchtigt sie die Kommunikation eher nicht, oder führt eine Häufung zu einer eingeschränkten Verständlichkeit?
– Deuten die Fehler auf eine Unkenntnis oder Unsicherheit hinsichtlich relevanter grammatischer Regeln hin?

Kommunikative Relevanz typischer Fehler

Die folgenden Beispiele zeigen **Fehler, die die Kommunikation beeinträchtigen** und somit zu Abzügen führen. Die Auflistung ist nicht vollständig, sondern vermittelt einen exemplarischen Überblick:

– korrupte Syntax durch Fehlerhäufung
– falsche Bezüge
– uneinheitlicher bzw. falscher Tempusgebrauch (vgl. *summary*)
– falscher Tempusgebrauch bei eindeutigen Signalwörtern (z. B. *last year*)
– fehlende Umschreibung mit *to do* bei Frage und Verneinung
– falsche Präpositionen in *phrasal verbs*
– Germanismen
– falscher Gebrauch von Infinitiv und Gerundium
– *contact clause* im nicht notwendigen Relativsatz
– *that* im nicht notwendigen Relativsatz

Folgende Fehler beeinträchtigen die Kommunikation nicht oder nur in geringem Umfang:

– Rechtschreibfehler, wenn deutlich wird, welches Wort gemeint ist
– falsch gesetztes oder fehlendes Apostroph (*Peters bike; its/it's*)
– fehlerhafte Partizipialkonstruktionen
– Flüchtigkeitsfehler wie gelegentliches Fehlen des *3rd-person singular present -s* oder Plural-s
– ungebräuchliche Präposition bei klarer Aussageabsicht (z. B. *typical for*)
– *progressive* anstatt *simple* (z. B. *The author is dealing with …*)
– fehlerhafte Zeichensetzung

Operatoren für das Fach Englisch[1]

Die Liste der Operatoren gibt einen Überblick über die wichtigsten Arbeitsanweisungen, die in den Prüfungen vorkommen.

---

[1] Quelle: https://www.nibis.de/uploads/1gohrgs/za2021/2018_Erlass_ZA_Bewertung_FS.pdf (Zugriff: 01.04.2023, gekürzt)

Anforderungsbereich I

describe	give a detailed account of
outline	give the main features or general principles of a text; leave out minor details
state	specify clearly
summarise	give a concise account of the main points

Anforderungsbereich II

analyse	describe and explore in detail certain aspects of the text and how they are presented
compare	show similarities and differences
contrast	emphasise the differences between two or more things
examine	describe and explore in detail certain aspects of the text and how they are presented
explain	show causes and effects in a given context

Anforderungsbereich III

comment	state clearly your opinion on the topic in question and support your views with evidence
discuss	investigate and give reasons for and against
justify	present reasons for decisions, positions or conclusions
assess/evaluate	consider in a balanced way points for and/or against something

TIPP zum Punktesammeln

Denken Sie daran, die Zusammenfassung mit einem Einleitungssatz zu beginnen. Er muss den Titel des Textes, den Namen der Autorin / des Autors, das Jahr der Veröffentlichung sowie seine Kernaussage enthalten.

Aufgabenarten

Es können auch Aufgaben gestellt werden, die eine **kreative Lösung** erfordern, um dem Anforderungsbereich III zu genügen. Denkbar sind u. a. das Schreiben eines Briefes oder einer E-Mail an einen Freund oder an die Herausgeberin einer Zeitung, ein Schreiben zur Erlangung von Informationen oder auch ein Beschwerdebrief.
Weiterhin sind Aufgabenstellungen möglich, die das Verfassen eines Artikels, eines **Berichtes**, eines **Drehbuches,** eines **Tagebucheintrags** oder eines **Dialogs** erfordern. Das Schreiben einer **Fortsetzung** oder eines **alternativen Endes einer Geschichte** ist ebenso eine mögliche Aufgabenstellung wie die **Schilderung einer Begebenheit** aus einer anderen Perspektive, um nur einige mögliche Beispiele zu benennen.

Strukturiertes Vorgehen in der Abiturprüfung

Bei der Bearbeitung der Aufgaben in der Abiturprüfung empfiehlt sich ein systematisches Vorgehen in klar definierten Einzelschritten:

Lesen Sie sich zunächst den Text in Ruhe durch und unterstreichen Sie mit Bleistift Wörter, die Sie nachschlagen möchten. Konzentrieren Sie sich dabei auf solche Wörter, die bedeutungsrelevant und zentral für Ihr Verständnis des Textes sind. Verlieren Sie keine wertvolle Zeit mit dem Nachschlagen von Füllwörtern. Schlagen Sie dann die wichtigsten Wörter nach und lesen Sie den Text ein zweites Mal – nun zügiger – durch. Wenden Sie sich danach den Aufgaben zu: Lesen Sie zuerst alle Teilaufgaben genau durch. Machen Sie sich nochmals klar, dass die Bearbeitung der *comprehension task* (Anforderungsbereich I) weitgehend am Ausgangstext orientiert erfolgen soll, gegebenenfalls unter Einbindung vorhandenen Hintergrundwissens. Die *analysis* (Anforderungsbereich II) erfordert die detaillierte Betrachtung von Einzelaspekten unter Anwendung Ihrer Kenntnisse aus dem Bereich Zitieren und Argumentieren. In der *evaluation* (Anforderungsbereich III) wird schließlich nach Ihrer persönlichen Einordnung und Bewertung gefragt. Konzentrieren Sie sich anschließend auf die erste Teilaufgabe und kennzeichnen Sie gezielt unmittelbar relevante Textpassagen mit einem Marker. Machen Sie sich auf einem separaten Blatt stichpunktartige Notizen zur Bearbeitung der ersten Aufgabe und verfahren Sie so mit allen weiteren Teilaufgaben. Strukturieren Sie nun Ihre Stichpunkte durch Nummerieren und prüfen Sie unmittelbar vor dem Ausformulieren noch einmal die Aufgabenstellung, um sich rechtzeitig zu vergewissern, dass Ihre Bearbeitung auf den Kern der Frage abzielt. Nehmen Sie sich genug Zeit für diese Vorarbeiten (etwa ein Drittel der Zeit ist nicht zu viel), da Sie mit gut vorsortierten Inhalten umso schneller schreiben und sich dabei stärker auf die sprachlichen Aspekte im Englischen konzentrieren können. Es wird als positiv im Sinne der Textkohärenz bewertet, wenn Sie sich bemühen, Ihre Antworten zu den einzelnen Teilaufgaben sprachlich miteinander in Verbindung zu setzen. Betrachten Sie nicht jede Aufgabe als isolierten Einzelaspekt, der jeweils mit einem Satz für Leserinnen und Leser ohne Vorwissen eingeleitet wird.

TIPP zum Punktesammeln

Gehen Sie professionell vor und lesen Sie Ihre gesamte Arbeit vor der Abgabe noch einmal gründlich durch. Planen Sie dafür etwa 15 bis 20 Minuten ein. Bei diesem Arbeitsgang werden Ihnen selbst ganz sicher sprachliche Fehler auffallen. Achten Sie besonders auf die Bezüge bei den Pronomina, das -s in der 3. Person Singular Präsens, die Zeitenfolge sowie Rechtschreibung und Zeichensetzung.

TIPP zur Zeitplanung

1. Schritt: Text lesen, bedeutungsrelevanten Wortschatz klären	20 Min
2. Schritt: Fragen lesen, Stichpunkte machen und vorsortieren	20 Min
3. Schritt: Fragen unter Verwendung der Gliederung beantworten	80 Min
4. Schritt: Korrekturlesen	15 Min

(Diese zeitlichen Richtlinien gelten für Grundkurse; bei Prüfungen im Leistungskurs verlängern sich die Zeiten entsprechend.)

Wortschatzerschließung

Viele scheinbar unbekannte Wörter lassen sich problemlos ableiten. Hierzu kann man den Kontext oder andere bekannte Wörter aus derselben Wortfamilie zurate ziehen. In manchen Fällen helfen auch fächerübergreifend die Kenntnisse in anderen Fremdsprachen oder der Muttersprache. Insbesondere auf das Lateinische bzw. Französische kann man hier häufig zurückgreifen.

Textgestaltung

Kohärenz, Adressatenorientierung, Leserleitung

Kohärenz

TIPP zum Punktesammeln

Bemühen Sie sich, Ihren Text kohärent, also auch sprachlich zusammenhängend, zu gestalten. Schaffen Sie sinnvolle inhaltliche Verknüpfungen zwischen Satzteilen, Sätzen und Sinnabschnitten. Verwenden Sie dazu die sogenannten **Konnektoren,** die als Verbindungsglieder zum besseren Textverständnis beitragen.

Hier ist eine Liste der wichtigsten Konnektoren, geordnet nach ihrer Funktion im Satz.

Reihung von Argumenten

and	und
first(ly)/second(ly)/third(ly)	erstens/zweitens/drittens
furthermore/moreover	außerdem / darüber hinaus / überdies
in addition to	zusätzlich zu
not only … but also …	nicht nur …, sondern auch
as well as	sowie
finally	schließlich

Gegensatz

but	aber/sondern
although	obwohl
however	jedoch
despite the fact that	trotz der Tatsache, dass
in spite of	trotz
nevertheless/nonetheless	nichtsdestoweniger

even so	selbst dann
on the contrary	im Gegensatz dazu
on the one hand, … on the other hand,	einerseits …, andererseits
unlike	anders als
whereas	während/wogegen/indessen
while/whilst	während (dagegen)
yet	dennoch

Bedingung

if	falls/wenn
unless	wenn nicht
otherwise	ansonsten

Folge

because	weil
since	da
so	daher
consequently	folglich
as a result	demzufolge
therefore	daher/deshalb
due to	infolge
according to	zufolge
that is why	deshalb

Vergleich

like	wie
in comparison to/with	im Vergleich zu
similarly	ähnlich
equally	gleichermaßen

Zielgruppenorientierung

Schneiden Sie Ihren Text genau auf den Adressaten zu und drücken Sie sich präzise aus. Bewegen Sie sich in der Abiturklausur auf einer neutralen Sprachebene, vermeiden Sie also Stilbrüche wie Slangwörter und *spoken English*. Auch *contracted forms (they're, he's got)* sind nur in privater Kommunikation angebracht.

Lesendenleitung: *Writing a paragraph/comment*

Hier soll insbesondere der *argumentative comment* näher betrachtet werden, in dem Argumente für und gegen eine Behauptung erläutert werden. Die Form des *comment,* der eine These stützt bzw. nur antithetisch arbeitet, ist ein Teilbereich eines *argumentative comment.*

TIPP zum Punktesammeln

Entwickeln Sie in Ihrem Text eine für die Lesenden nachvollziehbare Argumentation.

Ein *comment* folgt einer klaren Struktur: Er beginnt mit einem *topic sentence* zur Einleitung, in dem eine Aussage zum Thema gemacht wird. Anschließend führt er das Argument aus (**These**), geht über zur Darstellung der Gegenargumente (**Antithese**), um mit einer **Schlussfolgerung** bzw. der **Darstellung der eigenen Meinung** abzuschließen. In jedem Teil sollten spezifische Formulierungen zur logischen Verknüpfung eingesetzt werden, um den Lesenden die Redeabsicht zu signalisieren.

Eine Sicherheit ausdrücken

The fact is that …	Es ist eine Tatsache, dass …
It cannot be denied that …	Man kann nicht leugnen, dass …
It goes without saying that …	Selbstredend …
Undoubtedly, …	Zweifellos …
I am convinced that …	Ich bin überzeugt davon, dass …
It is indisputable/obvious that … There is no doubt that …	Es ist unbestreitbar / offensichtlich / nicht zu bezweifeln, dass …
It is inevitable that …	Es ist unvermeidbar, dass …

Eine Vermutung ausdrücken

Apparently, …	Anscheinend …
They will probably …	Sie werden wahrscheinlich …
It seems highly likely that …	Es scheint äußerst wahrscheinlich, dass …
It may be the case that …	Es kann sein, dass …

Einen Zweifel ausdrücken

It is doubtful whether …	Es ist zweifelhaft, ob …
I wonder if …	Ich frage mich, ob …
There is no proof/evidence that …	Es gibt keine Beweise, dass …

Einen Sachverhalt betonen

In order to stress that …	Um hervorzuheben, dass …
to emphasise	betonen
I would like to make it clear that …	Ich möchte klarstellen, dass …

Eine Meinung ausdrücken

In my opinion, … / In my view, …	Meiner Meinung nach …
My thoughts on the subject are …	Meine Meinung zu diesem Thema ist …
Personally, I think that …	Ich persönlich denke, dass …
As far as I am concerned, …	Was mich angeht …
From my point of view, …	Aus meiner Sicht …
I assume that …	Ich vermute, dass …
I am (not) convinced that …	Ich bin (nicht) überzeugt davon, dass …
I cannot help thinking that …	Ich kann nicht umhin zu denken, dass …
I get the impression that …	Ich habe den Eindruck, dass …
I am afraid that …	(abschwächend) Ich fürchte, dass …
Honestly, … / To be honest, …	Ehrlich gesagt …
I cannot judge whether/if …	Ich kann nicht beurteilen, ob …
I am in no position to say …	Es steht mir nicht zu, zu sagen …

Einen Widerspruch einräumen

in contrast to …	im Gegensatz zu …
On the contrary, …	Ganz im Gegenteil …
whereas	(gegenüberstellend) während
I strongly object to …	Ich spreche mich deutlich gegen … aus.
One could argue that …, but …	Man könnte argumentieren, dass … , aber …
Although it is true that … it would be wrong to claim that …	Obwohl es wahr ist, dass …, wäre es falsch zu behaupten, dass …

Zustimmung ausdrücken

Fortunately, …	Glücklicherweise …
I entirely agree with / I share the opinion that …	Ich stimme vollkommen mit … überein.

I support his view.	Ich unterstütze seine Meinung.
I share her views.	Ich teile ihre Meinung.
I am of the same opinion (as) ...	Ich bin der gleichen Meinung (wie) ...
I approve of his/her opinion.	Ich bin mit seiner/ihrer Meinung einverstanden.
I take your point about ...	Ich akzeptiere Ihre Meinung über ...
I am in favour of ...	Ich bin für ...
He rightly mentions that ...	Zu Recht betont er, dass ...
I will not object to ...	Ich widerspreche ... nicht.
It cannot be justified that ...	Es gibt keine Rechtfertigung für ...
Nobody would disagree with that statement.	Niemand würde dieser Behauptung widersprechen.
This statement is very convincing.	Diese Aussage ist sehr überzeugend.
I have to admit that the author ...	Ich muss zugeben, dass der Autor / die Autorin ...

Ablehnung ausdrücken

It is only partly true that ...	Es entspricht nur teilweise der Wahrheit, dass ...
I disagree completely with ...	Ich muss widersprechen.
I see things differently.	Ich sehe den Sachverhalt anders.
I must/have to disagree on this matter.	Ich bin in dieser Angelegenheit anderer Meinung.
One cannot possibly accept that ...	Man kann unmöglich akzeptieren, dass ...
I must object to ...	Ich muss ... widersprechen.
I have to criticise strongly that ...	Ich muss scharf kritisieren, dass ...
I doubt whether ...	Ich bezweifle, dass ...
This statement entirely contradicts ...	Diese Behauptung widerspricht ganz und gar ...
However, ...	Jedoch ...
It is not as simple as it seems.	Es ist nicht so einfach wie es scheint.
Unlike the author, I think ...	Anders als der Autor / die Autorin glaube ich ...
I cannot share the author's view on ...	Ich kann die Meinung des Autors / der Autorin über ... nicht teilen.

Einen Grund angeben

As/Since ...	Da/Weil ...
In view of the fact that ...	Angesichts der Tatsache, dass ...
The reason for this lies in ...	Der Grund dafür liegt bei ...
This causes confusion.	Das sorgt für Verwirrung.
That is why ... / Therefore / For this reason ...	Aus diesem Grund ... / Deshalb
Given that ...	In Anbetracht der Tatsache, dass ...
That was caused by ...	Das wurde verursacht durch ...

Eine Folge darstellen

Consequently, ... / As a consequence, ...	Folglich (am Satzanfang)
In view of this statement, ...	In Anbetracht dieser Behauptung ...
in order to	um zu
as a result of	als Folge von

Vergleiche anstellen

to be comparable	vergleichbar sein
compared to / in comparison with	im Vergleich zu
to be different from	sich unterscheiden von
distinguish between (A and B)	(A von B) unterscheiden
to be considerably better than	wesentlich besser sein als
to get more and more difficult	immer schwieriger werden
Nowadays, it is less and less common ...	Heutzutage ist es immer weniger üblich ...
superior/inferior to	überlegen/unterlegen
The former ..., the latter	Der erstere ..., der letztere ...
They have little in common.	Sie haben wenig gemeinsam.
They are equal in price.	Sie haben den gleichen Preis.

Beispiele anführen

for example/instance	zum Beispiel
Let me give you an example.	Lassen Sie mich ein Beispiel anführen.
such as	wie (zum Beispiel)
Look at ...	Sehen wir uns einmal ... an.

Conclusion

To sum up, … / To summarise, …	Zusammenfassend kann man sagen …
I come to the conclusion that …	Ich komme zu dem Schluss, dass …
in short	kurz gesagt
To put it in a nutshell …	Um es auf einen Nenner zu bringen …
I can support the author's view on …	Ich kann die Ansicht des Autors / der Autorin über … unterstützen.
All in all, I believe that …	Insgesamt glaube ich …

Intention der Autorin / des Autors

An mehreren Stellen in Ihrer Abiturklausur werden Sie Ihre eigenen Aussagen in Relation zur Meinung der verfassenden Person setzen müssen. Dafür empfiehlt es sich, eine Reihe von sprachlichen Ausdrücken parat zu haben, z. B.:

He/She points out / argues that …	Er/Sie weist darauf hin / führt an, dass …
He implies/claims/states that …	Er behauptet, dass …
He/She believes/suggests …	Er/Sie glaubt/schlägt vor …
He/She lays emphasis on …	Er/Sie betont …
His/Her idea was to …	Er/Sie wollte …
He/She writes with the intention of (+ gerund) …	Er/Sie schreibt mit der Absicht, …
His/Her aim is to …	Sein/Ihr Ziel ist es …
His/Her attitude towards …	Seine/Ihre Einstellung gegenüber …
When he/she says/writes …, he/she means that …	Wenn er/sie sagt/schreibt …, meint er/sie …
According to the author, …	Dem Autor / Der Autorin zufolge …

Verweise und Zitate

Um Ihre Aussagen zu belegen, fügen Sie geeignete Zitate aus dem Originaltext in Ihre Antworten ein. Setzen Sie diese in englische Anführungszeichen – diese beginnen und enden oben. Da es sich in der Abiturklausur um einen relativ kurzen Ausgangstext handelt, genügt als Quellenangabe die Zeilennummer in Klammern direkt hinter dem Zitat.

Beispiel zu Shakespeare, Romeo and Juliet:
In his speech Prince Escalus speaks about the Montagues and the Capulets as "enemies to peace" (l. 1) and finishes by even menacing them with "pain of death" (l. 23).
Verwenden Sie nicht das ganze Zitat, können Sie die ausgelassenen Passagen mit eckigen Klammern kennzeichnen. Genauso können Sie ein Bezugswort in eckigen Klammern einfügen, wenn dies aufgrund der Satzkonstruktion notwendig ist.

Die wörtliche Übernahme von Formulierungen aus dem Ausgangstext bzw. einem anderen Text ohne entsprechende Kennzeichnung ist nicht zulässig und wird negativ bewertet. Da mit Zitaten Aussagen belegt oder gefestigt werden, stehen sie normalerweise nach der entsprechenden Behauptung. Diese sollten Sie zunächst mit eigenen Worten paraphrasieren. Nehmen Sie dabei Ihr einsprachiges Wörterbuch zur Hilfe, um nach Synonymen zu suchen.

Textstruktur und Absätze

Formalia

TIPP zum Punktesammeln

Achten Sie darauf, dass Sie formale Nachlässigkeiten vermeiden. Hier Punkte zu verschenken, ist unnötig.

Zunächst eine generelle Bemerkung: Die Lesenden Ihrer Englischprüfung werden Ihnen grundsätzlich wohlgesonnen sein und werden Sie gerecht bewerten wollen. Dazu ist es natürlich gerade in einer Fremdsprache eine wichtige Voraussetzung, dass Ihre Handschrift gut lesbar ist, sowie dass die Buchstaben und die Wortgrenzen deutlich erkennbar sind, damit die Leser nicht raten müssen, ob Sie nun das für den jeweiligen Kontext passende Wort benutzt haben oder nicht. Wenn Sie also wissen, dass Ihre Handschrift schlecht lesbar ist, bemühen Sie sich zu Ihrem eigenen Vorteil darum, besonders groß und deutlich zu schreiben! Reduzieren Sie nachträgliche Ergänzungen auf ein Minimum. Lassen sich diese nicht vermeiden, nummerieren Sie sie fortlaufend und deutlich und listen Sie den eingefügten Text entweder jeweils am Seitenende oder nach Abschluss des Textes in chronologischer Reihenfolge auf.
Rücken Sie zur besseren Lesbarkeit zwei bis drei Zentimeter ein, wenn Sie einen neuen Absatz beginnen. Erlauben Sie wie gefordert die Hälfte der Seite als Rand für Korrekturzeichen und Bemerkungen der Lehrkraft.

Satzzeichen

Natürlich sollen Sie in der Englischprüfung im Abitur zeigen, dass Sie mit komplexen Satzgefügen umgehen können. Vermeiden Sie allerdings Schwerfälligkeit! Allzu lange Sätze mit vielen Nebensätzen machen Ihren Text schwer lesbar und erhöhen die Wahrscheinlichkeit, dass Sie sich in Ihrer Satzkonstruktion verzetteln. Achten Sie auf sinnvolle Strukturierung durch Satzzeichen; sie helfen dem Leser / der Leserin, Ihren Gedanken zu folgen und sich in Ihrem Text zurechtzufinden. Wechseln Sie ab: Verwenden Sie nicht nur Punkt und Komma, sondern auch Strichpunkt oder Gedankenstrich. Auch durch den Einsatz von Fragen können Sie Ihre Texte ansprechender gestalten.
Interpunktion wird in den Bewertungskriterien nicht aufgeführt und in der Schule großzügig gehandhabt. Bedeutungstragende Satzzeichen, z. B. bei *non-defining relative clauses,* werden jedoch verlangt.

Ausdrucksvermögen / Verfügbarkeit sprachlicher Mittel

Klarheit und Präzision

Die Formulierung der Abituraufgaben folgt klar definierten Regeln. So kommen als Arbeitsanweisungen nur bestimmte Verben in Frage, die sogenannten **Operatoren**. Eine Aufstellung der Operatoren finden Sie auf den Seiten 99 f. und 127 f. in diesem Buch. Lesen Sie die Formulierung der Fragen genau und machen Sie sich klar, welche Art der Antwort von Ihnen im konkreten Fall erwartet wird. Der Operator drückt deutlich aus, was von Ihnen verlangt wird.

Nachdem also die Art der Fragestellung aufgrund der Formulierung mittels der Operatoren klar definiert ist, können Sie Ihre Antwort entsprechend ausrichten. Achten Sie beim Verfassen auf Fehlerquellen, die leicht vermieden werden können. Im Folgenden werden einige typische Fehlerquellen genannt und erläutert. Diese Hinweise mögen auf den ersten Blick selbstverständlich erscheinen, doch durch die notwendige Konzentration auf den Inhalt oder das Arbeiten unter Zeitdruck schleichen sich oft unnötige Fehler ein.

Textökonomie

Schreiben Sie nach dem Grundsatz der Textökonomie „Jeder Satz ein Statement". Vermeiden Sie Wiederholungen im Wortschatz und umständliche inhaltliche „Schleifen". Zum einen leidet darunter der Stil und zum anderen wird die korrigierende Person diese Taktik wahrscheinlich durchschauen.

Vermeiden Sie die Formulierung von Allgemeinplätzen.

(Beispiel: *It is well-known that Europe is suffering from many problems these days.*)

Stellen Sie sicher, dass die sprachlichen Bezüge korrekt sind: Wählen Sie also bewusst die passenden Personal-, Possessiv-, Demonstrativ- und Relativpronomen, um Ihre Leserschaft eindeutig durch den Text zu führen. Verwenden Sie zusätzlich **signal words** *(Firstly, secondly, thirdly, …)* als Gliederungssignale, um den Text sinnvoll zu strukturieren. Achten Sie auf die Verwendung der Zeiten! Wenn Sie im **past tense** beginnen, müssen Sie diese Zeitebene auch durchgängig beibehalten.

Wortschatz

Der in Ihren Texten verwendete Wortschatz sollte sachlich und stilistisch angemessen sein. Demonstrieren Sie, dass Sie über einen differenzierten allgemeinen Wortschatz verfügen, und variieren Sie in Ihrem Ausdruck.

Ausdrucksmöglichkeiten im Wortfeld „sagen"

to say, to tell, to relate, to describe, to let somebody know, to state, to speak, to talk, to answer, to respond, to reply, to inform, to advise, to recommend, to brief, to update somebody, to promise, to lie, to whisper, to shout, to scream, to yell, to report, to repeat, to argue, to converse, to allude to something, to articulate, to suggest, to demand, to insist, to urge, to ask, to question

---

Achten Sie dabei besonders auf gängige Fehlerquellen. Die Beispiele sollen Sie für die Problematik sensibilisieren, aus Platzgründen werden jeweils nur einige genannt.

Seien Sie in Alarmbereitschaft bei potenziellen **false friends.**
Hier ist eine Liste der gängigen Fallen:

deutsch	englisch	false friend
bekommen	to get	*nicht:* become
die Kritik	criticism	*nicht:* critic – die Kritikerin / der Kritiker
die Politik	politics	*nicht:* policy – persönliche Stra*tegie, außer in Begriffen wie* foreign policy – Außenpolitik
sensibel	sensitive	*nicht:* sensible – vernünftig
meinen/ glauben	to think	*nicht:* mean – bedeuten *(oder Adj.* mean – gemein)
aktuell	current	*nicht:* actually – in der Tat
also	so	*nicht:* also – auch
Chef	boss	*nicht:* chef – der Küchenchef
engagiert	committed	*nicht:* engaged – verlobt; besetzt
eventuell	possibly	*nicht:* eventually – schließlich
Handy	mobile phone (AE: cell phone)	*nicht:* handy – handlich, praktisch
Konfession	denomination	*nicht:* confession – die Beichte
Konkurrenz	competition	*nicht:* concurrence – Übereinstimmung
konsequent	consistent	*nicht:* consequently – folglich
mobben	to bully	*nicht:* mob – das gemeine Volk
prägnant	concise	*nicht:* pregnant – schwanger
prinzipiell	fundamentally, basically, in/on principle	*nicht:* principally – hauptsächlich
Prospekt	brochure, leaflet	*nicht:* prospect(s) – die Zukunftsaussichten
Protokoll	minutes	*nicht:* protocol – die Etikette (außer bei EDV)
Publikum	audience	*nicht:* public – die Öffentlichkeit
rentabel	profitable	*nicht:* rentable – zu mieten
Rückseite	back	*nicht:* backside – Hinterteil
spenden	to donate	*nicht:* to spend – ausgeben

Verwendung der richtigen Präposition nach Verben oder Adjektiven
Orientieren Sie sich hier nicht am Deutschen, das kann leicht zu einem falschen Ergebnis führen.

Collocations

Bestimmte Wörter treten immer in einer **festen Verbindung** auf, einer **Kollokation**. Der Austausch eines der Bestandteile ist nicht möglich. (Beispiele: *a quick shower, strong tea, to drive so. crazy, fully aware*)

Darüber hinaus wird von Ihnen die Verwendung eines angemessenen **thematischen Wortschatzes** erwartet. Prägen Sie sich die Glossare zu den lehrplanrelevanten Themen der vorangegangenen Kapitel ein, um den thematischen Wortschatz bei Bedarf zur Verfügung zu haben (vgl. Kapitel „Basiswissen", S. 16 ff.).

Zu guter Letzt sollten Sie über einen präzisen **fachmethodischen Wortschatz** verfügen. Das Handwerkszeug dazu bekommen Sie im Kapitel „Methoden der Textarbeit" (S. 98) dieses Buches, wo Sie geeignetes Vokabular zum Thema finden. Sie sollten sich sowohl Vokabular für literarische Texte als auch für Sach- und Gebrauchstexte aneignen.

Differenzierte Satzgestaltung

Neben der Gewandtheit im Wortschatz wird natürlich auch Ihr Können im Bereich Syntax bewertet. Wechseln Sie also je nach Kontext ab zwischen Parataxe und Hypotaxe, d. h. einer Reihung von Hauptsätzen bzw. komplexen Satzgefügen mit Nebensätzen. Verbinden Sie diese entsprechend mit Konnektoren (s. Liste S. 130 f.); erwähnen Sie Bezüge in temporaler, kausaler, konzessiver, konditionaler und resultativer Hinsicht.

Übersicht über die möglichen Konjunktionen

temporal	while, before, after, until
kausal	since, because, as, for
konzessiv	(al)though, while/whilst, whereas
konditional	if, unless
resultativ	so (that)

Integrieren Sie Partizipial-, Gerundial- und Infinitivkonstruktionen sowie Passivkonstruktionen. Wechseln Sie zusätzlich durch Inversion sowie gelegentliche Verwendung von (rhetorischen) Fragen mit anderen Satzformen ab.

Eigenständigkeit (Paraphrase)

In der Abiturklausur werden Ihr Textverständnis und Ihre Ausdrucksfähigkeit bewertet. Ihr Ziel muss es deshalb sein, dem Korrektor ein umfassendes Bild von Ihrer Ausdrucksfähigkeit im Englischen zu geben. Greifen Sie dabei häufig auf längere Textpassagen des Originaltexts zurück, kann die Eigenständigkeit der Leistung nicht ausreichend bewertet werden. Denken Sie also daran, Zitate nur zum Belegen Ihrer eigenen Thesen zu verwenden.

Sprachliche Richtigkeit (Fehlerschwerpunkte vermeiden)

Orthografie, Grammatik
Orthografie

Rechtschreibfehler passieren leicht als Flüchtigkeitsfehler beim Schreiben. Um dem entgegenzuwirken, sollten Sie sich eine funktionierende Zeitplanung aneignen, die Ihnen genug Spielraum lässt, nach Abschluss der produktiven Phase den Text noch einmal durchzulesen und eventuelle Rechtschreibkorrekturen vorzunehmen. Achten Sie dabei besonders auf Interferenzen mit dem Deutschen.

Grammatik

Wie bereits zu Eingang des Kapitels erwähnt, kann in diesem Rahmen keine umfassende Grammatikwiederholung stattfinden. Gehen Sie also Ihre individuellen Problempunkte selbst an.

Trotzdem können an dieser Stelle einige gängige Fehlerquellen genannt werden, auf die Sie ein besonderes Augenmerk legen sollten:

Verben

Sehen Sie sich vor der Prüfung noch einmal die Liste der unregelmäßigen Verben an und prägen Sie sich die Formen ein, die keinem gängigen Schema folgen, z. B. *lie, lay, catch.*

Denken Sie darüber hinaus auch an *phrasal verbs,* deren Bedeutung zum Teil nicht aus den Bedeutungen der Einzelwörter erschließbar ist, z. B. *turn down* (etwas ablehnen).

Adverbien

position of adverbs in the sentence: Adverbien können im englischen Satz an verschiedenen Stellen stehen, die oft nicht mit dem Deutschen übereinstimmen. Sie können folgende Positionen einnehmen: Satzanfang oder -ende sowie vor und nach dem Verb, das sie näher bestimmen (bei zusammengesetzten Verbformen nach dem Hilfsverb).

Beispiele:
Unfortunately, the turnout for the country's first free election was very low.
*They had counted the votes **carefully.***
***Nevertheless,** the bad news weighed **heavily** on them.*
*I **often** wonder what became of him.*
*My sister **also** came.*
*We must **also** consider the opposite case.*

Beispiele für Prüfungsaufgaben

Die Beispielaufgaben sind vom Umfang und vom Schwierigkeitsgrad her teilweise für Leistungskurse, teilweise für Grundkurse konzipiert.

Um den verschiedenen Vorgaben für die beiden Kursarten gerecht zu werden, wurden überwiegend Texte ausgewählt, die den Vorgaben beider Kursarten entsprechen. Von Fall zu Fall werden Aufgabenstellungen ergänzt oder angepasst. Eine gute Möglichkeit, sich auf diesen Teil der Prüfung vorzubereiten, sind die TED talks: www.ted.com.

Aufgaben mit Beispiellösungen

Hörverstehen

Beispielklausur: *Immigration in Britain*

You can listen to the audio file by scanning this QR code:

Source: http://www.marketplace.org/2013/08/08/world/britains-immigration-crackdown-sparks-anger
(published on 8 August 2013, accessed on 1 April 2023)

> You will hear a radio programme called *Marketplace*, dealing with the topic of immigration in Britain. While listening, tick the right answer (a, b, c, or d). Do not tick more than one answer. You will hear the recording twice. You have 2 minutes to look at the task. You will have 30 seconds to finalise your answers after the second listening.

1. The British government is planning to reduce illegal immigration because
a) illegal immigrants are too expensive. ☐
b) residents living in Britain legally don't get enough jobs. ☐
c) illegal immigrants are known for their drug abuse. ☐
d) British citizens have racial views. ☐

2. The billboard carried by a van in the northeast corner of London
a) made most people who saw it smile. ☐
b) diverted other drivers' attention. ☐
c) caused a lot of anger. ☐
d) was created by illegal immigrants ☐

3. Neemal Patel claims that
a) Black people have raided a supermarket. ☐
b) Black people were asking for a place to live. ☐
c) the official's behaviour was illegal. ☐
d) some of the Black people refused to give their names. ☐

4. Immigration minister Mark Harper says that
a) the billboard campaign must be stopped. ☐
b) the officials acted legally. ☐
c) Black people have to be checked. ☐
d) immigration status must be controlled. ☐

5. James Goddard from Ilford complains that
a) the reporter's English is rather poor. ☐
b) only a few people in Ilford speak English. ☐
c) nobody speaks English accurately. ☐
d) in Ilford it is dangerous to walk along the street. ☐

6. According to Goddard, life in Ilford has changed because
a) whites are now a minority. ☐
b) the press only reports about positive aspects of immigration. ☐
c) the media ignore the immigrants. ☐
d) the white people have left the immigrants behind. ☐

7. James Goddard's reaction to the billboard campaign shows that
a) he is in favour of it. ☐
b) he wants to see another campaign like that. ☐
c) he likes the idea of stirring up trouble. ☐
d) he is against campaigns like that. ☐

Lösungen

1. b	5. b
2. c	6. a
3. c	7. d
4. b	

Beispielklausur: *British Asians are Living in Fear*

You can listen to the audio file by scanning this QR code:

Source: https://www.bbc.co.uk/sounds/play/p01hn2xg
(accessed on 1 April 2023)

You will hear a radio programme dealing with the topic of Asians in Britain. While listening, complete the table below. Write your answers in the boxes. You do not have to write complete sentences. There is one example answer (0). You will hear the recording twice. You have 90 seconds to look at the table. You will have 2 minutes to finalise your answers after the second listening.

0	The Runnymede Trust made a survey and argues that, due to race and religion, 60 % of members of ethnic minorities are worried about … (Give two examples.)	*a) personal safety* *b) discrimination in education services (and the workplace)*
1	As a means to stop the harassment, one woman says she had to … (Give two examples.)	*a)* *b)*
2	Being British, she says, has always been …	
3	The leader of a Meena women's project says the massive media coverage has led to … (Give two examples.)	
4	The fear of Asians to leave their homes and their immediate area has been creating …	
5	The Runnymede Trust claims that even the British government has been using racist rhetoric, telling ethnic minorities to …	
6	A survey has shown that the colour of people's skin has had a negative impact on … (Give two examples.)	*a)* *b)*
7	It is feared that a change will only happen in something like …	

Lösungen

1. a) change her (personal) appearance
   b) stop wearing certain clothes
2. a part of their lives
3. a) a sense of concern
   b) anxiety
4. enclaves
5. go home
6. a) their life chances
   b) their security
7. 50 years

Beispielklausur: *Mum's Cooking Makes Jobs*

You can listen to the audio file by scanning this QR code:

Source: https://www.bbc.co.uk/sounds/play/p018zgpl
(accessed on 1 April 2023)

> You will hear a radio programme dealing with the topic of Asians in Britain. While lis-
> tening, complete the table below. Write your answers in the boxes. You do not have to
> write complete sentences. There is one example answer (0). You will hear the recording
> twice. You have 90 seconds to look at the table. You will have 2 minutes to finalise your
> answers after the second listening.

0	The speaker's mother has always wanted to start a food business but did not do it because of … (Give two examples.)	a) lack of confidence b) lack of formal qualifications (and language barriers)
1	Things started to change when the speaker … (Give two examples.)	a) b)
2	Together with some friends, the idea of home delivery made him …	
3	In the South Asian community, after the children have left the house, women consider themselves …	
4	Women of these ethnic minority backgrounds are not usually found in the statistics and do not claim …	
5	They are so scared that they lack everything, so they do not even start …	
6	Irene motivated herself to be a part of 'Mummy's Cooking' because she thought she … (Give two examples.)	a) b)
7	How she was going to be perceived was something that she at first …	
8	That training would be for young people only is what Irene considered … at first.	

Lösungen

1. a) was studying at university
   b) had to eat bad food there
2. found a company with friends
3. too old
4. unemployment benefit
5. the process of getting benefit
6. a) was a good candidate
   b) could be independent
7. feared
8. a barrier

Kombinierte Aufgabe – Sachtext und Politische Rede

Part 1: Mediation

AUFGABENSTELLUNG

Together with your English partner school, you are participating in an international project on climate change. Your task is to write an article on the results of the Glasgow Climate Change Conference 2021 (COP 26) to be published on the project's website. Write this text using the article below and focussing on the perspective of the African nations.

Materialgrundlage

M1 Andrea Böhm, „Klimaschutz oder grüner Kolonialismus? – Eine Kolumne von Andrea Böhm", *ZEIT online,* 06.01.2022, https://www.zeit.de/politik/ausland/2022-01/cop-26-globaler-sueden-klimawandel-gerechtigkeit-5vor8 (Zugriff: 01.04.2023, gekürzt).

Hilfsmittel

Den Prüflingen stehen einsprachige sowie für den schulischen Gebrauch geeignete zweisprachige Wörterbücher der Allgemeinsprache (Deutsch–Englisch/Englisch–Deutsch) zur Verfügung.

M1 „Klimaschutz oder grüner Kolonialismus?" *Andrea Böhm*

[...]

Die Konferenz in Glasgow im vergangenen November, in Deutschland schon fast wieder vergessen, hat in Staaten des globalen Südens enorme Verbitterung hinterlassen. Erneut wurde ihre zentrale Forderung abgebügelt: Klimagerechtigkeit.

Natürlich war COP26 kein totaler Reinfall. Der schrittweise Abschied aus der Kohleenergie steht im Abschlusspapier, über 140 Regierungen haben den Schutz und die Wiederaufforstung der Wälder versprochen, über 100 Länder wollen bis 2030 den Methanausstoß um ein Drittel reduzieren und alle sollen ihre Klimaziele bis zur nächsten Konferenz nachbessern. Was in Glasgow nicht passierte: die Verantwortung für die Erhitzung unseres Planeten ehrlich zu benennen und Rechenschaft abzulegen.

Dass die Ärmsten am wenigsten zur Erderwärmung beigetragen haben, aber schon seit Langem den höchsten Preis zahlen, ist längst eine Binsenweisheit. Bloß empfindet sie in unseren Breitengraden kaum jemand als Skandal. 23 reiche Staaten mit heute zwölf Prozent der Weltbevölkerung (darunter die USA, Deutschland, Kanada und Japan) haben seit Beginn der Industrialisierung die Hälfte aller CO_2-Emissionen ausgestoßen.

Die andere Hälfte verteilt sich auf über 150 andere Länder – und wird angeführt von China, das inzwischen fast 14 Prozent der Emissionen verursacht hat. Subsaharaafrika ist für gerade mal 1,85 Prozent verantwortlich, wird aber schon seit Jahrzehnten weit dramatischer von den Folgen der Klimakrise getroffen als Europa. Gleiches gilt für die kleinen Inselstaaten, denen buchstäblich der Untergang droht.

Deswegen fordern ärmere Staaten seit Jahren einen Fonds für Schäden und Verluste (*loss and damage*) gefüllt von den Hauptverursachern des Klimawandels. Aus diesem Fonds sollen von Dürren, Fluten, Hungersnöten oder Unwettern Betroffene im Zusammenhang mit der Erderwärmung unterstützt werden. Der Außenminister von Bangladesch, AK Abdul Momen, hat das Konzept unlängst mit dem Vorgehen gegen die Tabakindustrie in den Neunzigerjahren verglichen, als sich die US-Regierung von den Konzernen vor Gericht einige der Milliarden Dollar zurückholte, die durch die Gesundheitsschäden des Rauchens entstanden waren.

Die Entwicklungsländer fühlen sich verprellt

Nun, der Fonds wurde in Glasgow nicht beschlossen, vor allem aufgrund des Widerstands der USA und der EU, die fürchten, für Klimaschäden haftbar gemacht zu werden. Auch bei anderen Zahlungen fühlen sich Entwicklungsländer verprellt. 100 Milliarden US-Dollar jährlich ab 2020 wollten Industrienationen für Klimaprojekte im globalen Süden bereitstellen, um beim Übergang zu grüner Energie und bei der Anpassung an die Krise zu helfen – zum Beispiel durch Frühwarnsysteme oder Küstenbefestigungen. Die Summe wird frühestens 2023 zum ersten Mal erreicht.

Zum Vergleich: Der Hilfsfonds für die Opfer des Hochwassers in Rheinland-Pfalz und Nordrhein-Westfalen ist auf 30 Milliarden Euro angelegt.

Viel des internationalen Geldes wird laut einer Studie von Oxfam auch gar nicht als Zuschuss geleistet, sondern als Kredite, die oft mit Zinsen zurückgezahlt werden müssen. Soll heißen: Was vonseiten der Industriestaaten als Hilfe angeboten wird, ist für die Empfänger oftmals eine Schuldenfalle.

85 Natürlich gibt es auch kleine Lichtblicke: So gaben die EU, Großbritannien, Deutschland und Frankreich während der Glasgower Konferenz bekannt, Südafrika mit 8,5 Milliarden Euro beim Ausstieg aus 90 der Kohle helfen zu wollen.

Prima. Aber es mindert nicht die Wut unter Politikern wie Aktivistinnen auf dem Nachbarkontinent über europäische und US-amerikanische Heuchelei. In Glasgow 95 versprachen westliche Industrienationen, die Finanzierung weiterer Projekte zur Öl- und Gasförderung zu stoppen. Im Ausland, aber nicht daheim. Großbritannien subventioniert weiter seine Erdölindustrie, die 100 USA wollen ihre Inlandsproduktion sogar noch steigern.

Kein afrikanisches Land sieht seine Zukunft in fossilen Energieträgern

Und während westliche Staaten sowie 105 internationale Finanzinstitutionen den Geldhahn für Erdgasförderung in afrikanischen Ländern zudrehen, stempelt sich die EU Atomkraft und Gas klimafreundlich. Der Vorwurf des "grünen Kolonialismus"

afrikanischer Aktivisten mag in europäischen Ohren harsch klingen, verständlich ist er allemal: Hier warten Abermillionen darauf, dass endlich Strom aus der Steckdose kommt. Gerade Afrika braucht Erdgas für seine wirtschaftliche Entwicklung – als 115 Übergang. Denn kein afrikanisches Land sieht seine Zukunft in fossilen Energieträgern. Kenia oder Sambia beziehen schon heute über 50 Prozent ihrer Energie aus nachhaltigen Quellen. Das Ölland Nigeria, 120 das 2050 mehr Einwohner haben wird als die USA, will seine Stromproduktion bis dahin verachtfachen – überwiegend mit Solarenergie. Zur Absicherung braucht es, wie gesagt, Erdgas. Und mehr finanzielle 125 Hilfe.

Die Forderung nach einer gerechteren Beteiligung und Entschädigung durch Industriestaaten wird nach Glasgow nicht leiser, sondern lauter werden. Immerhin: Die 130 Deutschen sehen ihr Land in der Verantwortung. Über 70 Prozent erklärten in einer Umfrage des Instituts für Demoskopie Allensbach im vergangenen Sommer, dass die Industrieländer eine "große" oder "sehr 135 große" Verantwortung für die Klimakrise in Entwicklungsländern tragen.

[...]

Part 2: Politische Rede

AUFGABENSTELLUNG Writing

1 Outline the main points in Kamala Harris's speech.
2 Imagine you are a member of a journalist club in your school. Write an article expressing your own views towards the possibility of change in the USA, referring to Kamala Harris's visions and to information you have gathered during your English lessons.

Materialgrundlage

M2 „Senator and Vice-Presidential Nominee Kamala Harris' 2020 Democratic National Convention (DNC) speech on August 19", 19.02.2020, General Counsel, Austin; https://www.rev.com/blog/transcripts/kamala-harris-2020-dnc-speech-transcript (Zugriff: 01.04.2023, gekürzt)

M2 Kamala Harris: 2020 Speech at the Democratic National Convention (extract)

Aug 20, 2020

That I am here tonight is a testament to the dedication of generations before me, women and men who believed so fiercely
5 in the promise of equality, liberty, and justice for all. [...]

My mother instilled in my sister Maya and me the values that would chart the course of our lives. She raised us to be
10 proud, strong Black women, and she raised us to know and be proud of our Indian heritage. She taught us to put family first, the family you're born into, and the family you choose. [...]

15 And even as she taught us to keep our family at the center of our world, she also pushed us to see a world beyond ourselves. She taught us to be conscious and compassionate about the struggles of all people, to
20 believe public service is a noble cause, and the fight for justice is a shared responsibility. [...]

I accept your nomination for Vice President of the United States of America.

25 I do so committed to the values she taught me, [...] and to a vision passed on through generations of Americans, one that Joe Biden shares. A vision of our nation as a beloved community, where all are
30 welcome, no matter what we look like, no matter where we come from, or who we love. A country where we may not agree on every detail, but we are united by the fundamental belief that every human being is

of infinite worth, deserving of compassion, 35 dignity, and respect. A country where we look out for one another, where we rise and fall as one, where we face our challenges and celebrate our triumphs together.

Today, that country feels distant. Don- 40 ald Trump's failure of leadership has cost lives and livelihoods. [...] And while this virus touches us all, we got to be honest. It is not an equal opportunity offender. Black, Latino, and Indigenous people are suffering 45 and dying disproportionately. And this is not a coincidence. It is the effect of structural racism, of inequities in education and technology, healthcare and housing, job security and transportation. [...] 50

So we're at an inflection point. The constant chaos leaves us adrift. The incompetence makes us feel afraid. The callousness makes us feel alone. It's a lot, and here's the thing. We can do better, and 55 deserve so much more. We must elect a president who will bring something different, something better, and do the important work. A president who will bring all of us together, Black, White, Latino, Asian, 60 Indigenous, to achieve the future we collectively want. We must elect Joe Biden. [...]

Right now, we have a president who turns our tragedies into political weap- 65 ons. Joe will be a president who turns our challenges into purpose. Joe will bring us together to build an economy that doesn't leave anyone behind, where a good paying job is the floor, not the ceiling. [...]

That's the vision that our parents and grandparents fought for. The vision that made my own life possible. The vision that makes the American promise, for all its complexities and imperfections, a promise worth fighting for. So make no mistake, the road ahead is not easy. We may stumble. We may fall short, but I pledge to you that we will act boldly and deal with our challenges honestly. We will speak truths, and we will act with the same faith in you that we ask you to place in us. We believe that our country, all of us, will stand together for a better future. [...]

In this election, we have a chance to change the course of history. We're all in this fight. You, me, and Joe, together. What an awesome responsibility. What an awesome privilege. So let's fight with conviction. Let's fight with hope. Let's fight with confidence in ourselves, and a commitment to each other, to the America we know is possible, the America we love. And years from now, this moment will have passed, and our children and our grandchildren will look in our eyes. And they're going to ask us, "Where were you when the stakes were so high?" They will ask us, "What was it like?" And we will tell them. We will tell them not just how we felt. We will tell them what we did. [...]

Erwartungshorizont

Überprüfte Kompetenzen	
Mediation	Strategien
Aufg. 1)	Zusammenstellen der wichtigsten Inhalte, Verfassen eines Internetartikels mit passender Überschrift, Verwendung von thematisch passendem Vokabular
Schreiben	
Aufg. 1)	Zusammenfassen der wichtigsten Inhalte
Aufg. 2)	In einem Artikel die eigene Meinung darlegen und begründen und sie in Beziehung zu den Aussagen des Textes setzen

Beispiellösung
Part 1: Mediation

North vs. South: The Climate Injustice of COP 26

The conference in Glasgow may seem a success story for a lot of states in the Northern hemisphere: 140 countries signed a treaty to phase out of fossil fuels, to protect forests and to reduce methane emissions by a third.

However, in her review of COP 26 in the German newspaper "ZEIT", Andrea Böhm points out that it has left many nations in the South feeling bitter, as the conference once again failed to address one pressing issue: climate justice. While 23 states with 12 % of the world population are responsible for half of all CO_2 emissions, these suffer comparatively little from the effects of climate change. On the other hand, sub-Saharan nations, for example, which contribute less than 2 % of global CO_2 emissions, are hit particularly hard by climate change. Hence, these southern nations demand that those mainly responsible for CO_2 emissions create a special fund to pay for the damages caused by climate change. Due to resistance from the US and the EU, COP 26 failed to implement this fund. In addition, financial aids promised by these richer nations for climate projects in the global south not only appear relatively small compared to money that is spent on climate-related damages nationally. A lot of these payments are also planned as loans, making further debt likely.

Another injustice has led some African activists to speak of "green colonialism": While the EU labels natural gas as climate-friendly within its sphere, it has stopped financial support for its exploitation further south. This decision hits African nations hard since they rely on gas for their economic growth, even though some of these states already gain over 50 % of their energy from sustainable sources and no African country sees its future in fossil fuels.

In any case, the calls for more climate justice are growing louder even in Western nations such as Germany. Luckily, COP 27 is just around the corner.

Part 2: Politische Rede

Aufgabe 1

The text is from Senator Kamala Harris's acceptance speech, given at the Democratic National Convention on 20 August 2020 after her nomination as democratic vice presidential candidate for the forthcoming election. As the first woman of colour to run for vice presidency of the USA, she emphasises her pride in her Indian heritage and her gratitude to her mother, who brought her up to be compassionate and conscious of other people's problems.

Harris touches upon liberty, equality and justice for all: this is the "shared responsibility" (l. 21 f.) she and Joe Biden accept. She pictures the USA as a "beloved community" (l. 29) where everybody is welcome, irrespective of ethnic heritage or sexual orientation. Everyone deserves respect; every individual is of inestimable value.

Harris calls on her fellow Democratic Party members to show unity and loyalty to Joe Biden and herself in the task of reversing Trump's white-supremacy policy, which has politically polarised and socially divided the country. She holds out the prospect of Joe Biden as a healing and unifying head of state, building an economy that provides jobs for all and in this way re-establishes the "American promise" (l. 75). But at the same time she admits that this may be a path of trial and tribulation.

Harris ends her speech by emphasising her belief in the country standing together to achieve a better future for all American citizens and by again invoking Democratic Party unity. Underlining the opportunity to change the course of history by winning the Presidency, she calls the election a "fight" (l. 89) which should be undertaken confidently and convincingly.

Aufgabe 2

Kamala Harris gave a very interesting and inspiring acceptance speech as vice presidential candidate of the USA. In her speech, held before the Democratic National Convention on 20 August 2020, Harris mentions politically charged issues she wants to address during Joe Biden's and her term of office. These include the situation of minorities – for example people of colour or homosexuals. Furthermore, she pursues the idea of a "united" America as a country every American can love.

The latter is a noble and ambitious aim in a politically polarised society, where the Democratic Party nurtures ideas of equality, while conservative Republicans are often unwilling to give up on latent ideas of white supremacy. The Democrats will have a hard fight to enact their intended bills.

The situation is compounded by the fact that there is now, after the election, a standoff in the Senate between Democrats and Republicans. But this tricky situation might be resolved by Kamala Harris herself, as she will have a 'casting vote' as vice president when it comes to a 50:50 situation for and against a bill.

The Democrats might, then, be able to legally change situations for certain social groups. History shows, however, that laws can be implemented but are not necessarily observed by people who oppose them. Racism will not be removed by law alone: profound social and cultural change must occur, above all in countering the fear that drives self-aggrandisement, racism and violence.

As racist actions are often carried out covertly, it is hard to take adequate measures against them. To my mind, the vision of peaceful coexistence among groups of people with a widely different experience of everyday life, like WASPs and those from the LGBTQ community, may be difficult – or even impossible – to realise in today's societies.

Harris's speech is powerfully written and touches on topics of major importance for individual and social life in the USA. Her appeal for change in US society is positive and her ideas are contagious. Let us hope that she will succeed in achieving her political goals.

Cartoon – Globalisation

AUFGABENSTELLUNG

Globalisation – a fair chance for everyone?

With an international group of university students, you are preparing a weekend seminar on the effects of globalisation. You do these preparations via email.

You are responsible for the opening session and have been given the task of choosing a cartoon for it. You have found the cartoon at hand. Explain how it will best suit the purpose of introducing the issue and why it can be given to the participants as a means for stimulating their awareness.

After describing the cartoon, analyse what the students can learn from it and plan your seminar session, giving your partners some ideas of the main points you want to make. Write this email.

Copyright: Popa Matumula/toonpool.com

TIPP zur Beschreibung von Bildmaterial

Auch bei Aufgaben, in denen das Material nur eingebettet ist, ist es sinnvoll, dieses an der entsprechenden Stelle im Text zu beschreiben. In unserem Beispiel ist es notwendig, die Beschreibung des Bildes in der Einleitung aufzugreifen, um anschließend darauf eingehen zu können. Bei der Betrachtung von Bildern ist es ebenso wie bei Texten entscheidend, die Position des Fotografen, Künstlers, Karikaturisten etc. zu berücksichtigen. Bei jedem Bild sollte man sich die Frage stellen, mit welcher Absicht es angefertigt worden ist, und sollte dies sprachlich in der Darstellung berücksichtigen.

Lösungshinweise

- introduction: reasons for choosing this cartoon as eye-opener for weekend seminar
- possibly cover caption "Globalisation" to stimulate participation
- description of illustration: man riding giant wave that is about to crush another man; man on beach depicted with an empty bowl and in ragged clothes, symbolising poverty; man in boat ("The Rich") with Caucasian features
- enormous wealth gap between North and South; positive vs. life-threatening experience of globalisation; North riding the wave of exploiting the South
- but: wave will eventually break; rich North will suffer the consequences of globalisation
- personal questions:
  - Where do you personally notice the effects of globalisation?
  - Where do the products you use come from?
  - What negative effects of globalisation do you know about?
  - Have you ever been to countries that suffer negative effects from globalisation?
- ask for feedback

Sachtext – Politischer Zeitungsartikel

AUFGABENSTELLUNG

1 Point out the different measures the LAPD uses to fight crime. (30 %)

2 Explain the pros and cons of the concept of "predictive policing" (ll. 34 f.) on the basis of the given article and compare it to the police's work in the films you have seen. (30 %)

3 For many young people becoming a police officer is a dream job. *The Guardian* has invited young people like you to debate the new measures of policing in a conference held in London. As you have dealt with short stories which show police work and the problems officers face, you want to take part in it. In order to apply for participation in the conference, you have to write an essay outlining your idea of a modern police force. In your essay you should also refer to this article and to material studied in class. (40 %)

Materialgrundlage

Nate Berg, „Predicting crime, LAPD-style", *The Guardian*, 25.06.2014, https://www.theguardian.com/cities/2014/jun/25/predicting-crime-lapd-los-angeles-police-data-analysis-algorithm-minority-report (Zugriff: 01.04.2023, gekürzt)

Hilfsmittel

Den Prüflingen stehen einsprachige sowie für den schulischen Gebrauch geeignete zweisprachige Wörterbücher der Allgemeinsprache (Deutsch–Englisch/Englisch–Deutsch) zur Verfügung.

"Predicting crime, LAPD-style"   *Nate Berg*

[...]

The Los Angeles Police Department, like many urban police forces today, is both heavily armed and thoroughly computer-
5   ised. The Real-Time Analysis and Critical Response Division in downtown LA is its central processor. Rows of crime analysts and technologists sit before a wall covered in video screens stretching more than
10   10 metres wide. Multiple news broadcasts are playing simultaneously, and a real-time earthquake map is tracking the region's seismic activity. Half-a-dozen security cameras are focused on the Hollywood sign, the
15   city's icon. In the centre of this video menagerie is an oversized satellite map showing some of the most recent arrests made across the city – a couple of burglaries, a few assaults, a shooting.

On a slightly smaller screen the divi-   20
sion's top official, Captain John Romero, mans the keyboard and zooms in on a comparably micro-scale section of LA. It represents just 500 feet by 500 feet. Over the past six months, this sub-block section of   25
the city has seen three vehicle burglaries and two property burglaries – an atypical concentration. And, according to a new algorithm crunching crime numbers in LA, and dozens of other cities worldwide, it's a   30
sign that yet more crime is likely to occur right here in this tiny pocket of the city.

The algorithm at play is performing what's commonly referred to as predictive policing. Using years – and sometimes decades – worth of crime reports, the algorithm analyses the data to identify areas with high probabilities for certain types of crime, placing little red boxes on maps of the city that are streamed into patrol cars. "Burglars tend to be territorial, so once they find a neighbourhood where they get good stuff, they come back again and again," Romero says. "And that assists the algorithm in placing the boxes. [...] A really good officer would be able to go out and do the same, but this somehow makes the average guys' ability to find the crime a little bit better."

Predictive policing is just one tool in this new, tech-enhanced and data-fortified era of fighting and preventing crime. As the ability to collect, store and analyse data becomes cheaper and easier, law enforcement agencies all over the world are adopting techniques that harness the potential of technology to provide more and better information. But while these new tools have been welcomed by law enforcement agencies, they're raising concerns about privacy, surveillance and how much power should be given over to computer algorithms.

P. Jeffrey Brantingham is a professor of anthropology at UCLA who helped develop the predictive policing system that is now licensed to dozens of police departments under the brand name PredPol. "This is not Minority Report," he's quick to say, referring to the science-fiction story often associated with PredPol's technique and proprietary algorithm. "Minority Report is about predicting who will commit a crime before they commit it. This is about predicting where and when crime is most likely to occur, not who will commit it."

[...] Jennifer Lynch [senior staff attorney at the Electronic Frontier Foundation (EFF)] worries that there's too much submissive acceptance of these technologies by the public, without consideration of exactly how this data is collected and used. She says that predictive policing, with its claims of reducing crime, will be given something of a free pass.

"What starts to happen is people think the results that come out of that must be accurate because there's technology involved," Lynch says. "But what we forget is that the information that went in may have been the subject of bias, may have been based on inaccurate assumptions about people, may have been collected in certain communities more than other communities. The problem is technology legitimises somehow the problematic policing that was the origination of the data to begin with."

[...] "We're pretty careful about what people do here," Romero says. "I care about civil liberties and freedom. And I know that our constitution was not written to protect us from gang members and thieves and thugs; it was written to protect us from the government and overreach of the government."

But concerns persist. Gary T Marx, professor emeritus of sociology at the Massachusetts Institute of Technology, says technology such as predictive policing creates "categorical suspicion" of people in predicted crime areas, which can lead to unnecessary questioning or excessive stopping-and-searching. And as data-driven policing expands, Marx worries that analysis and decision-making by machine will lead to what he calls "the tyranny of the algorithm". "The Soviet Union had remarkably little street crime when they were at their worst of their totalitarian, authoritarian controls," Marx says. "But, my god, at what price?"

Lösungshinweise

Aufgabe 1

Measures used by LAPD to fight crime: CCTV (closed circuit television) surveillance; satellite map of LA showing recent arrests; zoom-in facility governed by "predictive policing" algorithms; conventional armed policing

Aufgabe 2

Predictive policing
- pros: crime tends to concentrate in hotspots which are identifiable by algorithms, which can process far more data far more quickly than the average police officer; this enables police to focus on these areas
- cons: people believe technology too easily; algorithms are only as reliable as the information fed into them; focus on a particular area can easily lead to focus on the particular people or ethnic group that live in that area; predicting crime is not the same as detecting or preventing crime and can even be counterproductive.
  The film "Crash", for example, is concerned more with the way the particular experience, background and circumstances of the individual police officer can affect their work. But the film is set before the "digital revolution", so has nothing directly to do with the scenario of the "predictive policing" article. The police in "Crash" are out on the streets and in their patrol cars and have to survive there in their job, with their colleagues and in their personal lives. They are more affected by problems like racism and xenophobia, criminals in the family and so on – i. e. personal problems.

Aufgabe 3

Here are some ideas for your application:
- purpose of policing is to make life safe for all citizens – a basic need of society;
- but this cannot be at the cost of equally basic liberties;
- policing can only be as fair as the laws governing society;
- fair policing presupposes fair and just laws and law courts;
- this principle must also govern the means the police use to maintain and protect people's safety;
- the reason for surveillance of all kinds is always suspicion, and suspicion may quickly interpret an action as illegal or threatening even if it is not so;
- after all, everyone is made of good and evil and there is an inherent human tendency to accuse anyone who is however slightly different from what we ourselves consider the norm
- algorithms have proven to suffer from racial bias, casting attention particularly on the black community; predictive policing likely to criminalise these members of our society
- cf. short story „Heads of the Colored People": Riley and Richard Simmons become just another two nameless black victims of racist police violence

Aufgaben mit Bewertungskriterien

Kombinierte Aufgabe – Mediation und Writing

Part 1: Mediation
Aufgabenart

Zielgruppengerechte Sprachmittlung – keine Übersetzung! Für die Aufgabe stehen 60 Minuten Zeit zur Verfügung. Es darf ein Wörterbuch verwendet werden. Nach Ablauf der Bearbeitungszeit wird der zweite Prüfungsteil ausgehändigt.

AUFGABENSTELLUNG

Your English partner school is planning an international work experience programme, which also welcomes applications from German students. The programme's supervising teacher found the article below online and has asked you for a contribution to the school's homepage. Write this text, summarising the article's key information.

Materialgrundlage

M1 Roland Preuß, „Anonyme Bewerbungen: Inkognito zum neuen Job", *Süddeutsche Zeitung*, 17.04.2012, https://www.sueddeutsche.de/karriere/anonyme-bewerbungen-inkognito-zum-neuen-job-1.1334284 (Zugriff: 01.04.2023, gekürzt)

M1 „Anonyme Bewerbungen: Inkognito zum neuen Job"   *Roland Preuß*

[...]

Ein Pilotprojekt zeigt nun auf, wie mehr Chancengleichheit in die Personalabteilungen einziehen kann. Eineinhalb Jahre lang haben fünf Unternehmen und drei öffent-
5 liche Arbeitgeber anonymisierte Bewerbungen getestet, unter ihnen die Deutsche Post, L'Oréal und das Bundesfamilienministerium. An diesem Dienstag stellt die Antidiskriminierungsstelle des Bundes in Berlin
10 die Ergebnisse vor. In dem Bericht, der der *Süddeutschen Zeitung* vorliegt, kommen die Autoren [...] zu dem Schluss, dass anonyme Bewerbungen denen, die sonst unter Pauschalurteilen leiden, zugutekommen.
15

[...]

Bei dem Großversuch mit gut 8500 Bewerbungen hatten die Arbeitgeber zunächst auf Angaben wie Foto, Name, Alter
20 und Geschlecht verzichtet. Mal mussten die Aspiranten einen Online-Fragebogen ausfüllen, mal wurden verräterische Zeilen geschwärzt. Für die Vorentscheidung zählten also nur die Fakten wie Abschlüsse und Berufserfahrung. Erst vor dem Bewer-
25 bungsgespräch durften die Chefs Namen und Zeugnisse sehen. Dann aber haben die Bewerber nach Einschätzung der Forscher bereits die entscheidende Hürde überwunden, denn im persönlichen Gespräch wu-
30 cherten Klischees weniger.

„Das Projekt hat gezeigt, dass anonymisierte Bewerbungen den Fokus auf die Qualifikation lenken", sagt die Leiterin der Antidiskriminierungsstelle des Bundes,
35 Christine Lüders. Zudem habe sich das Verfahren als praktikabel erwiesen. Laut Bericht sehen die Personalverantwortlichen das neue Verfahren „durchgängig positiv", nur das Schwärzen von Unterla-

40 gen wird als aufwendig kritisiert. Auch die Jobsuchenden befürworten das Verfahren überwiegend, allerdings glaubt ein gutes Viertel von ihnen, dass ihre Chancen bei herkömmlichen Bewerbungen höher sind.

45 Vier Arbeitgeber des Pilotversuchs haben sich bereits dafür entscheiden, weiter auf anonymisierte Bewerbungen zu setzen, darunter der Geschenkedienstleister Mydays und das Bundesfamilienministerium. [...]

50

Part 2: Literarischer Text – Zadie Smith, *White Teeth*
Aufgabenart

Analyse und Interpretation eines literarischen Textes im Rahmen eines situativen Kontextes. Für diesen Prüfungsteil stehen ca. 240 Minuten (auf erhöhtem Niveau) zur Verfügung.

AUFGABENSTELLUNG

You are taking part in an international seminar on the situation of Black immigrants in Great Britain. The basis of your studies is Zadie Smith's novel. In order to sum up the results of your group, you have been asked to write an article to be read by the other participants.

1 In your article you contrast the situation of immigrants in England with the situation of people of colour in America.

2 You interpret the author's intention when writing this passage and her possible personal opinion on the matter of immigration.

Materialgrundlage

M2 Zadie Smith, *White Teeth*, London: Hamish Hamilton, 2000. S. 326 f. (346 Wörter)

M2 White Teeth (excerpt) *Zadie Smith*

The following text is an extract from the novel "White Teeth" by Zadie Smith, which is set in contemporary London. The story focuses on three families with different cultural backgrounds whose lives become intertwined because of their children. One of the characters (Irie Jones, l. 8) has an English father and a Caribbean mother. She has fallen in love with a boy called Millat Iqbal, whose parents are from Bangladesh.

This has been the century of strangers, brown, yellow, and white. This has been the century of the great immigrant experiment. It is only this late in the day that you can walk into a playground and find Isaac Leung by the fish pond, Danny Rahman in the football cage, Quang O'Rourke bouncing a basketball, and Irie Jones humming a tune. Children with first and last names on a direct collision course. Names that secrete within them mass exodus, cramped boats and planes, cold arrivals, medical checkups.

5

10

It is only this late in the day, and possibly only in Willesden, that you can find best friends Sita and Sharon, constantly mistaken for each other because Sita is white (her mother liked the name) and Sharon is Pakistani (her mother thought it best – less trouble). Yet, despite all the mixing up, despite the fact that we have finally slipped into each other's lives with reasonable comfort (like a man returning to his lover's bed after a midnight walk), despite all this, it is still hard to admit that there is no one more English than the Indian, no one more Indian than the English. There are still young white men who are angry about that; who will roll out at closing time into the poorly lit streets with a kitchen knife wrapped in a tight fist. But it makes an immigrant laugh to hear the fears of the nationalist, scared of infection, penetration, miscegenation, when this is small fry, peanuts, compared to what the immigrant fears – dissolution, disappearance. Even the unflappable Alsana Iqbal would regularly wake up in a puddle of her own sweat after a night visited by visions of Millat (genetically BB; where B stands for Bengaliness) marrying someone called Sarah (aa where 'a' stands for Aryan), resulting in a child called Michael (Ba), who in turn marries someone called Lucy (aa), leaving Alsana with a legacy of unrecognizable great-grandchildren (Aaaaaaa!), their Bengaliness thoroughly diluted, genotype hidden by phenotype. It is both the most irrational and natural feeling in the world.

Annotations:

8 to hum: summen; **10 to secrete:** to hide; **14 Willesden:** an area in North West London;

33 miscegenation: Rassenmischung; **36 unflappable:** unerschütterlich;

46 diluted: verdünnt; **46 f. genotype/phenotype:** genetische Veranlagung / äußere Erscheinung

Bewertungskriterien und Erwartungshorizont
Teil 1: Sprachmittlung

Dieser Teil wird in Abhängigkeit von Qualität und Klarheit der sprachlichen Vermittlung integrativ bewertet. Es erfolgt keine getrennte Wertung von Sprache und Inhalt.

Sprachmittlung
Die Schülerin / Der Schüler stellt im Rahmen der geforderten Textsorte zielgruppengerecht und sprachlich angemessen die wesentlichen Punkte des Textes dar: – pilot scheme that included the German mail service and companies like L'Oreal tested anonymous applications for 18 months – proved that otherwise disadvantaged applicants profit from this process – applicants either blacked out details like name, gender and age or completed an online application; these details were only provided to the potential employer shortly before interviews – process put greater focus on an applicant's qualifications instead of clichés – while a quarter of the applicants believed to have a better chance with a regular application, four of the five participating employers decided to continue with the anonymous application process

TIPP zum Punktesammeln

In Mediationsaufgaben wird generell erwartet, dass das Material nicht wortwörtlich übersetzt, sondern sinngemäß einbezogen wird. Dies erfordert einen souveränen Umgang mit der englischen Sprache, sodass deutsche Ausdrücke und Redewendungen nicht wörtlich übernommen, sondern in richtiges Englisch umgesetzt werden. Auch die kulturellen Unterschiede können bei diesem Aufgabentyp von Bedeutung sein, sodass beachtet werden muss, ob typisch deutsche Gepflogenheiten ggf. geklärt werden sollten oder ob es, wie in diesem Fall, darauf ankommt, auf im englischen Sprachraum bekannte Themen zurückzugreifen.

Teil 2: Schreibaufgabe

Aufgabe 1

Diese Aufgabe gehört zum Anforderungsbereich II.

TIPP zum Punktesammeln

Es wird hier erwartet, dass Sie einen Artikel verfassen, der den vorliegenden Text mit vorhandenem landeskundlichen Hintergrundwissen verknüpft. Beachten Sie die geforderte Textsorte! Wichtig ist auch hier eine geeignete Überschrift! Denken Sie auch daran, dass ein adressatenorientierter Text verfasst werden muss.

Aufgabe 1
In einem zielgruppengerechten Artikel werden Parallelen zwischen der Situation von Immigranten in Großbritannien und der der Afroamerikaner in den USA erarbeitet. Folgende Aspekte könnten erörtert werden:
– While immigrants have decided to move to a different country in order to live there, people of colour in America did not choose to live in the US – they were forced to live and work there as slaves.
– People of colour in the US were treated as second-class people for centuries; immigrants also often face prejudice and discrimination.
– Both immigrants and people of colour face everyday discrimination in education, jobs, housing, etc. This makes it difficult for them to accept the host society as their own; both groups tend towards ghettoisation and cultural isolation.
– While immigrants have the chance to blend in with their new surroundings, so long as they do not look too foreign (see names in the excerpt), people of colour cannot shed their skin – their heritage is always visible and they are therefore perceived as different; this also applies to many immigrant groups, whose members are visibly different.
– Despite being American citizens, people of colour in the US have long been outsiders in American society; with a growing number of prominent Black representatives (e.g. President Barack Obama), this role is changing.

Aufgabe 2

Diese Aufgabe gehört zum Anforderungsbereich III – *Interpretation.*

Aufgabe 2
Die Schülerin / Der Schüler interpretiert im Rahmen der geforderten Textsorte den Textauszug im Hinblick auf die mögliche Aussageabsicht der Autorin Zadie Smith.
– Smith wants to reveal how immigrants feel about living in Britain; she wants to **arouse empathy** for first-generation immigrants who are afraid that their children will lose their cultural identity.
– She points out that immigration has already led to a mix of cultures and states that "we have finally slipped into each other's lives with reasonable comfort" (ll. 20–22). With this comment, one gets a positive, consoling impression of immigration. It becomes evident that **integration is possible.**
– But Smith is also conscious of the **dangers of assimilation.** She describes the loss of cultural identity and parents' fear that integration into British society might mean their children **giving up their cultural heritage.**
– But Smith comments on this by saying, "[i]t is both the most irrational and natural feeling in the world" (ll. 47 f.). Here it becomes clear that, while she understands this feeling, **she is not afraid that cultural roots will be lost completely.**
– In this respect, Smith seeks to convey the positive aspects of immigration by showing the possibility of living together. She takes on a **critical and insightful** perspective, which enables the reader to understand that (first-generation) immigrants are just as afraid of a cultural and genetic mixing as are British nationalists.

Aufgaben zur Sprachmittlung mit Beispiellösungen oder Bewertungskriterien

Sachtext – *Gun debate*

AUFGABENSTELLUNG

You have just come back from an exchange year at an American high school in Massachusetts. Since your English class is discussing the American self-perception at the moment, your teacher has asked you to do a short presentation on the American self-image in terms of the gun debate. While searching the internet, you have found the following article online.

Write that part of the presentation that deals with this article.

Materialgrundlage

David Signer, „Nur ein bewaffneter Amerikaner ist ein richtiger Amerikaner", in: *Neue Zürcher Zeitung* (Zürich), 13.07.2022, https://www.nzz.ch/meinung/amoklaeufe-in-den-usa-die-liebe-zu-waffen-ist-teil-der-kultur-ld.1692477 (Zugriff: 01.04.2023, verändert)

Nur ein bewaffneter Amerikaner ist ein richtiger Amerikaner
David Signer

[...]

„Hey Joe, wohin gehst du mit dem Gewehr in deiner Hand?", heißt es in dem alten amerikanischen Song, der in der Ver-
5 sion von Jimi Hendrix berühmt wurde. „Ich erschieße meine Alte, weil sie mit einem andern rumgemacht hat." Nach vollbrachter Tat macht sich der Rächer im Lied auf in den Süden, „wo ein Mann noch frei
10 sein kann".

Da ist alles drin, was der Hälfte der Amerikaner heute solche Sorgen macht: Die Gewaltverherrlichung, der Preis [des] Waffenkult[s], die „toxische Männlichkeit",
15 die Frauenverachtung und eine seltsame Auffassung von Freiheit. Die andere Hälfte der Amerikaner sieht jedoch kein Problem darin, und das ist das wahre Problem.

[...]

20 Zwar führt ein Vorfall wie die Tötung von sieben Zuschauern einer Parade in Chicago, ausgerechnet am amerikanis-chen Unabhängigkeitstag, zu Schock und Empörung. Aber es wäre erstaunlich, wenn sich irgendetwas ändern würde. Die Patt-
25 situation bei den Gesetzgebern ist lediglich ein Spiegel der Bevölkerung. Unter Millionen von Amerikanern ist der „Kult um den Colt" tief verankert; schließlich ist das Recht, eine Waffe zu besitzen und zu tra-
30 gen, schon im Zweiten Zusatzartikel der Verfassung festgehalten. Für viele ist dieses Grundrecht praktisch gleichbedeutend mit Freiheit an sich. [...] Die Beziehung vieler Amerikaner zu ihrer Waffe ist geradezu
35 mythisch, vor allem auf dem Land und in kleinstädtischen Verhältnissen.

In diesem konservativen Milieu, „wo die Welt noch in Ordnung ist", und nicht in den Großstädten, finden die meisten Mas-
40 senschießereien statt. Die Knaben wachsen dort mit Spielzeugpistolen auf, spielen Cowboys, die Jagd auf Indianer machen, und später bekommen sie von ihrem Vater

feierlich ein Gewehr als Geschenk überreicht. Wenn man Erwachsene von diesem Moment erzählen hört, wird man an Initiationsrituale erinnert, an Konfirmation, Bar Mizwa[1], Matura[2] oder Rekrutenschule, die aus dem Knaben angeblich einen richtigen Mann machen.

Der Archetyp des amerikanischen Waffenträgers ist der Revolverheld, wie er in unzähligen Filmen gefeiert wurde und wird. Die klassische Ausprägung ist der einsame Cowboy mit seinem Colt, der sich im Wilden Westen in einer gottverlassenen Frontier-Siedlung und in der Prärie gegen Indianer und andere Bösewichte verteidigen muss. Jüngere Versionen werden verkörpert von Rambo und anderen Einzelkämpfern, zugleich Helden und Antihelden, die das Gesetz in die eigenen Hände nehmen, weil auf keinen anderen Verlass ist. [...]

Übrigens werden auch oft Hip-Hop-Videoclips mit ihrer Verherrlichung von Gangsta-Kultur und Machismo für die Bandenkriminalität vor allem unter Afroamerikanern verantwortlich gemacht. Am Phänomen selbst gibt es nichts zu rütteln, aber es handelt sich dabei um eine Subkultur. Der Kult um Waffenbesitz und Waffentragen als Ausdruck einer uramerikanischen Freiheit betrifft hingegen vor allem die Mainstream-USA und wird in erster Linie von weißen Männern (und auch Frauen) getragen.

Die verbreitete Kriminalität und die Brutalität der Polizei vor allem gegen Afroamerikaner, der konservativ-patriotische Stolz der „Rechtschaffenen" auf ihre Waffe und die Gewaltorgien der Amokschützen, die sich in ihren irren Manifesten oft zu furchtlosen Kämpfern hochstilisieren, gehören zusammen; sie sind die zwei Seiten derselben unglückseligen Medaille.

Die Bibel in der einen, das Gewehr in der anderen Hand

Erstaunlich ist die Symbiose, die die „gun culture" oft mit christlichem und vor allem evangelikalem Gedankengut eingeht, verkörpert in dem weitverbreiteten Bild des „rechtschaffenen Amerikaners" mit dem Gewehr in der einen und der Bibel in der anderen Hand. Eigentlich kann man sich den Jesus der Bergpredigt kaum als Revolverhelden vorstellen.

Davon abgesehen passt der Kult ums Töten auch nicht recht zur vehementen Ablehnung der Abtreibung in denselben Kreisen. Schutz des Lebens? Pro Life für Ungeborene, Pro Death für Geborene? Und die militante Verteidigung der individuellen Freiheit und der Selbstbestimmung kollidiert eigentlich mit der Jagd auf sexuelle Minderheiten, zu der die Konservativen zunehmend blasen. Aber Stringenz und Widerspruchslosigkeit waren noch nie typische Kennzeichen von Ideologien.

Wenn die Anbetung der Waffe tatsächlich so tief verwurzelt ist in der amerikanischen Geschichte, Mythologie und Kultur, bedeutet das, dass sie kaum verändert werden kann? Nicht unbedingt. In Ländern wie Kanada, Australien oder Neuseeland herrschte und herrscht vor allem unter der ländlichen Bevölkerung ein ähnlich konservativer, individualistischer und staatskritischer Unabhängigkeits– und Pioniergeist. Trotzdem ist es diesen Ländern nach ähnlich aufsehenerregenden Schießereien wie in den USA gelungen, die Waffengewalt einzudämmen. Die USA sind heute das einzige Land auf der Welt, in dem diese Art von Massenmorden, vor allem an Schulen, regelmäßig vorkommt.

[...]

Dieser Text wurde aus didaktischen Gründen gekürzt und verändert.

Annotations:

1 **Bar Mizwa:** jüdische Feier, die das Erreichen der religiösen Mündigkeit im Alter von 13 Jahren zelebriert

2 **Matura:** schulische Abschlussprüfung in der Schweiz, die etwa dem Abitur entspricht

Beispiellösung

Dear class,

I've just come back from my exchange year in Massachusetts. The right to bear arms is a very controversial topic in the United States because it is deeply linked to the American self-image. I would like to look at the fact that although tens of thousands of Americans are killed by guns every year because of easy access to weapons, many Americans still don't support gun control. In addition to my personal experience, I've also found an interesting article on this topic in the "Neue Zürcher Zeitung".

So let's start with the fact that it's an erroneous assumption that the majority of Americans rejects stricter gun laws. Many consider their country's arms policy to glorify violence and a symbol of toxic masculinity and misogyny. Furthermore, it reflects a strange concept of freedom for many people. However, half of the Americans see no problem in the handling of weapons, which is an even bigger issue according to David Signer, the author of the article.

Even though incidents such as the killing of seven spectators at a parade in Chicago on Independence Day lead to shock and public outcry, it doesn't change anything because the public holds on to their right under the 2nd Amendment to own a gun. As you know, for many Americans this is synonymous with freedom itself. According to Signer, many Americans are in a mystic relationship with their weapons, in particular people from rural or provincial areas. In these places one is likely to find a conservative environment in which boys grow up surrounded with toy guns. As little children they play cowboys hunting Native Americans and are solemnly presented with a gun by their fathers later on. Furthermore, the archetype of American arm bearers seems to be the gunslinger, who is presented in pop-cultural contexts such as the lonely cowboy who has to defend himself against various villains in the wild west. In general, these characters take the law into their own hands because no one else can be relied upon.

Talking about cultural aspects: Weapon ownership is most likely to be seen as a cultural tradition and the ultimate expression of freedom among white men and women. African-Americans, on the other hand, are often victims of white police violence, while hip-hop subculture that glorifies violence is often wrongly mistaken as characteristic for the whole Black population.

Another inherent aspect of American identity forms an interesting symbiosis with gun culture, namely the religious faith of many Americans. Singer points out that the righteous American carries a gun in his one and a bible in his other hand. This seems to contradict the call for protecting life in all its stages, which is often made by precisely those people who are against any form of gun control.

But does this mean that gun control and gun culture cannot be changed because it is rooted deeply in American history and culture? Signer points out that the rural populations of Canada, New Zealand and Australia share certain similarities with their American counterpart, namely their conservative and individualistic pioneer spirit. However, those countries were able to drastically reduce cases of gun violence. So far, the United States remain the only country where mass killings occur frequently.

Now that you've heard about the American self-image in terms of gun control, it's up to you how you feel about the issue. From my personal experience I may add that guns belong to a cultural tradition that is shared by many Americans and is considered to be self-evident.

Sachtext – *Migration*

AUFGABENSTELLUNG

With an international group of university students, you are preparing a weekend seminar on current population developments in big cities.

You take part in the opening session of this international project, and you have been given the task of talking about different aspects of migration to major German cities. Using the notion of "good/bad migrants" from Sadigh's article, write an email to your professor and your fellow students, giving them an idea of the main points of your presentation.

Materialgrundlage

Parvin Sadigh, „Die guten, bösen Einwanderer", in: *ZEIT online,* 20.06.2013, http://www.zeit.de/wirtschaft/2013-06/einwanderung-migration-mythen-fakten/seite-5 (Zugriff: 01.04.2023, gekürzt)

„Die guten, bösen Einwanderer"   *Parvin Sadigh*

[...] Mythos 5: Es gibt genug Parallelgesellschaften in deutschen Städten. Kommen mehr Einwanderer, ist der gesellschaftliche Zusammenhalt gefährdet.

Jeder kennt die Straßenzüge in Berlin-Neukölln, Hamburg-Wilhelmsburg oder Duisburg-Marxloh: Straßen, in denen alle Läden türkisch sind und Frauen mit Kopftuch herumlaufen. Diese Bilder werden oft mit der Vorstellung verknüpft, hinter den Wohnungs- und Moscheetüren habe sich eine autonome fremde Gesellschaft gebildet, die ihren eigenen Regeln folgt.

Der Historiker Jochen Oltmer findet jedoch schon das Wort falsch. Parallelgesellschaft sei ein Kampfbegriff, sagt er. Meist seien damit nur türkisch-muslimische Communitys gemeint. Die Elite, die in Dahlem oder Blankenese unter sich bleibt und deren Mitglieder sich gegenseitig Vorteile verschaffen, wird nicht so bezeichnet. Freiwillig ist die Konzentration der ungebildeten, armen Einwanderer in bestimmten Stadtteilen ohnehin nur bedingt. Sie brauchen bezahlbare Wohnungen. Und natürlich leben nicht nur Türken und Muslime in Neukölln. Eigene Schiedsgerichte oder Schulen gibt es sehr selten. Die meisten

25 türkischstämmigen Einwanderer nutzen die deutschen Institutionen und arbeiten in deutschen Firmen.

Tatsächlich aber nutzen Einwanderer soziale oder ethnische Netzwerke, denn 30 es nützt ihnen. Der Politikwissenschaftler Thomas Meyer spricht von einer „hilfreichen Schleusenfunktion". Bereits hier lebende Verwandte oder Freunde erklären, zu welcher Behörde die neu Eingewanderten 35 ten gehen müssen, wie man eine Wohnung findet. Sie sprechen die gleiche Sprache und sorgen für ein wenig Geborgenheit in der Fremde. Oltmer sagt, diese Netzwerke seien charakteristisch für Migration, sogar 40 verantwortlich für ihr Ausmaß. Man denke an Kolonien in New York wie Little Italy, Little Germany oder China Town.

Nur wenn das Netz sehr groß ist, die Einwanderer einheitlich aus einer unge- 45 bildeten armen Schicht kommen und sie sich von der Mehrheitsgesellschaft diskriminiert fühlen, kann das für sie zur Falle werden, sagt Meyer. Die neuen Migranten lernen nicht Deutsch, können ihren Kin- 50 dern in der Schule nicht helfen, sie kon-

sumieren nur türkischsprachige Medien. Eine Spirale entsteht, die die Einwanderer am Aufstieg und an der Integration in die Mehrheitsgesellschaft hindert. Wer arbeitslos ist, verkehrt nur noch mit Arbeitslosen, 55 der Hilfsarbeiter mit Hilfsarbeitern.

Besteht also die Gefahr, dass sich neue Kolonien bilden? Neue Einwanderer in Deutschland kommen zu 60 Prozent aus europäischen Ländern. Polen, Rumänen 60 und Bulgaren nutzen natürlich ihre Netzwerke. Spanische Studenten ziehen in eine WG mit befreundeten Spaniern. Doch diese Netze werden sich nicht zu sogenannten Parallelgesellschaften verfestigen. Die 65 meisten der aktuellen Einwanderer sind gebildet – und „je höher der Bildungsgrad, desto größer ist die Tendenz, dass sich Kolonien wieder auflösen", sagt Oltmer. Auch die Gefahr, dass sich sogenannte Parallel- 70 gesellschaften von ungebildeten Bulgaren und Rumänen bilden, sei nicht sehr groß. Viele der Einwanderer bleiben nicht lange in Deutschland, sagt Oltmer, und sie sind zu wenige, um eigene Kolonien zu bilden. 75

Bewertungskriterien

Formale Aspekte

E-Mail-Form, um Information bezüglich eines Themenkomplexes (Einwanderung) an den Professor und an Studienkollegen weiterzugeben:
- Sprachregister: gepflegtes Englisch (aber nicht zu formell, aufgrund des Adressaten)
- Einleitung (um Anlass, Kontext und Adressat zu nennen) sowie Quelle (Erklärung, was ZEIT online ist)
- Hauptteil bestehend aus für die Fragestellung wesentlichen Aspekten aus dem Text

Inhaltliche Aspekte
- Einleitung – Adressat: Professor und Studienkollegen
- Kontext: E-Mail zur Vorbereitung einer Präsentation zum Thema Einwanderung
- Verweis auf Quelle und Gesamtkontext des Textauszuges
- Hauptteil
- Assoziationen in Bezug auf Alltagsbilder mit vermeintlichen Parallelgesellschaften aus Neukölln, Hamburg etc.

– tatsächlicher Ist-Zustand: es wird nur der ärmere, bildungsferner Teil der Migranten mit diesem Begriff bezeichnet, nicht die gebildete Elite, äußere Faktoren wie Mietpreise spielen eine Rolle
– Bedeutung der Netzwerke, Vergleich zu den USA
– Gefahr nur bei zu großem, einheitlichem Netz und Gefühl der Diskriminierung: kaum Spracherwerb, soziale Kontakte bleiben im bekannten Umfeld, kein Aufstieg
– Gefahr neuer Kolonienbildung ist gering, da Anteil der gebildeten Migranten höher ist
– Schluss mit Bezug zum Kontext

Original-Prüfungsaufgaben 2022 gA

Quelle der Aufgabenstellung

Niedersächsisches Kultusministerium

Hinweis: Bei den Musterlösungen zu den Prüfungsaufgaben handelt es sich um nicht amtliche Lösungen.

Hinweise:

Die zentrale schriftliche Abiturprüfung im Fach Englisch besteht aus einer kombinierten Aufgabe:

Prüfungsteil 1:	a) **Hörverstehen**	**Prüfungsteil 2:** **Textaufgabe**
	b) **Sprachmittlung**	

Ablauf und Bewertung der Prüfung:

Ausgabe der **Aufgaben für den Prüfungsteil 1a**

Prüfungsteil 1a:	**Hörverstehen**
Gewichtung:	20 %
Bearbeitungszeit:	30 Minuten
	Abgabe sämtlicher Unterlagen des **Prüfungsteils 1a**

Ausgabe der **Aufgaben für den Prüfungsteil 1b**
und der zugelassenen **Hilfsmittel**

Prüfungsteil 1b:	**Sprachmittlung**
Gewichtung:	25 %
Bearbeitungszeit:	60 Minuten
	Abgabe sämtlicher Unterlagen des **Prüfungsteils 1b**

Ausgabe der **Aufgaben für den Prüfungsteil 2**

Prüfungsteil 2:	**Textaufgabe**
Gewichtung:	55 %
Prüfungszeit:	210 Minuten
	Die Prüfungszeit setzt sich zusammen aus 30 Minuten Auswahlzeit und 180 Minuten Bearbeitungszeit.

Hilfsmittel für alle Prüfungsteile:

Den Prüflingen stehen einsprachige sowie für den schulischen Gebrauch geeignete zweisprachige Wörterbücher der Allgemeinsprache (Deutsch–Englisch/Englisch–Deutsch) zur Verfügung (s. Erlass zur Nutzung von [elektronischen] Wörterbüchern in Prüfungen: https://www.nibis.de/uploads/mk-bolhoefer/2022/202111Elektronis cheWoerterbuecher.pdf).

Hinweis

- Jedes einzelne Blatt ist mit dem Namen zu versehen.

Hinweise zum Prüfungsteil 2
- Von den zwei Aufgaben ist eine auszuwählen und zu bearbeiten.
- Bei jeder Teilaufgabe ist die inhaltliche Gewichtung angegeben.

gA Listening Comprehension   24 BE

AUFGABENSTELLUNG

You will hear each recording twice. After each listening, you will have time to complete your answers.

Task 1: Turning Pollution into Art   9 BE
Preparation time: 1:30 minutes
You will hear an interview with Angela Haseltine Pozzi, an artist living in Oregon.
While listening, tick the correct answer (a, b, or c). There is only one correct answer.

1. The Southern Oregon coast is known for its

a	flat islands.	☐
b	dramatic scenery.	☐
c	recreational value.	☐

2. It is Angela's aim to

a	gather lots of plastic.	☐
b	make people collect plastic on shore.	☐
c	locate plastic items bitten into by animals.	☐

3. Angela's pieces of art feature

a	extinct sea animals.	☐
b	fantasy sea animals.	☐
c	endangered sea animals.	☐

4. Angela's intention of creating large sculptures is that

a	people notice them.	☐
b	stability can be ensured.	☐
c	a lot of waste is used up.	☐

5. With her project, Angela hopes

a	to encourage other artists.	☐
b	to appeal to society as a whole.	☐
c	to cooperate with youth workers.	☐

6. Angela's organisation Washed Ashore

a	gathers plastic waste from all over the US.	☐
b	puts together exhibitions throughout the nation.	☐
c	supports global campaigns for plastic-free oceans.	☐

7. The Beijing Olympics is mentioned to show that

a	plastic is a long-lasting problem.	☐
b	sports events create a lot of plastic trash.	☐
c	people find plastic products with logos attractive.	☐

8. Angela is aware that plastic

a	can be necessary.	☐
b	has to be replaced.	☐
c	should be disposed of properly.	☐

9. When it comes to single-use plastic items, Angela suggests that

a	they should be banned.	☐
b	engineers must solve the problem.	☐
c	the public is warned about the long-term effects.	☐

Now listen to the recording again.

Source:

Kirk Siegler, "On The Oregon Coast, Turning Pollution Into Art With A Purpose", *npr*, 4 December 2019, https://www.npr.org/2019/12/04/784416386/on-the-oregon-coast-turning-pollution-into-art-with-a-purpose (accessed on 1 April 2023).

Task 2: Sugar   5 BE

Preparation time: 30 seconds

You will hear five people talking about regulating sugar consumption.
Choose from the list (A–G) which heading best applies to which statement (1–5). For each
statement there is only one correct answer. There are two more headings than you need.

Headings	
A	Harming minors
B	Business principles
C	Prolonging life expectancy
D	Attitude towards authorities
E	Lowering the cost for health care
F	Impact of prices on consumer groups
G	Varied public health measures required

Statement	1	2	3	4	5	6
Heading						

Now listen to the recording again.

Sources:
- "Health Report: Is it time for a sugar tax?", *ABC*, 18 December 2017, http://www.abc.net.au/radio national/programs/healthreport/is-it-time-for-a-sugar-tax/9224258 (accessed on 1 April 2023)
  Statement 1: 13:16–13:41
  Statement 2: 08:07–08:31
  Statement 4: 04:54–05:16 + 05:37–05:41
  Statement 5: 04:04–04:34
- "Inside Health: Preventive HIV therapy, Sugar tax, Bowel cancer, Surgery", *BBC Radio 4*, 22 March 2016, https://www.bbc.co.uk/programmes/b07414dg (accessed on 1 April 2023).
  Statement 3: 02:43–03:11

Task 3: Modernising the Royal Family

10 BE

Preparation time: 1 minute

You will hear a radio programme on changes in the British Royal Family since 1992. Lucy Burns from the BBC speaks to Charles Anson, the former press secretary of the Royal Family.

While listening, answer the questions. You need not write complete sentences. Unless otherwise specified, name one aspect.

1	What did the Royal Family do in reaction to the situation in the early 1990s?	
2	How does the Queen remember 1992?	
3	What family matters affected the Royals in 1992? (Name one.)	
4	How did the media react to the royal events? (Name two examples.)	• _____ • _____
5	What issue did the public raise?	
6	What happened in November 1992?	
7	What made Charles Anson's job more challenging at the time?	
8	How does Anson characterise the Queen during her long reign?	
9	Which change did Queen Elizabeth declare that affected the public directly?	

Now listen to the recording again.

Source:

"The Way Ahead group: Modernising the Royal Family", *BBC World Service*, 27 January 2020, https://www.bbc.co.uk/sounds/play/w3csywyp (00:09–04:08) (accessed on 1 April 2023).

Lösungen

Task 1: Turning Pollution into Art

1	2	3	4	5	6	7	8	9
b	a	c	a	b	b	a	a	c

Task 2: Sugar

1	2	3	4	5
D	B	F	G	A

Task 3: Modernising the Royal Family

No.	BE	*Lösungsvorschlag:*
1	1	set up group to plan for the future
2	1	as a difficult/horrible year
3	1	separations/divorces
4	1 1	*two of the following:* relentless interest / leaked tapes of intimate phone calls / offered phone lines to listen to recordings
5	1	cost of royal family to taxpayers
6	1	fire at Windsor Castle
7	1	people wanted to talk about private lives of royal family, which they weren't allowed to discuss
8	1	offered steadiness / very calm
9	1	started paying income tax / public would not need to pay for certain members of royal family

gA Sprachmittlung

David Gutensohn, „Fast niemand zieht mehr aus Überzeugung in eine WG" (2019)

AUFGABENSTELLUNG

In your social studies class, you and students at your American partner school are working on the joint e-learning project "Changing Lifestyles".

Write an article for the project website, outlining why people have lived in shared accommodation in the past and present.

Materialgrundlage:

David Gutensohn (Interview mit Clemens Albrecht), „Fast niemand zieht mehr aus Überzeugung in eine WG", in: *ZEIT Campus Online,* 19.04.2019, zitiert nach: https://www.zeit.de/campus/2019-04/wohngemeinschaften-studierende-bezahlbarer-wohnraum-clemens-albrecht (Zugriff: 01.04.2023).

Hilfsmittel:

Ein- und zweisprachiges Wörterbuch der Zielsprache

„Fast niemand zieht mehr aus Überzeugung in eine WG"
David Gutensohn

ZEIT Campus ONLINE: Immer mehr Menschen leben in Wohngemeinschaften. Seit wann liegt die WG im Trend?

Clemens Albrecht: Menschen, die nicht
5 miteinander verwandt sind, aber einen Haushalt teilen, gab es schon im Römischen Reich. Das ganze europäische Mittelalter war geprägt von Lebensformen, in denen Familien, ihr Dienstpersonal und an-
10 dere Personen sich ein Haus teilten. Eigentlich ist die Wohngemeinschaft die normale Lebensform.

Seit wann leben Familien nicht mehr in Wohngemeinschaften?

15 Zumindest bis in die Mitte des 19. Jahrhunderts war das die Regel. Danach lebte die Kernfamilie verstärkt im eigenen Heim, allerdings in der Oberschicht immer noch mit Personal. Als die Dienstboten dann in
20 den 1950er- und 1960er-Jahren durch Maschinen ersetzt wurden, wurde die Kernfamilie mit eigenem Haushalt zum Standard. Die Männer gingen arbeiten, die Frauen blieben zu Hause und kümmerten sich um die Kinder. 25

Wie hat das Modell der Wohngemeinschaft trotzdem überlebt?

Wie so viele gesellschaftliche Strukturen wurde auch diese von der 68er-Bewegung aufgebrochen. Ihre Wohngemeinschafts- 30 projekte läuteten das Comeback der alten Wohnform ein. Das damals Neue an der Wohngemeinschaft war, dass sie egalitär organisiert wurde. Es gab keine patriarchalen Strukturen innerhalb von Wohnge- 35 meinschaften. Das ist bis heute so geblieben, wenn man mal davon absieht, dass es Haupt- und Untermieter gibt. Die Wohngemeinschaft der 68er war immer ein gesellschaftsreformerisches Projekt. Doch die 40

Hoffnung, dass irgendwann alle Menschen frei und gleich zusammenleben würden, erwies sich als große Illusion.

Wieso ist die Idee gescheitert?

45 Heute entscheiden sich Studierende pragmatisch statt politisch für eine Wohngemeinschaft. Ist das Studium beendet und die Familie gegründet, verlässt man die WG und zieht ins Reihenhaus. Einige Jah-
50 re später wird der Nachwuchs denselben Kreislauf durchlaufen. Die WG ist zu einer Lebensform auf Zeit geworden – vor allem für gut gebildete 20- bis 30-Jährige. Fast niemand zieht mehr aus Überzeugung in
55 eine Wohngemeinschaft.

Warum sonst? Eine Studie vom Centrum für Hochschulentwicklung (CHE) zeigt, dass die WG-Quote kontinuierlich steigt und mittlerweile jeder und
60 **jede dritte Studierende in einer Wohngemeinschaft lebt. Für sie ist die WG zur beliebtesten Wohnform geworden.**

Rein pragmatisch ist die WG für viele Studierende einfach die beste Lösung. Sie
65 haben oft zu wenig Einkommen, um sich eine eigene Wohnung leisten zu können. Vor allem in angesagten Städten sind Ein- oder Zweizimmerwohnungen besonders teuer. Dort sind nicht nur Studierende auf
70 Wohngemeinschaften angewiesen. Auch Erwachsene, die im Berufsleben stehen, bleiben oder ziehen heute in Wohngemeinschaften. Oft nur, weil das finanzierbar ist und sie ohnehin mobiler und flexibler ar-
75 beiten und leben als früher.

Entscheiden sich Menschen heute nur noch aus finanziellen Gründen für eine WG?

Zum Teil. Es ist aber auch ein anderer Trend zu beobachten: Einige Menschen 80 leben explizit asketisch und minimalistisch. Es gibt eine ganze Bewegung von Menschen, die bewusst Verzicht üben und möglichst wenig besitzen möchten. Da kann man sich mit keiner Wohnform bes- 85 ser identifizieren als mit der Wohngemeinschaft. Die WG kann also auch Teil eines Lebensstils sein und Identifikation schaffen. Einige machen damit aus der Not eine Tugend: Sie bloggen über ihren Lebensstil 90 und integrieren das kleine WG-Zimmer in ihr positives Selbstbild.

Andere wiederum wünschen sich nur, dass abends jemand zu Hause ist, oder? 95

Wohngemeinschaften können auch eine Art Familienersatz sein. Wir Soziologen unterscheiden zwischen Gemeinschaft und Gesellschaft. Gemeinschaft, das sind Freunde und Familie, unsere engsten Be- 100 ziehungen, die immer mit sozialer Kontrolle verbunden sind. Daraus möchten viele fliehen, ohne in die völlige Anonymität der großen Städte zu geraten. Ihnen kann die WG wiederum Gemeinschaft bieten, ohne 105 so eng wie Familie zu sein: Menschen, die da sind und sich um einen kümmern, vor denen man sich aber nicht für den alltäglichen Lebenswandel verantworten muss. [...] (585 Wörter)

Anmerkungen:

4 Clemens Albrecht – Professor für Kultursoziologie, Universität Bonn

29 68er-Bewegung – *hier:* die westdeutsche Studentenprotestbewegung der späten 1960er-Jahre

Beispiellösung

Shared accommodation now and then

As Clemens Albrecht, a professor in the sociology of culture, points out in an interview in the German magazine *ZEIT Campus ONLINE* on 19 April 2019, all throughout history there have been people sharing accommodation. Already in the time of the Roman Empire, people who were not related shared living quarters. During the Middle Ages households often comprised servants and the persons who employed them. It was not until modern history that living arrangements started to be concentrate on core families which, unless in the case of the wealthy, did not include attendants.

Later on, the late 1960s heralded a revitalisation of shared accommodation, as its politically motivated proponents rejected patriarchal structures and sought to organise communal living on an equal footing for all residents.

Nowadays, nearly nobody becomes part of a community due to their political opinion but rather because of pragmatic considerations like a student's financial situation. Young professionals likewise appreciate living in a flatshare, as they can pursue their professions more flexibly, enjoy the advantages of being more mobile and save money due to small rents.

On the other hand, there are also people who share a household as a deliberate decision to cultivate a frugal lifestyle. And finally, to some people, shared accommodation offers company without any commitment or family pressure.

Whatever the reasons – shared living space remains a successful, well-tried model.

(231 words)

gA Aufgabe I mit Beispiellösung

Text: Ayad Akhtar, *Homeland Elegies* (excerpt, 2020)

AUFGABENSTELLUNG

1 Describe the situation presented in the excerpt. (30 %)

2 Examine how Ayad behaves in the conversation with Officer Matthew. (30 %)

3 You are taking part in an international youth project on "Finding Your Place." You have been asked to write an article for the project website in which you comment on the following statement by author Charles Yu: "You came here, your parents and their parents and their parents, and you always seem to have just arrived and yet never seem to have actually arrived."
Write the article, also referring to the text at hand and materials studied in class, such as the short stories "Loose Change" and "She Shall Not Be Moved." (40 %)

Materialgrundlage:

Ayad Akhtar. *Homeland Elegies*. 2020. London: Tinder Press, 2021. 90–92.

Hilfsmittel:

Ein- und zweisprachiges Wörterbuch der Zielsprache

Homeland Elegies (2020, excerpt)   *Ayad Akhtar*

On a highway in Pennsylvania, Ayad, the main character, has been stopped and alerted to problems with his car by a police officer.

[...] He was bone-white, his features boyish, though there was something ancient about his vaulted cheekbones and the Tartar slant to his eyes. Polish or Serbian,
5 I thought, though the last name on his tag betrayed no obvious ethnic origin: MAT-THEW. As we stepped away from the car, he pointed ahead at an exit. We weren't far from Clarks Summit, he said, where
10 there was a garage. He suspected that was where AAA would take me, though he had to admit he'd only ever heard bad things about the service there. "I know a garage in Scranton where I always go. It's a little
15 farther, but they'll come get you with their own truck. I know the owner. They do great work. I'd be happy to call him for you."

It was a bright, mild day in late Octo-ber. The surrounding hills were ablaze with
20 autumn color. As Trooper Matthew and I waited for the tow truck, his cruiser be-tween us and the traffic's noisy ebb and flow, he turned to me and asked – entirely benignly, I thought – where my name was
25 from. I knew from experience that an hon-est answer to this not infrequent question could raise suspicions where there might otherwise have been none, my well-inten-tioned interlocutors suddenly beclouded by
30 some reflexive evocation of terror. In the

trying months after 9/11 – when the simple act of mounting the city bus and paying my fare had become a provocation, met with fearful, watching glares – I'd settled on a pro-
35 phylactic strategy: "India," I would say. It was a lie. The name wasn't Indian. But I knew the question usually masked a curiosity about my origins [...]. This answer had the obvious advantage of connoting not the referents of
40 terror, murder, and rage that most associated with Pakistan but rather the bright colors and spicy tastes of delightful dishes like tik-ka masala, gyrating flash mobs in Bollywood movies, and yoga pants. To complicate all
45 this further, my name is actually Egyptian, and depending on the political moment – in the wake of attacks like those on tourists at Luxor and Sharm el Sheikh, or two years later, during the misleading months of the
50 so-called Arab Spring – mentioning Egypt can become a prompt to more questions, each riddled with a particular pitfall that often leads to the very sort of mistrust I am ever keen to avoid in the first place. If all this
55 sounds somewhat paranoid, I am happy for you. Clearly you have not been beset by daily worries of being perceived – and therefore treated – as a foe of the republic rather than a member of it.
60   Standing alongside Officer Matthew, surrounded by the painted hills, grateful for his charitable interest in my vehicle's proper repair, disarmed by gratitude, I opt-ed for the complicated truth. "The name is
65 Egyptian," I said.
    "Really?"
    "My parents aren't from Egypt, but when my father first came to this country, he had an Egyptian friend who had my
70 name. He'd never heard it before and really liked it. So when I was born, he used it for me. Funny thing is, he doesn't say it right. Or at least not how he heard it said by his friend ..."

"How are you supposed to say it?"   75
    I joked my way through the various pro-nunciations of my name – the original Ara-bic, which sounded nothing like how my parents said it and which was different still from the way my kindergarten teacher had   80
coined the American pronunciation, which had stuck ever since.
    "So why couldn't your parents say it right?"
    "They don't speak Arabic."   85
    "They're not Arabs?"
    "Well, no, they're from Pakistan, so – ac-tually, they were born in India. But that's a long story."
    "And you all moved here from Pakistan   90
when you were in kindergarten?"
    "I was born here."
    He paused for a moment, picking lint off the stiff felt dome of his wide-brimmed trooper hat. From somewhere upwind of us,   95
the sweet smell of burning apple wood was pouring into the air. "So where were you born?" he asked, suddenly tentative.
    It was clear I'd made a mistake.
    "Wisconsin," I said. It was another lie.   100
Though I spent almost the entirety of my childhood and adolescence in Wisconsin, I was born on Staten Island. "Wisconsin," though, felt like a stronger move in this ne-gotiation around the impression forming   105
inside him.
    "Never been," he said. "I just read this book, The Looming Tower. You heard of it?"
    "It won the Pulitzer last year, didn't it?"
    "It's pretty incredible."   110
    "I know the writer. Lawrence Wright. Great guy."
    [...] I was misrepresenting both my af-fection for – and proximity to – this famous writer in an obvious attempt to signal sta-   115
tus and amiability, to get Trooper Matthew off whatever suspicions I worried he was now harboring.   (793 words)

Annotations

4	**Tartar** – member of an ethnic group from Central Asia
11	**AAA** – abbreviation for American Automobile Association, an organization providing roadside assistance
20	**Trooper** – officer of the state police
48	**Luxor and Sharm el Sheikh** – holiday destinations in Egypt
50	**Arab Spring** – series of anti-government protests against corruption and lack of democracy
93	**lint** – *German:* Fussel
109	**Pulitzer** – reference to the Pulitzer Prize, a prestigious literary award

Beispiellösung

Aufgabe 1

Ayad and an officer of the state police are on a highway where they are waiting for a tow service recommended by the officer. In order to pass the time, they start a conversation. Ayad eyes the trooper trying to work out his heritage but cannot clearly make up his mind, ultimately guessing him to be Polish or Serbian.

During their conversation the Trooper asks where Ayad's name derives from. This triggers a train of thought in Ayad, who has found that a truthful answer – that his parents hail from Pakistan and gave him an Egyptian name – often causes suspicion because people associate it with terrorism. So, Ayad normally lies about his heritage, but this time he decides to tell the truth. When he mentions where his parents originally came from, this causes noticeable reservations with the officer. Due to this, Ayad gives a wrong place of birth and pretends to know an author they are talking about in order to allay the trooper's concerns. (165 words)

Aufgabe 2

Ayad is a second-generation immigrant whose parents originally came from Pakistan. During the whole scene on the highway, he seems to try hard not to arouse resentment and suspicion (cf. ll. 53 f., 117 f.). For this reason, he immediately examines Trooper Matthew, attempting to discern his ethnicity while they are waiting for the tow service (cf. ll. 1–4).

During their conversation the officer asks Ayad about his name, seemingly without any ulterior motives. Ayad however immediately recalls all the uncomfortable experiences he made after 9/11 and the Arab Spring, which left him feeling helpless, as many, particularly white Americans became suspicious of everyone with Middle Eastern origins (cf. ll. 25–34; "a prompt to more questions, each riddled with a particular pitfall that often leads to the very sort of mistrust I am ever keen to avoid in the first place", ll. 51–54). On account of these incidents and the openly shown mistrust towards his person (cf. ll. 51–55, ll. 58 f.), he is reluctant to disclose his heritage and ponders how to react to the trooper's question (cf. ll. 25 ff.).

It becomes clear that Ayad takes this issue into consideration all the time because he wants to prevent being discriminated against (cf. ll. 54–59). Consequently, he has developed various strategies to avoid both the truth as well as awkward questions and situations. For example, he lies about where he was born ("'Wisconsin,' I said. It was another

179

lie. Though I spent almost the entirety of my childhood and adolescence in Wisconsin, I was born on Staten Island", ll. 101–104). For the same purpose, he makes fun of his heritage when he describes the various mispronunciations of his first name (cf. ll. 76 f.). Eventually, however, Ayad decides to tell the officer the "complicated truth" (l. 64) about his name since he is grateful for Matthew's help (cf. ll. 61–63). It thus becomes obvious that Ayad is very cautious and strictly avoids standing out but that he is also a well-meaning person who is able to trust others. Nonetheless, he remains highly receptive to other people's reactions towards him. This is why Ayad quickly adopts his strategy to lying when the officer's tone appears to change ("'So where were you born?' he asked, suddenly tentative. It was clear I'd made a mistake", ll. 97–99). Again, he seeks to prevent Matthew from putting forward more questions and in order to resolve upcoming doubts (ll. 100–106). He even starts pretending to like and know a certain author more than he actually does in order to take the officer's mind off any alleged suspicions and to show that he is knowledgeable and amiable.

Finally, looking at all these points, it can be concluded that Ayad is permanently striving to be seen as a "regular" American and painstakingly trying not to rub people the wrong way by employing evasive strategies like glossing over or lying about details of his heritage. (497 words)

Aufgabe 3

Dear members,

While reading various texts for our project "Finding Your Place", I also found an interesting statement by Charles Yu: "You came here, your parents and their parents and their parents, and you always seem to have just arrived and yet never seem to have actually arrived". This seems to hit the nail right on the head, as not only first-generation immigrants struggle to integrate themselves into a new society, but also the following generations still face difficulties in being acknowledged and accepted as "regular" members of the community their parents moved to.

Most significantly, second-generation immigrants are still exposed to little or unconcealed resentment and sometimes verbal or even physical hate attacks. This can be seen in the short story "She Shall Not Be Moved", when the Somali woman is verbally abused and openly discriminated against by the two elderly white women refusing to give up their seats as well as antagonised by the black bus driver who yells at her instead of taking her side. Another example of such discrimination can be found in the nameless narrator of the short story "Loose Change", who even though she is a grandchild of immigrants herself, eventually decides not to host Laylor out of fear for her family's safety. Looking at *Homeland Elegies*, it becomes clear that negative reactions can also be conveyed in a subtle way. Nevertheless, they are sensed by Ayad, as he has become accustomed to the fact that his Pakistani origins and his Egyptian name frequently arouse a feeling of unease or resentments in the people to whom he reveals these details.

Consequently, on the basis of these experiences, Ayad normally tries to keep his real identity secret to avoid complications and tries very hard to blend in. The Somali woman in "She Shall Not Be Moved" on the other hand openly shows that she will not be humiliated by others, no matter if black or white. Therefore, she strongly reacts towards the black bus driver, regarding him a "slave" for not standing up to every-day racism. Crucially, even second-generation immigrants suffer from a feeling of not really belonging to the society they live in. This can be seen in Ayad's case when he tries to hide his actual identity, as he constantly fears unjustified resentment. Similarly, the thoughts of the narrator in "She Shall Not Be Moved" betray a habitual apprehension that she may be thrown off the bus partially because of the colour of her skin; while she feels generally safe in Britain, she admits that anti-racism laws are rarely applied. Only the narrator in "Loose Change" feels fully integrated, considering herself a stereotypical Londoner. Even having achieved acknowledgment, second-generation immigrants are often anxious about their social status, which they want to keep at any price. Hence, the narrator in the short story "She Shall Not Be Moved" does not dare to take sides with the Somali woman, even though she knows the white women's impudent and provoking behaviour to be racist. Ayad's strategy is to evade potential conflicts by hiding his ethnic origins because he does not want to endanger the social status he has achieved.

Lastly, there is another central aspect that makes many second-generation immigrants feel they have not arrived yet, namely the lack of educational and hence also economic opportunities provided for them. Only well-educated people are able to get well-paid jobs and climb the social ladder in order to improve their standard of living, but many second-generation immigrants are deprived of such chances. It is thus no wonder that many of them feel neglected, abandoned and therefore "never seem to have actually arrived".

In my eyes, it can easily be seen that even as a second-generation immigrant finding one's place in a society can be very difficult if others make their lives miserable through subtle or obvious racism. To overcome this feeling of being unwelcome, it is very important that immigrants of any generation experience social and emotional support from their families and from those whose families have been part of that society for much longer.   (677 words)

gA Aufgabe II mit Beispiellösung

Marybeth Gasman, "The Shame of My Father's Racism" (2017)

AUFGABENSTELLUNG

1 Outline Marybeth Gasman's reactions to her father's racism. (30 %)

2 Compare the author's father with Walt Kowalski from the movie *Gran Torino*. (30 %)

3 WHYY, a public news and media organization, has invited readers to share their ideas about "Living Cultural Diversity" on its website. You have decided to contribute a blog entry in which you assess the relevance of dealing with questions of cultural diversity for members of your generation. As a starting point, you take the following statement by author Audre Lorde: "It is not our differences that divide us. It is our inability to recognize, accept, and celebrate those differences."
Write the blog entry, also referring to the text at hand and materials studied in class, such as the movie *Gran Torino*. (40 %)

Materialgrundlage:

Marybeth Gasman, "The Shame of My Father's Racism", in: *WHYY.org*, 20.05.2017, zitiert nach: https://whyy.org/articles/essay-the-shame-of-my-fathers-racism (Zugriff: 01.04.2023).

Hilfsmittel:

Ein- und zweisprachiges Wörterbuch der Zielsprache

"The Shame of My Father's Racism" (2017)   *Marybeth Gasman*

It took me years to talk about the racism perpetuated by my father in public settings. I was ashamed and embarrassed by him most of my early life. He was angry,
5 verbally abusive, and looked down upon others regularly.

When I was a child, he attempted to fill my head with racist ideas about various people. He used racial slurs regularly and
10 called me and members of our family these same names. As I grew older and began to read books in school, I started to push back at him and challenge his racist notions. He told me I was ignorant.

I couldn't understand why my father 15 hated most racial and ethnic minorities, even though he had never met any member of these groups in his entire life. His hate was deep and angry, and he used "evidence" to try to persuade me that whites 20 were better than others. He would tell me that African Americans "caused riots and destroyed cities," and point to pictures from the Civil Rights Movement. He left out most of the details. He would tell me that Afri- 25 can Americans were "stupid and preferred to live in poverty," and point to examples that he saw on television in shows such as

"Sanford and Son." He would tell me how cruel Asian Americans were, citing their efforts to defend their own nations during wartime. He neglected to tell me about the cruelty that has cut across our own nation both during wars and at times of peace. He would tell me how Hispanics were "lazy and took advantage of the government," citing stereotypical pictures drawn by whites of Mexican Americans.

My father was an uneducated man, living in dire poverty most of his life. Instead of seeing the commonalities that he had with others oppressed in our nation and looking for ways to bridge those commonalities, he chose to blame others for his poverty and lack of success. It's important to note that my father often worked two jobs – one in a lumberyard and another on our small animal and vegetable farm; he also looked for odd jobs to make extra money. However, he could never get ahead, making less than minimum wage in many cases. Instead of hurling insults at the systems that perpetuated poverty, or becoming more active locally to change these systems, he decided to funnel his anger into hate for racial and ethnic minorities.

I spent years trying to change his mind – talking with him, trying to educate him, sometimes yelling at him. I even pursued a career as a professor who concentrates on race and class issues in American society, to better understand the hate that my father held in his heart. However, it wasn't until my father was older, in a nursing home, and had met someone African American, that he let go of his hate and our nation's original sin.

The pathway for my father was friendship, and the eventual understanding that he and his friend had much in common and were equally frustrated with their lot in life. It was at this point that my father confided in me that he was unhappy with his life and chose to blame racial and ethnic minorities – African Americans in particular – for his pain and failure. It was easier to blame those who so many others blamed rather than take responsibility or fight the systems that had helped maintain his place in society.

My father's story is one of hope in many ways, because he realized his wrongs, but it is also hopeful for me as a scholar. Many of my faculty colleagues throughout the country don't believe that we can make progress on racial issues and racism. However, I do – but only by engaging others in conversation and encouraging them to assist in dismantling systems. People dismantle systems, not systems themselves.

I have spent hours upon hours talking to people on planes, trains, in hotels, at conferences, in classrooms, etc. about race and have with each conversation tried to get people to consider the perspectives of others and examine their own biases. When people ask me if I get tired or frustrated by these conversations, I often respond by noting that I worked with and on my father for nearly 20 years, knowing that eventually he would turn a corner. What I realized in the end, however, is that it was not my intellectual ideas that changed him but the friendship of another and my having heart-to-heart conversations in which I listened to him openly. We need to do more listening to each other's stories to move our nation to a better and more equitable place for all.

(777 words)

Annotations:

29 "Sanford and Son" – American sitcom TV series (1972–1977)

Beispiellösung

Aufgabe 1

In her article "The Shame of My Father's Racism", published on WHYY.org in 2017, Marybeth Gasman recounts how she has been upset by and concerned with her father's obvious racism and hatred towards ethnic minorities for decades.

Forced to endure her father's verbally abusive behaviour towards ethnic minorities in public and even towards his family, she feels unable to understand or address his racism at first. Through her education and as she gets older, however, she begins to take issue with him on his insulting notions and challenges him. She investigates the reasons for his hatred, tracing it back to a lack of education and resulting extreme poverty that caused him to scapegoat minorities. Finally, driven by her wish to understand her father's attitude, she chooses a career as a professor focusing on race and class issues. Moreover, she dedicates a lot of her time and energy on trying to educate people she meets on these matters. (157 words)

Aufgabe 2

When comparing Marybeth Gasman's father with Walt Kowalski, it becomes clear that both men at first share certain characteristics concerning their hostile convictions about ethnic minorities, but after experiencing unexpected friendship, they eventually change their minds.

Gasman and Kowalski spend most of their lives as inveterate racists, which can be seen in their openly displayed contempt towards other ethnic groups. Gasman uses racial slurs frequently and even abuses his family members with the same insults (l. 9–11). Kowalski likewise despises his Hmong neighbours, treating them with disrespect – for example, when he bangs the door into Thao's face – and slurring insults at them. Both Gasman and Kowalski are quick to draw on stereotypes in order to underline their firm convictions: Gasman "point[s] to examples that he saw on television" (ll. 27 f.), whereas Kowalski accuses Asians as a whole of allegedly eating dogs.

Both men are to some degree alienated from their family. Kowalski is widowed and estranged from his two sons, living alone with his dog. Gasman "was angry, verbally abusive, and looked down upon others" (ll. 4–6), including his own family, whom he also regularly bullied with racist epithets (cf. ll. 9–11). The text does not give any details about Gasman's family life, but most likely it was overshadowed by his antagonising behaviour. Another similarity is the fact that both of them project their personal frustrations on members of ethnic minorities, which eases their minds about their dissatisfying circumstances of life. Gasman particularly blames African Americans for his poverty (ll. 50–56). Kowalski, on the other hand, seems to be distressed by his changing neighbourhood, where he feels white middle-class families are being replaced by Hmong immigrants, whom he automatically associates with his traumatising experiences in the Korean War and his own lifelong guilt. Therefore, he murmurs insults and shows scornful behaviour like spitting in their direction.

Eventually, both Gasman and Kowalski open their minds to the people they despised so deeply before. The reason for sparking this process in both cases is making friends with a member of a different ethnic group. Gasman does so with an African-American man he meets in his nursing home (cf. ll. 63–67). Kowalski, on the other hand, is befriended by the Hmong family's daughter, opens up to their culture and becomes a substitute father figure for Thao. As a result, both Gasman and Kowalski eventually admit that their convictions were wrong. They open up and seem to achieve reconciliation, but their ways of doing so are completely different. Gasman confides to his daughter that it was his unhappiness about his life that fostered his racism (ll. 72–80). Kowalski, on the other hand, confesses to Thao to having killed an Asian boy during the Korean War, which has been haunting him ever since.

However, there are also dissimilarities to their situations. Gasman's social background differs from Kowalski's with respect to education and social class. Whereas Gasman belongs to the lower working class and suffers from lack of education (cf. ll. 39 f.), Kowalski is part of the middle class. In addition, their occupations show different qualities. Gasman's menial jobs were badly-paid (cf. ll. 45–49) and so deprived him of a sufficient income, a fact he proceeded to blame on immigrants. Kowalski, on the other hand, is bitter and disaffected by the decline of the automobile industry in Detroit that has also led – in his view – to a social decline of his environment. In addition, his experiences in the Korean War have left him traumatised and battling both guilt and a simplistic world view.

Lastly, their ways of redeeming themselves are likewise dissimilar. Gasman recognises the root of his racism and admits his wrongs to his daughter. Kowalski does not directly renounce his racist ideas. Instead, he acts as a mentor for Thao and eventually willingly and calculatingly sacrifices his own life in order to save Thao and his family by making sure that the gang members will be imprisoned for a long time.

All in all, the conclusion can be drawn that while Gasman and Kowalski share a path from racism to redemption, a closer look at the motives for their hatred and the personal insights causing their respective changes of mind reveals enormous differences.

Aufgabe 3

Dear fellow bloggers,

After reading so many blog entries on "Living Cultural Diversity", I have decided to write an entry based on a statement by Audre Lorde: "It is not our differences that divide us. It is our inability to recognize, accept, and celebrate those differences". I feel that this quote fittingly sums up our topic because it truly expresses the fact that people from different ethnic backgrounds do not easily find their way towards each other because we fear our cultural differences.

Lorde argues that the fact that people are different is of minor importance and that we need to learn to embrace cultural diversity. This seems a valuable idea taking into account that many people are intimidated by the unknown, which unfortunately makes them avoid new experiences. In order to overcome such obstacles and to reduce both apparent and subconscious fears, it is necessary to reconsider our everyday attitudes towards other ethnicities. If we manage to do so, we will be able to accept different cultures more easily and welcome each other with open arms.

Cases of people overcoming their prejudicial or even racist ideas through forming bonds with a person from a different culture can often be found in literature and film. Two such impressive examples are Marybeth Gasman's father, whose journey she describes in

"The Shame of My Father's Racism" (2017), and the protagonist Walt Kowalski in the film *Gran Torino*. Gasman's father, who had been quick to blame his own destitution on other ethnicities, finally makes friends with an African American in his retirement home and realises that people of colour face the same problems as he does. A similar development can be found in Kowalski: After initially showing open contempt towards his new Hmong neighbours, based in part on his own guilt-ridden experiences in the Korean War, he becomes a mentor to one of the family's boys and starts protecting the whole Hmong family, who is terrorised by a gang.

Aside from that, it can be very fortunate to give up one's reservations and approach situations of intercultural contact with open-minded curiosity. For Walt Kowalski, doing so enables him to gradually enjoy the Hmong family's hospitality when he is invited to share their meals and to get to know their customs.

Another advantageous way of approaching other cultures is actively looking for similarities, which definitely brings people together. This is underlined by both Gasman's father, who finds out that he and his African-American friend share a similar economic situation, as well as Kowalski, who eventually considers himself closer to the Hmong family than to his own.

In addition, it is vital that everybody tries to free themselves from prejudices and stereotypes as they represent considerable obstacles to a peaceful coexistence. Accordingly, Marybeth Gasman consistently tries to subvert not only her father's but also others' racist views.

Besides, as cultures of homogeneous ethnic roots are increasingly becoming a phenomenon of the past, it is important to recognise that changing ethnic structures of communities have been on their way for several decades and that we have to accept and assist this development by actively learning about each other's cultures in order to gain a closer insight into others' customs and traditions. Doing so should be considered the norm in order to give everybody an intercultural understanding. This way, we should be prepared to address critical situations, which could otherwise cause cultural conflict, in a constructive way.

However, a much better solution to many problems evoked by cultural clashes is to initiate systemic changes which, at best, could lead to a constant peaceful coexistence of different cultural communities. Movements such as Black Lives Matter can be seen as a significant step towards raising awareness and achieving equality.

And what about us younger people? What can we do for a closely-knit community consisting of various cultures? In my eyes, we must try to make this a better world by vehemently opposing stereotypes and prejudice, as Gasman lays out in her text. We must not let up and keep these issues alive and burning. And we must be fearless to "recognize, accept, and celebrate those differences", as Lorde puts it. It is high time that we, the young generation, took a stand against racism in order to heal painful wounds scarred by history and to prevent future wars. Consequently, we need to stick together in order to enable us all to live together peacefully.

Original-Prüfungsaufgaben 2022 eA

Hinweise:

Die zentrale schriftliche Abiturprüfung im Fach Englisch besteht aus einer kombinierten Aufgabe:

Prüfungsteil 1:   a)   **Hörverstehen**
                    b)   **Sprachmittlung**
Prüfungsteil 2:   **Textaufgabe**

Ablauf und Bewertung der Prüfung:

Ausgabe der **Aufgaben für den Prüfungsteil 1a**

Prüfungsteil 1a:	**Hörverstehen**
Gewichtung:	20 %
Bearbeitungszeit:	30 Minuten

Abgabe sämtlicher Unterlagen des **Prüfungsteil 1a**
Ausgabe der Aufgaben für den **Prüfungsteil 1b**

Prüfungsteil 1b:	**Sprachmittlung**
Gewichtung:	25 %
Bearbeitungszeit:	60 Minuten

Abgabe sämtlicher Unterlagen des **Prüfungsteil 1b**
Ausgabe der Aufgaben für den **Prüfungsteil 2**

Prüfungsteil 2:	**Textaufgabe**
Gewichtung:	55 %
Prüfungszeit:	240 Minuten
	Die Prüfungszeit setzt sich zusammen aus 30 Minuten Auswahlzeit und 210 Minuten Bearbeitungszeit.

Hilfsmittel für alle Prüfungsteile:

Den Prüflingen stehen einsprachige sowie für den schulischen Gebrauch geeignete zweisprachige Wörterbücher der Allgemeinsprache (Deutsch–Englisch/Englisch–Deutsch) zur Verfügung (s. Erlass zur Nutzung von [elektronischen] Wörterbüchern in Prüfungen: https://www.nibis.de/uploads/mk-bolhoefer/2022/202111ElektronischeWoerterbuecher.pdf).

Hinweis
- Jedes einzelne Blatt ist mit dem Namen zu versehen.

Hinweise zum Prüfungsteil 2
- Von den zwei Aufgaben ist eine auszuwählen und zu bearbeiten.
- Bei jeder Teilaufgabe ist die inhaltliche Gewichtung angegeben.

eA Listening Comprehension   25 BE

AUFGABENSTELLUNG

You will hear each recording twice. After each listening you will have time to complete your answers.

Task 1: Book reviews   5 BE

Preparation time: 40 seconds

You will hear the beginnings of five book reviews.
Choose from the list (A–G) which description best applies to which book review (1–5).
For each book review there is only one correct answer. There are two more descriptions than you need.

Descriptions	
A	Dealing with characters' secrets
B	Describing a character's dreams
C	Tracing a character's self-exploration
D	Inspired by very different historical events
E	Presenting the lives of prominent individuals
F	Telling the story of formerly overlooked people
G	Based on historical events and connected to current issues

Book review	1	2	3	4	5
Heading					

Now listen to the recording again.

Sources:
BBC Radio 4 – Bookclub.
Audio 1: James Meek – The People's Act of Love, 2 February 2020,
        https://www.bbc.co.uk/sounds/play/m000dxtp (00:12–00:16 + 00:29–00:42);
Audio 2: Owen Sheers – I Saw A Man, 4 August 2019,
        https://www.bbc.co.uk/sounds/play/m0007b4t (00:12–00:15 + 00:25–00:39);
Audio 3: Don DeLillo – Underworld, 8 September 2016,
        https://www.bbc.co.uk/sounds/play/b07sxttn (00:00–00:28);
Audio 4: Michael Holroyd – A Strange Eventful History, 6 March 2016,
        https://www.bbc.co.uk/sounds/play/b072htqw (00:00–00:24);
Audio 5: Marian Keyes – Rachel's Holiday, 1 March 2020,
        https://www.bbc.co.uk/sounds/play/m000fw1j (00:12–00:45).
(All audio files accessed on 1 April 2023.)

Task 2: Baroness Trumpington   14 BE

Preparation time: 1:30 minutes

You will hear a radio report about Lady Jean Trumpington (born Jean Campbell-Harris, 1922–2018, a British politician).
While listening, fill in the missing information. You need not write complete sentences. Unless otherwise specified, name one aspect.

1	Why did Lady Trumpington's departure from politics attract so much attention?	
2	Why does the host of a TV show mention the invention of television?	
3	Which incident made Lady Trumpington widely known?	
4	What is said about her education?	
5	In which two different fields of work was she active during World War II?	• _____ • _____
6	Why did she return to Great Britain?	
7	What did she change in her life during her time in Cambridge?	
8	Why did she choose the title "Baroness Trumpington"?	
9	What was special about her holding her governmental position at the end of the 1980s?	
10	What did she do in Downing Street that helped her keep her position?	
11	What was her duty as Baroness in Waiting?	
12	Which interest will she continue to pursue after retiring?	

Now think of the text as a whole. Tick the correct answer (a, b or c). There is only one correct answer.

13. In the radio report, Lady Trumpington's personality is presented as being

a	charitable and caring.	☐
b	cautious and level-headed.	☐
c	self-confident and unconventional.	☐

Now listen to the recording again.

Source:

Edward Storton, "Baroness Trumpington", *BBC Radio 4*, 15 October 2017, https://www.bbc.co.uk/sounds/ play/b098bqr1 (00:00–01:12 + 01:19–01:26 + 02:22–02:50 + 03:00–03:12 + 04:42–05:27 + 05:56–06:06 + 06:33–06:37 + 07:01–07:17 + 07:25–07:56 + 08:46–09:00 + 09:56–10:38 + 13:05–13:21) (accessed on 1 April 2023).

Task 3: Sea otters   6 BE

Preparation time: 1:30 minutes

You will hear a radio report about research on sea otters in Canada.
While listening, tick the correct answer (a, b or c). There is only one correct answer.

1. The research focusses on the

a	effects of sea otter populations on the local economy.	☐
b	behavioural patterns of sea otters living close to humans.	☐
c	consequences of climate change for sea otter populations.	☐

2. There was more seafood in the area after the Europeans had arrived because

a	sea otters were exterminated.	☐
b	Europeans relied mainly on farming.	☐
c	the native population was moved inland.	☐

3. The scientists have chosen Vancouver Island for their research project because

a	university facilities are readily available.	☐
b	a particular species of sea otters lives there.	☐
c	the place is suitable for comparative field studies.	☐

4. The sea otters affect the ecosystem because

a	they tend to destroy habitats of other species.	☐
b	their feeding behaviour fosters the growth of fish.	☐
c	they help to reduce the impact of invasive species.	☐

5. Ecologist Edward Gregr addresses the issue that

a	visits to the area need to be regulated.	☐
b	not everyone in the area profits in the same way.	☐
c	too many sea otters threaten the fragile ecosystem.	☐

6. Native Canadians living in isolated communities perceive the growing population of sea otters as

a	a potential threat.	☐
b	a minor nuisance.	☐
c	a welcome source of income.	☐

Now listen to the recording again.

Source:

Nell Greenfieldboyce, "What Happens When Sea Otters Eat 15 Pounds of Shellfish A Day", *npr*, 22 June 2020, https://www.npr.org/2020/06/11/873885445/sea-otters-can-be-money-makers-but-not-everyone-benefits?t=1593091818232 (accessed on 1 April 2023).

Lösungen

Task 1: Book reviews

1	2	3	4	5
G	A	D	E	C

Task 2: Lady Trumpington

No.	BE	Lösungsvorschlag:
1	1	part of the House of Lords for very long / difficult to imagine House of Lords without her
2	1	to show how long she has lived / to give her a humorous introduction
3	1	made a V sign / rude gesture at another peer
4	1	one of the following: limited education (typical for women of her time) / never took an exam / finishing school in Paris / good French and German
5	1 1	two of the following: worked on a farm / as a land girl; as a cipher clerk / at code-breaking centre
6	1	followed husband's career to Eton and Cambridge / because of her husband's career
7	1	became interested in politics / started a career in politics / became councilor, then mayor of Cambridge
8	1	village nearby / didn't like other names ("Barker"/"Six Mile Bottom")
9	1	she was the first female minister
10	1	cried / made Prime Minister feel sorry for her
11	1	representing the Queen on formal occasions
12	1	horse racing
13	1	c

Task 3: Sea otters

1	2	3	4	5	6
a	a	c	b	b	a

eA Sprachmittlung

AUFGABENSTELLUNG

You are taking part in a German-American youth project in which the participants share information about changing traditions. You have decided to focus on the role of porcelain in Germany.

Based on the interview below, write an article for the project website in which you describe the current situation of manufacturing and using porcelain in Germany and the developments responsible for it.

Materialgrundlage:

Kerstin Hergt / Sophie Hilgenstock (Interview mit Christoph René Holler), „Zurück zur Tischkultur: Ein Besuch in der Manufaktur Fürstenberg", in: *Redaktionsnetzwerk Deutschland,* 08.12.2018, zitiert nach: https://www.rnd.de/panorama/zuruck-zur-tischkultur-ein-besuch-in-der-manufaktur-furstenberg-6Q25QP5JTSRYF2QA24GC55VY5Q.html (Zugriff: 01.04.2023)

Hilfsmittel:

Ein- und zweisprachiges Wörterbuch der Zielsprache

„Zurück zur Tischkultur" – Interview von Sophie Hilgenstock (2018)

[...]

Herr Holler, ist das nur so ein Gefühl, oder erlebt Porzellan tatsächlich gerade eine Renaissance?

Nein, anhand der Zahlen können wir leider nicht erkennen, dass es eine Renaissance gibt. In diesem Jahr hatten die deutschen Porzellanhersteller im Vergleich zum Vorjahr einen Umsatzrückgang von 5,1 Prozent. Ähnlich sah es im letzten Jahr aus. Daher ist es schwierig zu behaupten, Porzellan erlebe eine Renaissance. Lediglich im Projektgeschäft, also im professionellen Bereich, ist die Nachfrage zuletzt gestiegen. In Gaststätten, Seniorenwohnanlagen und Krankenhäusern wird neuerdings wieder mehr Wert auf gutes Geschirr gelegt, dort konnten die deutschen Porzellanhersteller in den vergangenen Jahren große Erfolge feiern.

Wie sieht es in Privathaushalten aus? Spätestens zu Weihnachten ist gutes Geschirr doch der Renner.

Das ist richtig. Je näher Weihnachten rückt, umso besser läuft das Geschäft. Viele Kunden haben es dabei vor allem auf die Weihnachtskollektionen abgesehen, die viele Hersteller im Angebot haben. Gemeint ist Porzellan mit Weihnachtsdekor, also mit Tannenbäumen, Glocken und Nikoläusen. Diese Porzellanlinien funktionieren gut, speziell bei Familien mit Kindern.

Woran liegt es, dass Porzellan ansonsten aus der Mode ist?

Das hat mehrere Gründe. Der wohl wichtigste Faktor ist, dass jüngere Generationen weniger Wert auf hochwertiges Porzellan und Essen am gedeckten Tisch legen. Die sonntägliche Kaffeetafel, Familienfeiern zu Hause, Gäste zum Abendessen – die Anlässe, das gute Geschirr aus dem Schrank zu holen, sind aus der Mode gekommen. Wer greift heute noch zur Kaffeekanne aus Porzellan? Man stellt seinen Becher direkt unter den Kaffeeautomaten oder läuft mit Thermobecher aus dem Haus. Das ist ein Kulturwandel, den man nur in Teilen auffangen kann – etwa, indem die Geschirrhersteller Coffee-to-go-Becher aus Porzellan herstellen, die man immer wieder verwenden kann. Aber den Trend halten wir nicht auf.

Einst war die Porzellanmarke identitätsstiftend. Gilt Porzellan heute noch als Statussymbol?

Nicht mehr so wie früher. Es ist nicht mehr die Regel, dass jede Familie ein gutes Geschirr besitzt oder auf eine bestimmte Marke schwört. Porzellan gehört auch nicht mehr typischerweise zur Aussteuer. Es gibt zwar noch Hochzeitspaare, die zur Trauung ein bestimmtes Service bekommen, aber die sind aus unserer Sicht viel zu selten geworden – die meisten wünschen sich Geld für die Hochzeitsreise. Schaut man sich an, wofür junge Menschen heute Geld ausgeben, liegen die Prioritäten ganz klar woanders: Es ist kein Problem, sich für 800 Euro ein Handy zu kaufen, bei hochwertigem Porzellan sieht es oft anders aus.

Wie wollen Sie das ändern?

Mit modernem Design, guter Qualität und pfiffigen Ideen. Das Ziel muss es sein, sich von den Billigimporten aus Asien abzuheben. Außerdem müssen wir Online als Vertriebsweg ausbauen. Uns sterben zunehmend die Fachhändler weg – gab es früher in jeder Kleinstadt ein klassisches Haushaltswarengeschäft, machen heute etwa 40 Fachgeschäfte pro Jahr in den In-

nenstädten dicht. Aber Porzellan will man anfassen, bevor man es kauft. Der Onlinehandel ist damit eine Herausforderung.

Deutschland war einmal Porzellanland. Was ist schiefgelaufen?

Deutschland ist in Europa weiterhin der größte Standort der Porzellanherstellung, und ich bin sicher, das wird auch so bleiben. Die Herausforderungen allerdings werden nicht kleiner. Der Endverbraucher greift oft lieber zur Dumpingware aus China – also zu Porzellan, das weit unter Herstellungskosten auf den Markt geschwemmt wird. Inzwischen gibt es deshalb auf chinesische Importware Strafzölle. Aber damit sind die Probleme nicht vom Tisch: Die politischen Rahmenbedingungen für die deutschen Porzellanhersteller sind schwierig. Sie haben europaweit die höchsten Energiekosten und die höchste Abgabenlast. [...]

Wie schaffen es altehrwürdige Häuser wie Meissen, KPM oder Fürstenberg, sich am Markt zu halten?

In den letzten Jahren sind mit Russland oder dem Vorderen Orient wichtige Exportmärkte weggebrochen. Je mehr Krisen und Kriege die Welt erschüttern, umso schwieriger wird es auch für die Produzenten von kunsthandwerklich hergestelltem Porzellan. Nichtsdestoweniger gibt es weiterhin ein großes Interesse an individuellen, hochwertigen Produkten – von Porzellanfiguren über handbemalte Vasen bis hin zu aufwendig gestalteten Tellern. Wer heute noch am Markt ist, hat bewiesen, dass er sich trotz schwierigster Rahmenbedingungen mit seinen Produkten durchsetzen kann – von daher sehe ich nicht schwarz.

(645 Wörter)

Anmerkungen:

2   **Christoph René Holler** – Hauptgeschäftsführer des Bundesverbands Keramische Industrie

39   **Kaffeetafel** – ein festlich gedeckter Tisch für Kaffee und Kuchen am Nachmittag

60   **Aussteuer** – Ausstattung für den künftigen Haushalt, die eine Braut traditionell von ihrer Familie zur Hochzeit geschenkt bekam

102   **KPM** – Königliche Porzellan-Manufaktur Berlin

Beispiellösung

Germans and their porcelain – a changing tradition?

Germany has been the leading producer of quality porcelain for a long time with a lot of well-known and renowned producers such as Meissen, KPM or Fuerstenberg. But due to changing traditions, trends and markets sales, numbers have declined over the past few years. Formerly, families were proud of having a particularly valuable set of porcelain that they would lay out on festive occasions like Sunday lunch, evening invitations of guests or the famous "Kaffeetrinken" – an afternoon invitation offering coffee and cake. Hosts would show off their choice of porcelain often given to them as a marriage present. Today, however, good porcelain is no longer a common marriage gift or a symbol of social status. In addition, markets have crumbled due to international crises and wars. Moreover, the coffee-to-go-culture does not need a porcelain mug.

In an interview from 2018 for a newspaper from Leipzig, Christoph Holler, managing director for an association of the German ceramics industry, suggests that it is restaurants, residences for senior citizens and hospitals that increasingly decide to offer good porcelain to their guests, leading to a success for porcelain-producing companies. Another sales-boosting niche is Christmas-related porcelain with special seasonal designs for private households.

In light of these developments, Holler says, companies need to revive the interest in porcelain with younger people by changing their designs into more modern ones and inventing clever new concepts. They also need to stick to their level of quality since they are forced to fight cheap products from China. Holler argues that the online retail market needs to be increased even though consumers usually want to touch porcelain before buying it. Finally, German manufacturers face a difficult market as the production there is troubled by high energy costs and additional fees.

On the whole, however, Holler remains optimistic that German porcelain will have its market share despite the difficult circumstances.   (321 words)

eA Aufgabe I mit Beispiellösung

Joseph Azam, "Last, First, Middle" (2018, excerpt)

AUFGABENSTELLUNG

1 Outline the autobiographical information given by Joseph Azam. (30 %)

2 Examine the significance the author's names have for him. (30 %)

3 You are taking part in a workshop titled "Displacement and Identity in Literature." You have to hand in an article about the struggles of integration, discussing the statement "It is not easy to be stranded between two worlds, the sad truth is that we can never be completely comfortable in either world" by the novelist Sharon Kay Penman.
Write the article, also referring to the text at hand and materials studied in class, such as the short stories by Lahiri, Levy, Pandit, and Shahraz. (40 %)

Materialgrundlage:
Joseph Azam. "Last, First, Middle." The Displaced: *Refugee Writers on Refugee Lives*. Ed. Viet Thanh Nguyen. New York: Abrams, 2018. 29–33.

Hilfsmittel:
Ein- und zweisprachiges Wörterbuch der Zielsprache

"Last, First, Middle" (2018, excerpt) *Joseph Azam*

The writer Joseph Azam and his family fled Afghanistan in the early 1980s when he was still a baby.

[...]

Growing up, my name – Mohammad – caused me to dread the fall. While some kids fretted about months of monotony, my angst was focused squarely on the first moments of the school year when roll would be taken out loud for the first time. By the first grade, I had come up with a routine designed to ensure that my teacher wouldn't even utter the name Mohammad. [...]

I had a lot of friends from immigrant families with strange sounding names and most of them went even further than I did in trying to fortify their Americanness. Instead of going by their given names, many of them took on noms de guerre like Michael, or Danny, or Jessica in the struggle to fit in. I never had the courage or the permission to go that far myself. I had abandoned Mohammad, but I never asked to be called Joseph or Joe, in part because it felt dishonest but mostly because I was worried about my parents somehow finding out and seeing it as a rejection of who we were. Ironically enough, years later they would do it for me. [...]

When it came time to enroll me in [high] school, my father made a choice that short-

circuited my unrest, at least for a time. As
we stood there at the registrar's counter, he
very casually, and without so much as turning to me, registered me as Joseph Azam.
To this day I don't know what went into
his decision. Perhaps he and my mother
had noticed my mushrooming anxiety, and
perhaps they realized it had something to
do with how I thought I was going to fare
in this new place. In any case, my father's
decision liberated me from the immigrant
self-gaze that had consumed me for so
long, but it also felt like a death.

So much of what I had been through
with my parents over the years – Kabul, India, Germany, our early days in New York –
seemed to fall instantly out of focus as the
name Yousuf faded. Being known as Joseph
or Joe outside of my family brought with it
the ordinariness and anonymity that I had
so desperately wanted at age six, but at fif-
teen it brought me discomfort and waves of
guilt at home.

[…] I wondered whether it stung my
parents that on top of the many things they
lost and left behind in Kabul, a decade and
a half later they felt compelled to surren-
der my name as well. More than anything,
I brooded over what my grandfather would
have thought of the way in which I had
treated his exquisite gift to me.

I'll never know exactly how or to what
extent going through high school under an
alias colored my experience, or whether or
not it somehow helped clear a path for me
– to college back in New York, to graduate
school, to law school, to a career in corporate America. What it did do was leave me
with an entirely new dilemma over what
was worse: being identifiably foreign or
secretly false. It was a question I tortured
myself with throughout high school and
one that was thrown into relief not long
after I graduated at a U.S. Citizenship and
Immigration Services Center just south of
Los Angeles.

My parents had become naturalized U.S.
citizens when I was very young but hadn't
gotten around to filling out the paperwork
for me to claim my derivative citizenship
until we had moved to California. I was
eighteen years old by the time my application was up for review, which meant
I had to go in for a citizenship interview
as part of the process. I remember breez-
ing through my interview and sitting in a
drab corridor in the immigration center as
I waited to submit my passport application
that same day. The fluorescent lights above
my head had lulled me into a trance when
my eyes suddenly fixated on the first fields
of the still blank application: Name (Last,
First, Middle); Place of Birth; Address; List
All Other Names You Have Used.

No sooner had I realized the choice that
lay in front of me than my number was
called; I found myself standing with my
father at a counter once again being asked
to register my name. This time the decision was mine alone to make, he made sure
of that. At a loss for what to do and with
an impatient clerk scowling at my empty
form I panicked and dropped the stack of
documents that I had been toting around
all morning. Realizing that she had fraz-
zled me, even if she was unsure of why, the
clerk behind the counter told me to take my
time gathering myself and cleaning up my
mess. She had no idea how many years I
had spent trying to do just that.

As I knelt down to pull together the
papers that had fallen around my feet, I
was confronted by the dissonance that I
had lived with for so many years. I picked
up the green card with the photo of Yousuf, the wide-eyed asylum seeker. I picked
up the California driver's license with the
awkward photo of Joseph, the gangly teen-

ager who had just barely passed his driving test. I picked up my parents' citizenship certificates. I picked up duplicate after duplicate I had brought of my various citizenship forms that outlined in detail the places we had lived. I picked up my passport application and I picked up my pen.

What I did next is simply what felt most honest. Instead of choosing between my names, I chose all of them.

Joseph Mohammad Yousuf Azam. It was disjointed, redundant perhaps, but it made whole again the hopes of my grandfather and added to them my own. It didn't fit in the space provided on the form that day but it fit the moment and it fit me.

This was my American name.

(793 words)

Annotations:

10   Azam asked his teachers to address him by his middle-name Yousuf only.

16   **nom de guerre** – *German:* Deckname

59   **gift to me** – His grandfather in Kabul named the new-born baby Mohammad Yousuf.

62   **alias** – a fake name used to conceal one's identity

65 f.   **corporate America** – the world of large American businesses

78   **derivative citizenship** – a type of citizenship for children born abroad whose parents are U.S. citizens

103 f.   **to frazzle s. o.** – to make s.o. nervous

Beispiellösung

Aufgabe 1

Joseph Azam comes from a refugee family and was born in Kabul, Afghanistan, which he left when he was very young.
Fleeing their home in the 1980s, his parents emigrated with him first to India, then Germany and finally to the US, where they became naturalised citizens. Since this form of citizenship did not extend to Joseph, he applied for derivative citizenship aged 18, shortly after graduating high school. Doing so enabled Joseph to attend college, followed by graduate school and law school, and resulted in a successful professional career.

(90 words)

Aufgabe 2

On the one hand, Joseph Azam's three given names symbolise various aspects of his identity, on the other, they represent a source of ongoing inner conflict which he attempts to resolve when he applies for US citizenship.
Joseph's first given name, Mohammad, was an idea of his grandfather, "his exquisite gift to me" (l. 59), as he calls it. It reminds him of his family and cultural roots in Afghanistan. However, the name also marks him out as an outsider in the US since it is "identifiably foreign" (l. 68). Joseph dreads the moment of the roll call at the beginning of each school year (cf. ll. 4–7). While some of his classmates have adopted more American-sounding names (cf. ll. 15–17), he develops a routine that would make his teachers say his middle name, Yousuf (cf. ll. 8–10). In his mind, he abandons Mohammad altogether (cf. ll. 19 f.),

which frees him from continuously being identified as an immigrant ("liberated me", l. 39) but also feels like a betrayal of his identity ("it [...] felt like death", l. 41).

The name Yousuf comes back to Joseph when he claims American citizenship: in his mind, it is that of the "wide-eyed asylum seeker" (l. 114). When it was replaced by Joseph and gradually faded, the memory of the different stages of being a refugee faded with it (cf. ll. 42–46).

Perhaps noticing his son's discomfort with his first name, his father seemingly casually chooses the name Joseph for him in the registry office of high school (cf. ll. 30–32) as an Americanisation of Yousuf. It allows Joseph to blend in, to become Americanised (cf. ll. 46–49), even though he does not feel neutral about this "alias" (l. 62): it feels "secretly false" (l. 69) as it seems to deny Joseph's cultural and familial roots, to constitute a "rejection of who we were" (l. 24). However, this name makes it possible for him to fit in and follow his own version of the American dream. In retrospect, he wonders how much this name contributed to his professional success (cf. ll. 60–66).

When he applies for citizenship, Joseph is confronted by the past and these three identities as the form he needs to fill in requires him to give his name. In spite of the dissonance associated with them, he decides to be called Joseph Mohammad Yousuf Azam, uniting the three names into his "American name" (l. 133). Although this fusion appears "disjointed, redundant perhaps" (l. 128) even to Joseph, it allows him to assert his multicultural identity.   (431 words)

Aufgabe 3

Being completely comfortable is seemingly out of the question

"It is not easy to be stranded in two worlds, the sad truth is that we can never be completely comfortable in either world," says Sharon Kay Penman. Her statement suggests that people who have spent significant periods of time living in different cultures will usually face difficulties in feeling fully at home in any of them.

One of the most immediate aspects is that of naming. A name gives you an identity – it helps to anchor you in a cultural heritage, a language, a family, a region and a religion. Some names mean something specific, some are chosen by members of the family, some are inherited from older family members. You take your name with you into new surroundings, keeping you connected to your origins and aware of differences once you leave your country with its specific culture, language and religious conventions. Crucially, it serves as a marker not only for the person that has left their home but also for those in his new surroundings. Names can thus act as stumbling blocks on the way to assimilation, so that the individual feels forced to abandon previously given names and with them parts of their cultural heritage and identity. This conflict is effectively portrayed in Joseph Azam's essay "Last, First, Middle". He recounts how the adoption of an Americanised name felt like a rejection of parts of his identity but also paved the way to academic and personal success. Azam eventually resolves this conflict and makes a step towards being "comfortable" in both worlds when he decides to take on all his names – his Afghan and his Americanised one – when applying for citizenship.

This struggle for a unified cultural identity is a prevalent topic in many recent short stories written by immigrant writers, both in support of Penman's argument and against it. For instance, Samir in Qaisra Shahraz' story "The Escape" shares Azam's feelings of loneliness and alienation in both England and his native Pakistan. Mala in Jhumpa Lahiri's "The Third and Final Continent" finds it similarly hard to adjust to the new culture and is unwilling to give up her traditions. In addition, her lack of English language skills largely limits her social contact to her husband.

Protagonists in immigrant narratives are often confronted by various forms of discrimination and outright racism, even among themselves, e. g. the Somali woman not being given space on a bus, and who, in turn, calls the black bus driver a "slave" in Shereen Pandit's "She Shall Not Be Moved". Likewise, the narrator in Andrea Levy's short story "Loose Change" is torn between empathy and prejudice when she learns that the woman she is helping, Laylor, is a refugee, even though the narrator's grandmother shared a similar fate. Finally, the situation of the two cultures can lead to families being torn apart (e. g. Samir in "The Escape" or Mala and her husband in "The Third and Final Continent"). These depictions would thus support the "sad truth" of an ultimately doomed struggle for uniting cultural identities that Penman speaks of. However, another route is also presented in these short stories that contradicts her statement of continual discomfort. Firstly, the new surroundings may serve as a safe haven. This is the case, for example, for Azam in "Last, First, Middle", to whom America offers the chance of a successful law career, or for the narrator in "Loose Change", whose grandma was a refugee herself, or for Laylor, who sees London and the museum as a safe place.

The texts likewise often depict characters that successfully manage to knit together their various cultural identities: The author of "Last, First, Middle", for example, fits in after finding a compromise with his names, while the narrators in "Loose Change" and "The Third and Final Continent" have been integrated into British and American society respectively. Many of them, like Azam, show that a multicultural identity is possible. Finally, Lahiri shows us what a heartfelt international citizenship could look like, when her narrator in "The Third and Final Continent" truly mourns the death of his former landlady. Being accepted and integrated into a society and into a cultural environment is surely a difficult and long process that may be successful but will always have to overcome obstacles and sometimes just lead to discomfort within either world – the one the person comes from and the one he or she wants to fit in. Whether someone will be left "stranded" in between or become "completely comfortable", as Penman puts it, will be a matter of personal strength as well as an accommodating and supportive environment.

(773 words)

eA Aufgabe II mit Beispiellösung

Kazuo Ishiguro, *Klara and the Sun* (2021)

AUFGABENSTELLUNG

1 Sum up the excerpt. (30 %)

2 Compare the scientist Capaldi with Victor Frankenstein from Mary Shelley's novel. (30 %)

3 As a contribution to its monthly topic "Science Meets Literature," your online book club has asked its members to contribute a blog entry, commenting on the following statement by software programmer Justin Rosenberg: "[A]s the frontiers are pushed further and further, the unintended consequences of how science and technology are used could affect who we are as humans, the viability of our planet, and how society evolves."

Write the blog entry, also referring to the text at hand and materials studied in class, such as Mary Shelley's novel *Frankenstein*. (40 %)

Materialgrundlage:

Kazuo Ishiguro. *Klara and the Sun*. London: Faber & Faber, 2021. 205–210.

Hilfsmittel:

Ein- und zweisprachiges Wörterbuch der Zielsprache

Klara and the Sun (2021) *Kazuo Ishiguro*

The novel is set in a dystopian future, in which it has not only become common for wealthy people to buy human-like androids, so-called 'Artificial Friends' (or AFs), as companions for their teenage children, but also to have their children genetically modified in order to enhance their intellectual abilities. Due to this procedure, 15-year-old Josie has become seriously ill. She, her parents and her AF Klara are at the studio of Mr Capaldi, who is creating a 'portrait' of Josie at her mother's request. While walking through his studio, Klara has discovered that this 'portrait' is actually a life-size replica of Josie's body.

[...] I stepped out onto the balcony, now making no effort to conceal myself or to soften my footsteps. Leaning over the steel rail, I saw the Mother had sat down where earlier Josie had been sitting – on the metal chair in front of the charts. Mr Capaldi came across the floor till he was directly below me, and I could see the top of his bald head, but not his expression. He then con-tinued to walk slowly towards the Mother, as if slowness were a mark of his kindness, and stopped beside the tripod-stand lamp.

'I can see you're having misgivings,' he said in a new, soft voice. 'Let me tell you. I've seen this kind of thing happen many times before. And it's the ones who stick with it, keep faith, who win out.'

'Damn right I'm having misgivings.'

20 'You mustn't let Paul sway you. Remember. You've thought this through and he hasn't. Paul is confused.'

'It's not Paul. To hell with Paul. It's that ... that portrait up there.'

25 As she said this, she glanced up in my direction and saw me. She stared past the dazzle of the ceiling lights, then Mr Capaldi also turned and looked up at me. Then he looked at the Mother questioningly. The Mother continued to gaze at me, her hand 30 now raised to her forehead.

'Okay, Klara,' she said finally. 'Come on down.'

As I descended the metal steps, I was interested to see that instead of anger, the 35 Mother showed anxiety. I crossed the floor but stopped while still several strides away. It was Mr Capaldi who spoke first.

'What do you think, Klara? Am I doing a good job?'

40 'She resembles Josie quite accurately.'

'Then I guess that's a yes. By the way, Klara, how did you get on with the survey?'

'I completed it, Mr Capaldi.'

'Then I'm grateful for your cooperation. 45 And you stored the data safely?'

'Yes, Mr Capaldi. My responses are stored.'

There was a silence, while the Mother continued to stare at me from her chair and Mr Capaldi from beside his tripod light. I 50 realized they were waiting for me to say something further, so I continued:

'It's a pity Josie and the Father have left. Mr Capaldi's work on the portrait may be temporarily impeded.'

55 'It's okay,' he said. 'Not a serious setback.'

'I need to hear,' the Mother said. 'I need to hear, Klara, what you think. About what you saw.'

60 'I apologize for examining the portrait without permission. But in the circumstances, I felt it best to do so.'

'Okay,' the Mother said, and again I saw she was fearful rather than angry. 'Now tell us what you thought. Or rather, tell us what 65 you think you saw up there.'

'I'd suspected for some time that Mr Capaldi's portrait wasn't a picture or a sculpture, but an AF. I went in to confirm my speculation. Mr Capaldi has done an accu- 70 rate job of catching Josie's outward appearance. Though perhaps the hips should be a little narrower.'

'Thank you,' Mr Capaldi said. 'I'll bear that in mind. It's still a work in progress.' [...] 75

'Klara,' the Mother said. 'We came here today, the main reason. It wasn't so Josie could sit more. We came here because of you.'

'I understand,' I said. 'I understood about 80 the survey. It was to test how well I've come to know Josie. How well I understand how she makes her decisions and why she has her feelings. I think the results will show I'm well able to train the Josie upstairs. But 85 I say again, it's wrong to give up hope.'

'You still don't quite understand,' Mr Capaldi said. Although he was standing there before me, his voice seemed to come from the edges of my vision, because all I could 90 see still were the Mother's eyes. 'Let me explain to her, Chrissie. It'll be easier coming from me. Klara, we're not asking you to train the new Josie. We're asking you to *become* her. That Josie you saw up there, as 100 you noticed, is empty. If the day comes – I hope it doesn't, but if it does – we want you to inhabit that Josie up there with everything you've learned.'

'You wish me to inhabit her?' 105

'Chrissie chose you carefully with that in mind. She believed you to be the one best equipped to learn Josie. Not just superficially, but deeply, entirely. Learn her till there's no difference between the first Josie 110 and the second.' [...]

'So you see what's being asked of you, Klara,' Mr Capaldi said. 'You're not being required simply to mimic Josie's outward behavior. You're being asked to continue her for Chrissie. And for everyone who loves Josie.'

'But is that going to be possible?' the Mother said. 'Could she really continue Josie for me?'

'Yes, she can,' Mr Capaldi said. 'And now Klara's completed the survey up there, I'll be able to give you scientific proof of it. Proof she's already well on her way to accessing quite comprehensively all of Josie's impulses and desires. The trouble is, Chrissie, you're like me. We're both of us sentimental. We can't help it. Our generation still carry the old feelings. A part of us refuses to let go. The part that wants to keep believing there's something unreachable inside each of us. Something that's unique and won't transfer. But there's nothing like that, we know that now. *You* know that. For people our age it's a hard one to let go. We *have* to let it go, Chrissie. There's nothing there. Nothing inside Josie that's beyond the Klaras of this world to continue. The second Josie won't be a copy. She'll be the exact same and you'll have every right to love her just as you love Josie now. It's not faith you need. Only rationality. I had to do it, it was tough but now it works for me just fine. And it will for you.' [...]

(994 words)

Annotations:

19 Paul – Josie's father

Beispiellösung

Aufgabe 1

The excerpt from Kazuo Ishiguro's 2021 novel *Klara and the Sun* presents a discussion about a life-size replica of 15-year-old Josie. Josie's mother Chrissie has asked the artist/scientist Capaldi to create an artificial copy of her daughter because Josie is seriously ill. The two adults explain the portrait's purpose to Klara, Josie's AI companion, from whose perspective the story is told.

The scene starts with Klara observing a conversation between Capaldi and Josie's mother. The artist reassures Chrissie that she made the right decision to have him create her daughter's portrait despite the uncertainty of Josie's father Paul, who is not present. Klara, who had been tasked with filling out a survey in order to test how well she knows Josie, joins the two adults and apologises for having looked at the replica. She judges it to be very accurate and continues that she knows Josie very well and even understands her motivations and emotions. At this point Capaldi explains to her that Klara is supposed to make up for the vacuum inside the replica – that she will be asked to become Josie in case the girl dies. The scientist finally also assures Chrissie that Klara will not simply be a copy but a truthful continuation of her daughter. He explains that many of their generation need to let go of sentimental and false ideas such as the soul and that they need to learn that an AI can faithfully replicate and be as real as its biological original.

(249 words)

Aufgabe 2

The scientists Capaldi and Frankenstein hold very dissimilar views on experiments in general and are portrayed at very different historical times and with very different methods. However, both deal with artificially created individuals and seek to replicate human life, a power traditionally held only by God. Accordingly, both work at the limits of scientific thought established during their specific time.

Capaldi seems to be a successful scientist who works on special demand of Josie's mother: Chrissie has commissioned a copy of her daughter to help her deal with the pain and grief in case Josie dies from her illness (cf. ll. 119 f.). Within the narrative's world, it is common to make artificial friends to keep family members company (cf. introduction to the excerpt), and both Capaldi and Josie's mother talk to the AI with ease but from an employer's perspective. Capaldi expects Klara to be able to "continue" (l. 115) Josie for her mother as well as her family and friends (cf. ll. 115–117) by learning "Josie's impulses and desires" (l. 126): "The second Josie won't be a copy. She'll be the exact same" (ll. 38–140). His aim is thus slightly different to Frankenstein's: Capaldi wants to be able to replace human life, whereas the latter seeks to create life from dead matter. In addition, Capaldi's motivation is slightly vague: On the surface, his main incentive appears to be to help Chrissie (cf. "you'll have every right to love her just as you love Josie now", ll. 140 f.). On the other, his interests in the matter may at least partially be financial. Victor Frankenstein, on the other hand, is a university student and conducts scientific experiments for the sole purpose of proving himself. He experiments on human body parts that he stitches together and then tries to animate. His aim is to create a new living being out of dead material. Since his experiments are illegal – for example, because he gathers the body parts from dubious sources – Frankenstein works in secret. Both men thus use the materials available to them at their time: Frankenstein shapes his creature out of human body parts, Capaldi his android from synthetic materials. Furthermore, Capaldi's creation is based on a living blueprint ("She resembles Josie quite accurately", l. 40), while Frankenstein is not remaking a specific person.

Perhaps the relationship between the two scientists and their creation is the most revealing. Victor Frankenstein is so emotionally involved that he reacts with horror and panic once his creature is sparked into life, fleeing the scene. He is so abhorred by his creation that he does not go back while the creature is still in the laboratory but later hunts it. Capaldi, on the other hand, generally remains detached and impartial to the result of his work ("It's still a work in progress", l. 75), suggesting that Klara is little more to him than a product. Significantly, however, both men pay little attention to their creation's needs and feelings. Frankenstein abandons the "monster" several times over the course of the narrative, for example, when he fails to produce a mate. Capaldi, meanwhile, may not be treating her like an artificial being, but he ultimately has no respect for Klara's feelings, expecting her to forsake any intellectual or emotional life of her own in order to become Josie (cf. ll. 99 f.).

Finally, it can be argued that both scientists act unethically. Frankenstein wants to play God; Capaldi wants to prove that life can be faithfully recreated and that there is no such thing like a soul (cf. ll. 136 f.). Both men are unaware of or unwilling to accept the responsibilities this implies. (610 words)

Aufgabe 3

Is literature a wake-up call for the limits of science?

Our monthly topic "Science Meets Literature" is a very old but also a very current one. I'd like to talk about one of the world's most haunting science fiction novels and themes: Victor Frankenstein's story of making a humanoid creature out of dead body parts. This story galvanised and terrified people over two hundred years ago and still intrigues us today. At the other end of the line, I would like to look at Kazuo Ishiguro's *Klara and the Sun* from 2021 – a very recent novel about the artificial making of a human being.

Let me begin with the statement of the software programmer Justin Rosenberg who claims that because "frontiers are pushed further and further, the unintended consequences of how science and technology are used could affect who we are as humans, the viability of our planet, and how society evolves". Well, frontiers are indeed pushed further every day – AI (artificial intelligence) and robotics allow scientists to invent and reinvent. Ever since digitalisation has made it possible to gather and exploit large volumes of data, frontiers are continually shifting, and this could have serious effects on how mankind and its environment develop.

In former centuries, people respected the idea of God as the sole creator. However, the human condition has always fascinated people, trying to find something new, trying to improve ourselves. Scientists have continuously gone a little further and keep producing scientific developments in numerous ways. But there has ever remained this one frontier: the creation of one's own kind.

Literature, meanwhile, has helped to understand the thrill of science – mostly in science fiction stories (such as *Frankenstein*) but also in utopian texts. Mary Shelley is just one of many authors who deal with the taboo of creating a human being. And she tells us about the loss of control over this scientific discovery. As 21st century readers, we still shudder at the monstrosity of the undertaking: the creature Victor stitches together out of dead bodies and sparks into life but doesn't give education nor any moral understanding, indirectly causing the death of his friend and betrothed and ultimately his own undoing. As a contrast to this, in *Klara and the Sun* we meet a "portrait of a young lady", an artificial friend, that may take the place of the daughter when she dies. The scientist Capaldi creates humanoid replicas on demand – a process that seems to be socially accepted and undisputed. The artificial becomes real – it is the real thing. As a consequence, this novel establishes new forms of social contact between the artificial and the real. While Frankenstein's monster remains agonisingly separate from society, Klara shadows Josie in order to learn to be her, resulting in a complete lack of privacy.

The two texts also show different attitudes towards the idea of morality. In *Frankenstein*, the scientist's doings are continually subject to secrecy and frequently questioned. In Ishiguro's novel the question is not whether one should create artificial life but whether it would actually work, i. e. whether it could faithfully replace biological life. If everything is possible, why should we not do or use it? Our society has lost its taboos – the idea of being almighty is no longer viewed with same awe and dread as it used to be during Shelley's time.

The two texts also show how differently individuality is evaluated. To Frankenstein, his monster's identity and personality is of little concern; proving his ability to create any form of human-like life is all that truly matters to him. To Capaldi, faithfully recreating Josie's psychological individuality is crucial, arguably even more so than accurately matching her physical features.

Lastly, Ishiguro's novel also shows how easily science can be try to manipulate individuals to its needs. To Capaldi, the idea of a soul is inconvenient as he cannot measure it. He is therefore quick to try and manipulate Chrissie into abandoning this idea. The text thus warns us that science can also be used for an agenda.

Reading stories like the two I mentioned above can open our eyes to the fact that pushing the boundaries too far means that we as the human race not only have a lot to gain but also a lot to lose. Hence, I agree with Rosenberg. We always need to think about the consequences. (727 words)

Stichwortverzeichnis